William R. Watters

Formula Criticism and the Poetry of the Old Testament

William R. Watters

Formula Criticism and the Poetry of the Old Testament

Walter de Gruyter · Berlin · New York
1976

Beiheft zur Zeitschrift für die alttestamentliche Wissenschaft
Herausgegeben von Georg Fohrer
138

ISBN 3 11 005730 1

Printed in Germany

Satz und Druck: Hubert & Co., Göttingen
Bindearbeiten: Lüderitz & Bauer, Berlin 61

To Ginny

"Need we suppose that Shakespeare was indebted either to Jeremiah or to Job when he put into Hamlet's mouth the words:

O cursed spite
That ever I was born to set it right!"

A. Guillaume,
Studies in the Book of Job, with a New Translation, 15

Preface

Certainly in the completion of any published research, there are many persons, in addition to the author, who play significant roles at various stages. First, I must express my indebtedness to Dr. Jacob M. Myers (Gettysburg, Pennsylvania) who convinced me that the field of biblical Hebrew poetic composition was not exhausted in its entirety by Segert, Robinson and Lowth. And I would be remiss were I not to thank Drs. George Nickelsberg and Helen Goldstein (Iowa City, Iowa) for their advice and criticism of the manuscript at various stages. Foremost, however, was the concern and constant prodding of Dr. J. Kenneth Kuntz (Iowa City, Iowa) who oversaw the production of the manuscript in its final form. Without the constant encouragement of my wife, Virginia, who proof-read the manuscript at every point of preparation, the work would never have been completed.

Last, but in no small measure, I wish to show my indebtedness to Rabbi Leroy M. Diamond (Jerusalem) who taught me that it is not only important to examine the elements of the Hebrew poetic line, but also to appreciate the content of those lines. He has convinced me through study together that the poetry is central to the continuous Judaic tradition, and he has shown me through personal example that Jewry today is the embodiment of that tradition.

Jerusalem, Israel
December 25, 1975

William Watters

Table of Contents

List of Tables

Abbreviations

AJA	The American Journal of Archaeology
AJP	The American Journal of Philology
ALUOS	Annual of Leeds University Oriental Society, Leeds
ANVAO	Avhandlinger Utgitt av de Norske Videnskaps-Akademi i Oslo, Oslo
AO	Der Alte Orient, Leipzig
ArOr	Archiv Orientální, Prague
AcOr(L)	Acta Orientalia, Leiden
AcOr(R)	Acta Orientalia, Rome
ASNU	Acta Seminarii Neotestamentici Upsaliensis, Uppsala
BASOR	Bulletin of the American Schools of Oriental Research
BJPES	Bulletin of the Jewish Palestine Exploration Society
BS	Bibliotheca Sacra, Dallas
BWANT	Beiträge zur Wissenschaft vom Alten und Neuen Testament, Stuttgart
BZAW	Beihefte zur Zeitschrift für die Alttestamentliche Wissenschaft, Berlin
CBQ	The Catholic Biblical Quarterly
CL	Comparative Literature
CV	Communio Viatorum, Prague
ELH	English Literature and History
HSCL	Harvard Studies Comparative Literature
HSCP	Harvard Studies in Classical Philology
HUCA	Hebrew Union College Annual
ICC	The International Critical Commentary
JAOS	The Journal of the American Oriental Society
JBL	The Journal of Biblical Literature
JBLMS	Journal of Biblical Literature Monograph Series
JKLF	Jahrbuch für Kleinasiatische Forschung, Heidelberg
JNESt	Journal of Near Eastern Studies, Chicago
JPOS	Journal of the Palestine Oriental Society
JQR	Jewish Quarterly Review
JSSt	Journal of Semitic Studies, Manchester
JTS	Journal of Theological Studies, Oxford
LUÅ	Lunds Universitets Årsskrift, Lund
MP	Modern Philology
NM	Neuphilologische Mitteilungen
OBL	Orientalia et Biblica Lovaniensia, Louvain
RB	Revue Biblique, Paris
RGG	Religion in Geschichte und Gegenwart, Tübingen
RP	Revue de Paris
RQ	Revue de Qumran, Paris
SAOC	Studies in Ancient Oriental Civilization
SBT	Studies in Biblical Theology
SEÅ	Svensk Exegetisk Årsbok, Lund

StTh	Studia Theologica, Lund
SVT	Supplements to Vetus Testamentum, Leiden
ThLBl	Theologisches Literaturblatt, Leipzig
ThRv	Theologische Revue, Münster
TPAPA	Transaction and Proceedings of the American Philological Association
ThStKr	Theologische Studien und Kritiken, Berlin
VT	Vetus Testamentum, Leiden
WZKM	Wiener Zeitschrift für die Kunde des Morgenlandes, Wien
ZAW	Zeitschrift für die Alttestamentliche Wissenschaft, Berlin
ZDMG	Zeitschrift der Deutschen Morgenländischen Gesellschaft, (Leipzig) Wiesbaden
ZS	Zeitschrift für Semitistik und verwandte Gebiete, Leipzig

Introduction

Since this study has two objectives, it may be divided into two parts. First, it aims at explaining the origins of what we call formula criticism. The history of the criticism will be traced, mentioning as we go, the scholars who have contributed most to our own understanding. We shall not examine their work on all fronts, but rather shall treat their efforts as they converge directly upon our discussion. And we shall be interested in the antecedents of formula criticism only insofar as they will help us to isolate the ideas of each author so that we may establish the nature of formula criticism on our own.

Second, this study seeks to evaluate the central theories of formula criticism on the basis of the results of our own studies. Many long-standing and traditional questions will be posed, and the books of Isaiah, Job, Lamentations, and Ruth will be called upon to assist in the formation of the respective answers.

The aim of the whole, therefore, is to set formula criticism in proper perspective, and to show how it may assist the scholar as a useful tool in textual research.

Chapter I

Formula Criticism: An Historical Survey

A. INTRODUCTION

It is characteristic and a tragedy of modern scholarship that few writers in one field are aware of work being done in another. The man for all seasons, able to encompass all available knowledge, is certainly no longer with us. In the main, this is due to the difficulty of mastering one area of study, let alone two. Few students of Old Testament, for example, are aware of what is going on in the fields of world history, Romance languages, or the Classics, not to mention the sciences. And it is an unfortunate result of singular attention to one's own studies that discoveries in one field, especially with regard to new methodology, go completely unnoticed in another. And, as the student of the Old Testament might ask, "What has Beowulf or Odysseus to do with Isaiah?"

Yet as the following survey will show, ways of looking at texts developed in one field of study may go far in illuminating another field, specifically our own interests in Old Testament poetic criticism. We shall see how many different scholars from quite varied interests have developed a methodology for examining oral and written literature as different as the Song of Roland, Serbocroatian epics, Ugaritic poems, Cynewulf, and Job. By approaching these literatures from different angles and interests, the scholars have unwittingly come to very much the same conclusions. We shall trace the arguments of the scholars in their work, note the greatest weaknesses in their observations, and even more important, their contributions to the ongoing study of what we call formula criticism, a methodological term we now coin. In succeeding chapters, we shall reckon with specific aspects of the theories.

B. THE DISCOVERY OF FORMULA FROM CLASSICAL STUDIES

The study of formula, which we are now at great pains to describe, is considered a commonplace in Homeric scholarship, and has been so for over forty years [1]. Yet the work has gone wholly unnoticed in Old Testament

[1] In the 1930's the study of formula gained a foothold on scholarship. See M. Parry's: L'Epithete traditionelle dans Homere, 1928. This paper is rightly said to have

research until only recently. This situation we take to be the direct result of scholars' interest in encompassing only singular fields, which we have mentioned above.

1. *Milman Parry*

If not the first, M. Parry is certainly the most representative of those Homeric scholars who noted that repeated words and phrases exist within the Iliad and the Odyssey[2]. These repeated words and phrases in Homer, Parry called formulaic. By formulaic, he meant that the verse of Homer abounds in stock expressions which may be a word, phrase, or line in length. These formulas, said Parry, were the result of long-established tradition which recurred from time to time in the texts. By saying that these formulas were part of a traditional diction, he meant that these elements constituted a fund of characteristic speech useful in verse-making. In fact, Parry believed that much, if not all, of Homer's lines were formulaic. In his early work, Parry claimed, but without sufficient proof, that this traditional diction was due to an oral style in verse-making. His two articles: Studies in the Epic Technique of Oral Verse-Making, I and II, are concerned with oral composition in the Homeric narrative, and form the groundwork for his study[3]. These and others of his papers which have been until recently hard to find, are now collected into a one-volume work by his son. So influential was Parry's work with formulas, that Lattimore averred, "His methods and conclusions have revolutionized Homeric studies."[4] They certainly have. Today the formula is rarely overlooked in examining Homer.

---

begun the study of Homeric formula. The collected work of Parry is found in: The Making of Homeric Verse; the Collected Papers of Milman Parry, edited by his son A. Perry, 1971.

[2] The concordances of Homer compiled beginning in the 19th century allow us to see the repeated words, phrases, and lines. G.L. Prendergast's: A Complete Concordance to the Iliad of Homer, 1875, is perhaps the best example. C.E. Schmidt's: Parallel-Homer, 1965 (1885) is an equally valuable work.

[3] M. Parry, Studies in the Epic Technique of Oral Verse-Making I: Homer and the Homeric Style, HSCP 41 (1930), 73–147; and: Studies in the Epic Technique of Oral Verse-Making II: The Homeric Language as the Language of an Oral Poetry, HSCP 43 (1932), 1–50. A complete bibliography of Parry's work is found at the end of A.B.Lord, Homer, Parry, and Huso, AJA 52 (1948), 43–44. For the very best summary of Parry's views, see Albin Lesky in Pauly-Wissowa-Kroll, Paulys Real-encyclopädie, under the titles: Homeros, II. Oral Poetry, and: Homeros, III. Mündlichkeit und Schriftlichkeit.

[4] R. Lattimore, The Iliad of Homer: Translated with an Introduction, 1951, 39 note 1.

Especially interesting to Parry and noteworthy of the formulaic character of Homeric poetry were the often repeated epithets joined to the characters of the epics. The repeated epithets represent just one aspect of the Homeric formula, but they show us the nature of the formula in general. For example, that Achilles is called πόδας ὠκύς or ποδάρκης well over forty times in the Iliad is no accident. "Hector of the shining helm" (Il. 11.315; 8.326), "Swift footed Achilles" (Il. 1.84), and "Cloud gathering Zeus" (Il. 1.560), served two useful purposes for the Homeric poet as formulaic epithets[5]. These formulas first assisted in the characterization of the players, but second, and even more important, helped the poet in filling out the poetic line by providing standardized metrical lengths. The epithet, and so the formula, therefore, aided in composition of the verse.

These repeated words, phrases, and lines now termed formulas by Parry, were created to aid singers while they were composing songs in performance. For Parry believed that the Homeric poem had its origin and transmission in an oral verse-making society wherein poems were recomposed each time they were given for public performance. As the oral poetaster composed under the pressure of an audience before him, he was not bound to remembering the entire poem. Rather, he could draw upon stock formulas with which he could fill out the line. In a non-writing, oral society, Parry conjectured, a poet needed formulaic phrases upon which he could depend. In this we might say that the poet is much like the Christian clergyman today who composes prayers orally before an audience using Christian pious formulas: "Our heavenly Father, shepherd of the people; we come now before your altar ..." As the oral poet composed in public, the formula aided composition.

"Originality", Parry believed, insofar as we understand the word, had no meaning to the ancients. For them, what was best, what was acceptable, was that which was closest to tradition[6]. Each new poet received the traditional diction of formulas from previous poets; he used these formulas liberally, and then passed the tradition on to poets who followed him. When invited to make a new song, the bard did not struggle for originality in his verse-making. Rather, he stayed as close to tradition as possible. Hence he used the formula to help him remain within the traditional bounds. Because Greek meter requires that words be restricted to only a few places in the verse, these formulas constantly recurred in the same form. But for one instance, πολυμήτις, for example,

[5] Our text of the Iliad for these and other notations is the Oxford Classical Texts edition, *Homeri Opera*, edited by D.B. Monro and Th.W. Allen, 1966, Volumes I–II

[6] Parry, Studies in the Epic Technique of Oral Verse-Making I: Homer and the Homeric Style, HSCP 41 (1930), 138.

occurs in the nominative for Odysseus alone. As the epopoeist created the poem, the traditional formula helped him fill out the line when, in our example, the subject of Odysseus came up.

Because Parry's early work drew upon written texts of now dead Greek civilizations, many of his observations on oral verse-making were necessarily speculative. He could only guess that back of the Homeric texts was an oral composition. Before Parry, there had been little field work done with peoples who still composed poems orally. To remedy this void in the scholarship, Parry journeyed to Yugoslavia to record the songs of the South Slavonic peoples, an ethnic group which still orally recited and passed on their national songs. His purpose was to study the character of oral poetry firsthand, isolate oral poetic characteristics, and then determine if these oral characteristics were found in the texts of Homer.

Parry made a number of trips to Yugoslavia and gained much information on oral verse-making which largely supported his previous textual findings. But due to his untimely death, it was left for A. B. Lord, a student and field worker of Parry's, to sort through and publish portions of the oral poetry which they had discovered together[7].

2. *A.B. Lord*

The field techniques of dictation and recording used by Parry and Lord revealed many important results for oral poetic study. Their work has become a classic in the rapidly growing field of oral poetic research. From their examination of Serbo-Croatian poetry (as with Greek, an Indo-European language), Parry and Lord discovered that the long narrative poems, of which this people was so fond, were not sung from a memorized text. Rather, each performance of the same poetic subject was found not to be the same as the last. One lyrist, when asked to perform a given poem a number of times, did not sing the poem each time in exactly the same way[8]. Composed anew using traditional language, stock scenes and phrases, and typical descriptions, each performance had the same story line, but not exactly the same wording. Parry concluded, therefore, that the formulas assisted in the oral composition of the poem.

Lord's excellent volume, The Singer of Tales, an expansion of his 1949 Harvard dissertation, is considered the most eloquent and important

[7] Parry did publish some material. See: Whole Formulaic Verses in Greek and Southslavic Heroic Songs, TPAPA 64 (1933), 179–197. But the bulk of this work is found in: Serbocroatian Heroic Songs, Volume I: Novi Pazar: English Translations, collected by M. Parry and edited and translated by A.B. Lord, 1954.

[8] A.B. Lord, Homer and Other Epic Poetry, in: A Companion to Homer, edited by A. J.B. Wace and F.H. Stubbings, 1962, 188.

text on the subject of oral verse-making[9]. Because so much work on oral literature had been done between Parry's death and the book's publication, Lord was able to include the findings of many investigators who looked at various societies which still employed oral verse-making[10]. Observations made in widely different field locations were then drawn together and related to the Iliad and the Odyssey which were long suspected of hailing from an oral tradition. And Parry's earlier conjecture that Homer was orally composed was strongly confirmed by a comparison of the field work and the Homeric texts. While not accepted by all Homerists today, the concept of oral verse-making behind the text of Homer has been embraced by most[11].

To summarize: from Parry and Lord's work in Homer and verse-making in the field, it was agreed that the text of Homer is highly formulaic, and by that it is meant the poems contain words, phrases, and lines which are often repeated. It was further seen that this formulaic aspect of poetry came from the needs of an oral verse-making society in which these formulas bespoke a traditional diction in the language. These conclusions were reached by the scholars based upon field investigation of Indo-European peoples who still translated their verse orally.

3. Robert C. Culley

R. Culley is the first and most articulate of the few biblical scholars who have been introduced to the theories of Parry and Lord. Throughout his book: Oral Formulaic Language and the Biblical Psalms[12], Culley makes clear that he was very impressed by the work

---

[9] A.B. Lord, The Singer of Tales, 1954.

[10] The characteristics of oral verse-making which Lord discusses will be elaborated below under the work of R. Culley.

[11] The work of J.A. Notopoulos gives some idea of how formula study may be used with living languages. He deals with modern Greek poetry much as Parry dealt with Serbocroatian poetry. See: Homer, Hesiod, and the Achaean Heritage of Oral Poetry, Hesperia 29 (1960), 177–197; and Homeric as Oral Poetry: A Study of Post Homeric Oral Tradition, AJP 83 (1962), 337–368.

[12] R.C. Culley, Oral Formulaic Language in the Biblical Psalms, 1967. There are very few other Old Testament scholars who have as yet applied the study of oral verse-making to biblical texts. To our knowledge, W. Whallon, Formula, Character, and Context: Studies in Homeric, Old English, and Old Testament Poetry, 1969 is the only writer to approach Old Testament poetry from the work of Parry. W.F. Albright reveals his acquaintance with Parry's efforts in Some Oriental Glosses on the Homeric Problem, AJA 54 (1950), 162. J. Blenkinsopp, Structure and Style in Judges 13–16, JBL 82 (1963), 72 note 21, has read a little about the work of Parry, but misunderstands him in saying that formulaic poetry was both oral and memorized. Likewise, Th. Gaster fails to catch the drift of Parry's ideas when

of the two Homerists. In his first chapter, Culley reviews the efforts of Parry and Lord. He recalls that they determined the characteristics of living, orally composed and transmitted literature in field study, and they found these same characteristics in the Homeric epics. Parry and Lord went, as it were, from field work to Homer, from the examination of one Indo-European language to another Indo-European language. So Culley, drawing directly upon characteristics of a wide variety of verse-making peoples in addition to Parry and Lord's work, applied these same characteristics to the biblical psalms. He went, as it were, from field study to the biblical psalms, from the study of predominantly Indo-European literature to Northwest Semitic literature. His intention was to locate repeated phrases in the psalms, and determine, by their presence or absence, and by applying oral verse-making characteristics of other languages, to what extent the psalms were oral compositions.

Culley prefaces his investigation of the psalms with an excellent general discussion of oral verse-making drawing heavily upon the work of Parry and Lord. We shall look closely at Culley's observations on the results of Parry and Lord, since it is primarily the work of Culley in which we are interested, not that of Parry and Lord.

Oral transmission is of greatest importance to preliterate societies. And the oral transmission of the verse may be of two forms, fixed or unfixed[13]. In the former instance, verbatim memorization is the rule; the lines of the poem are memorized completely[14]. But also, oral poetry may be passed on in an unfixed form by poets who create poetry as they sing songs in public. In this unfixed form, fixed texts are not memorized. Rather, the poem is composed anew at each performance. The poets of the unfixed form knew story line, stock phrases, expressions, scenes and descriptions, and relied heavily upon them. By so using these "tools of their trade", the bards recomposed traditional poems at each performance. A given poem had the same general outline, but different wording each time it was given. Furthermore, this readymade tradition of phrases and scenes allowed poets of the unfixed form to create new poems when the need arose, employing the old time-honored stock

---

he cites Parry and Lord's Serbocroatian studies, but implies that the poetry was relegated to memory alone. See his: Prolegomenon, in R. Kittel's: Great Men and Movements in Israel, 1968 (1929), xlii.

[13] Culley, Oral Formulaic Language, 5.

[14] Culley's example of the early transmission of the Mishnah being passed in fixed form is probably wrong. Culley obtains his idea from B. Gerhardsson, Memory and Manuscript, 1961, 130ff. But see also L. Finkelstein, The Transmission of Early Rabbinic Tradition, HUCA 16 (1941), 115, who proposes a more "formulaic" passing of the early Mishnah, with key words memorized alone. And the views of S. Lieberman on the transmission of the Mishnah are not to be overlooked: Hellenism in Jewish Palestine, 1950.

forms. This method of creating poetry is now known as the "formulaic technique of oral composition". It is called formulaic, because that was the term used by Parry to describe the repeated words, phrases, and lines of Homeric verse[15].

Culley is certainly in a much better position to compare field studies with given textual evidence than was Parry or even Lord. Work with oral verse-making peoples has mushroomed between the time of Parry's death (1935) and the publication of The Singer of Tales (1954)[16]. Drawing upon world-wide field research, Culley emphasizes that such studies in this area are the only valid means of making a judgment in textual studies where civilizations have long since died out. Textual examination of Homeric and Anglo-Saxon poems, for example, serve to amplify and illustrate field studies[17]. Yet taken together, field and textual studies indicate that the unfixed oral formulaic technique occurs wherever oral literature exists. The technique is neither limited to time nor to type of poem[18].

This idea of the unfixed form of oral verse-making has many requirements. The primary ones are talent and practice on the part of the poet. While it has been found from field studies that even the average person in an oral verse-making society can compose short poems, the longer poems, considered national treasures by the people, are performed only by skilled, professional versemakers, expert in their craft.

The extensive use of the free form well reflects the ancient poet's interest in adhering as close to tradition as possible: the most acceptable poetry to the people was that which was closest to tradition in form and content; the most artistic poetry was that which was closest to tradition. The poet of the unfixed form is both a preserver of the tales handed down to him and a creative artist. The skilled poet strives to produce good versions of traditional poems. "He works creatively within traditional limits."[19] He is creative in varying his stock phrases and formulas in new situations. With the unfixed form of oral verse-

---

[15] Culley, Oral Formulaic Language, 7.

[16] To name but a few of the many Anglo-Saxon studies which reflect the work being done: R. Creed, The Making of an Anglo-Saxon Poem, ELH 26 (1959), 445–454; R. Creed, The Singer Looks at His Sources, CL 14 (1962), 44–52; F. P. Magoun, Jr., Oral Formulaic Character of Anglo-Saxon Narrative Poetry, Speculum 28 (1953), 446–467. And in the even more interesting area of Homeric studies, see: C.M. Bowra, Heroic Poetry, 1952; C.M. Bowra, Style, in: A Companion to Homer, 26ff.

[17] Culley, Oral Formulaic Language, 7–8.

[18] The Chadwicks report that the unfixed form is more common in oral literatures. H.M. and N.K. Chadwick, The Growth of Literature, 1932–40, III 868.

[19] Culley, Oral Formulaic Language, 9.

making, there is no real author of a poem, nor is there an original text. The singer must be seen as only the author of his performance alone, and the performance but one example of the poem.

Before Culley lists the characteristics of oral verse-making found in various field studies, he defines what he means by formula and formulaic system. "A formula in oral poetry is a repeated group of words the length of which corresponds to one of the divisions in the poetic structure, such as the line or the small divisions within the line created by some formal division such as the caesura."[20] Put more simply, formulas are "ready-made phrases in suitable metrical form"[21]. The definition of the formula implies, therefore, that its nature has to do with syntax, meter, and lines.

Formulas are present in oral poetry because they are useful. They are available to the poet to use while he is singing so that he need not invent them under the pressure of performance. Their usefulness is seen in the fact that formulas are used often, easily fit the structure of the given poetry, and can readily be grouped into what Culley calls "formulaic systems".

Parry's definition of the formula stressed the essential character of the formula as being its usefulness in oral composition. To Parry, a formula in the Homeric epic was "a group of words which is regularly employed under the same metrical conditions to express a given essential idea"[22]. But Parry saw the usefulness of the formula in terms of Homeric thrift, that is to say, that one formula supplied the same expression for a given idea. For example, the synonymous epithets of ἑκάεργος for Apollo, aid the poetaster with a readymade word which usefully fills out the line, and brings the noun to a standardized length[23].

Lord accepts the above definition of formula given by Parry. But he noted that the definition can be applied only to Homer where this aspect of thrift is present. Hence Culley observes that the definition of the formula must be modified to fit each new literature and tradition in which it is applied[24].

---

20 Ibid. 10.

21 Ibid. 10.

22 Parry, Studies in the Epic Technique of Oral Verse-Making I: Homer and the Homeric Style, 80.

23 That these epithets are not only useful, but fit the essential and unchanging character of the men whose names they augment, is the thesis of W. Whallon, The Homeric Epithets are Significantly True to Individual Character, in his: Formula, Character, and Context, 1–32.

24 Other authors recognize that the formula must be tailored to different traditions. See, for example, F. P. Magoun's definition of the formula in terms of Anglo-Saxon poetry in: The Theme of the Beasts of Battle in Anglo-Saxon Poetry, NM 56 (1955), 81.

Now scholarship is agreed that a repeated word, phrase, or line need not recur in exactly the same form each time in order to be included as a formula. In Greek, for instance, the metrics of the line limit the number of syllables within a certain latitude, but the syntax may vary within the meter: the aspect or gender may be changed, yet the word or phrase is still to be considered a formula. And more important in other poetic traditions where meter is not so significant, words and phrases recur with alterations, in the latter case, sometimes leaving only one word constant and a clue that it is formulaic. These phrases which are alike in some respect, but different in variations are what Culley calls the "formulaic system". His precise definition of a formulaic system is "a group of phrases having the same syntactical pattern, the same metrical structure, and at least one major lexical item in common"[25]. As הטה אלי אזנך (Psalm 31$_{3}$) is a formula because it repeats elsewhere (Psalms 71$_{2}$ 102$_{3}$), it is also a part of a formulaic system, for the phrase is found in larger contexts where some words are added. The phrase is found, for example, in Psalm 88$_{3}$ as הטה אזנך לרנתי. But the formula remains the same in all cases.

Formulaic systems support the view that formulas are functional and useful in the poetry because their patterns are easily modified. The creation of verse becomes for the poet simply a case of substitution within syntactical patterns. The lyrist need not know a formula for every idea; he need only know the systems which allow him to recompose formulas for less common ideas. As in the case above, the poet has only to remember הטה אזנך to fill out the above lines in all recurrences.

We must now list the characteristics of oral composition found in field studies before we can proceed further. The effect of formulas and formulaic systems on oral poetry is apparent in a number of ways[26]. First, often in oral poetry, several lines or phrases are found which recur together. The lines which are associated together, and are often repeated, are called runs or clusters. For instance, the two separate phrases, "Be not far off!" and "Hasten to my aid!" recur together in Psalms 22$_{19}$ 38$_{21-22}$ 71$_{12}$.

Second, there is a characteristic adding style in which lines are complete in formulaic oral poetry. The terms of a verse member stand in closer relation to one another than they do to any term in a preceding or in a following member. For example, Isaiah 2$_{4}$:

---

[25] Culley, Oral Formulaic Language, 12. See also Parry's definition of formulaic structure in: Studies in the Epic Technique of Oral Verse-Making I: Homer and the Homeric Style, 85.

[26] Culley, Oral Formulaic Language, 14ff. Most of the characteristics which he cites come from the work of Parry and Lord in: The Singer of Tales.

And he shall judge between the nations,
    and he shall decide for many peoples;
And they shall beat their swords into plowshares,
    and their spears into pruning hooks;

ושפט בין הגוים והכיח לעמים רבים
וכתתו חרבותם לאתים וחניתותיהם למזמרות

Such lines are complete in themselves, and do not depend upon preceding or succeeding lines. Enjambement or syncopation, the poetic situation where lines run on together in one continuous thought, is therefore rare in oral poetry[27]. There are no run-on lines in oral verse-making, and each line is usually complete in itself. The enjambement of Coriolanus and Lartius' lines in Shakespeare's Coriolanus (III 1.12–14) is unheard of in oral poetry:

Cor. Spoke he of me?
Lart. He did, my Lord.
Cor. How? what?

Here the meter and content of the three lines are completely bound together.

And third, inconsistencies and contradictions in adjective-noun relationships are an effect of the formulas, and so an indication of oral verse-making. C.M. Bowra, for example, cites the instance in Anglo-Saxon poetry of the adjective "fair-haired" applied to a Moor[28].

In addition to the effects of formulas and their systems in oral poetry, Culley notes a number of other characteristics. He believes, as does Lord, that formulas are traditional and handed down from generation to generation[29]. And this traditional locus of the formula is said to provide the formula with certain characteristics. First, for oral poetry, the sounds of words and phrases used in formulas are important for the oral presentation and the hearing of the audience. Strings of labials, gutterals, or dentals are frequent in the oral line. Sound seems to be used to heighten the total effect of the poetry upon its listeners. Old French, to cite one example, accented the end of the word and the clause, and thus produced its characteristic assonance. Old English, on the other hand, accented the beginning of the word which lent to the language's characteristic alliteration. Sound, in both cases, is very important to oral presentation.

Second, it has been found that oral formulas may preserve archaic words or ideas as well as foreign elements obtained from the inter-

---

[27] Culley, Oral Formulaic Language, 14. For Lord's view on enjambement, see: The Singer of Tales, 284, note 17.

[28] C.M. Bowra, Heroic Poetry, 239.

[29] Culley, Oral Formulaic Language, 15ff.

mingling of peoples. Indo-European languages seem to exchange words as time goes on. Third, field studies of oral verse-making tell us that if we think of formulas as being passed down in history from one poet to the next, then it is reasonable, says Culley, to conceive of "a common stock of traditional formulas"[30]. A group of poets in one area would use the same formulas, for instance, each artist relying primarily upon the group's stock of formulas and his own limited creativity. He would probably envision such groups as the Northern prophets, the wisdom poets, or the Attic rhapsodists, each with their own set of formulas. With this group idea in mind, the researcher might begin his studies with a single singer (poet), then broaden his field of examination by including all poets from a particular district, and finally encompass the whole tradition.

And along these same lines, Parry has suggested that there may be different stocks of formulas for different subject matters. A song, a narrative, or a lament may have formulas which are used exclusively in one type of poetry or the other. When called upon to sing a song of praise, the poet would select traditional formulas of praise which he knew would be appropriate to that occasion.

Fourth, Culley observes that traditional language may transcend social changes. This is to say that the formulas which had become traditional and part of the poet's stock in trade will continue even through great upheavals in society. If this observation is true in the Old Testament literature, we might expect, for example, that if an oral verse-making society existed before and after the fall of the Second Temple or the Babylonian exile, that the formulas found in the literature before and after these disasters would nevertheless remain the same[31].

Culley's third chapter deals with two very important questions regarding oral composition[32]. To posit the first question, Culley begins by noting that there are two types of texts for scholars to study. There are field study texts taken by dictation or recording in actual situations of oral verse-making, and so their origin is known. But also, there are written texts passed down to us of which the origin is not known. The question must be raised with respect to this second group of texts: Does the presence of formulas and oral characteristics in written texts whose origin is not known necessarily indicate oral composition?

In answering this question, Culley must deal with two problems. First, he says we must determine what is the "normal level" of formulas in known oral texts so that this criterion may be applied to texts of unknown origin.

---

[30] Ibid. 16.

[31] And if this is the case, the poetry of the Intertestamental Period and beyond should contain the same formulas. See Chapter VII below.

[32] Culley, Oral Formulaic Language, 21ff.

Surely, if formulas are a characteristic of the oral text, then the more formulas present in a questionable text, the more certain it is that the text must have once been oral. But if a phrase or word is a formula if used more than once, and without this repetition a phrase or word cannot be proven a formula, then our verdict on a text of unknown origin rests upon the physical factor of the amount of material available for study. The more lines of poetry in a text of unknown origin, the better is our chance of finding formulas (repeated words or phrases). The amount of poetry at our disposal is therefore critical. These observations lead Culley into his second problem area and the conclusion that "no percentage can be set which could be used to decide whether a text is oral or not"[33]. (Here he is speaking of the percentage of repeated versus nonrepeated words and phrases.) Percentages reflecting the amount of repeated material in a given poem are only relative. And when a shorter poem has few phrases or words repeated, we can only conclude that the poem is "non-formulaic with respect to the quantity of material present"[34]. If more verses were present, perhaps, believes Culley, we would find more formulas. Of course his view assumes that the text in question *was* oral, but given the few formulas found, we cannot prove it.

The second question which must be considered is the possibility of a written text exhibiting both oral and literary style. Can a written text at the same time exhibit both oral and written qualities? Turning our attention to Homeric studies for a moment, C.M. Bowra, for example, believes that Homer was a literate oral poet who both orally composed and then revised in writing[35]. He believes that Homer lived in the transitional period in his society between the stages of oral and written literature. This is to say that Homer was a skilled oral poet who wrote down his verse. But the weight of evidence, writes Lord, points to the fact that the transitional period in any given literature is so long between the oral and literary stage that no one master poet could have had great oral *and* literary skills at once[36]. For Lord, superb oral and written techniques are mutually exclusive: a text must be either written or oral[37]. No single poet can do both.

Therefore, Culley answers the question of whether the presence of formulas and oral characteristics in written texts indicate oral composition in the affirmative. But the amount of material available is critical

[33] Ibid. 22.

[34] Ibid 22.

[35] C.M. Bowra, Heroic Poetry, 240.

[36] A.B. Lord, The Singer of Tales, 128ff.

[37] But later Lord says that the mechanics of oral style persisted in written poetry and therefore the boundary between oral and literate style became blurred to all but the initiate, and by that he means himself. The Singer of Tales, 220.

in passing judgment upon a text. Verse with a great number of oral traits was probably orally composed originally. Conversely, poetry with few oral traits and few formulas was more than likely written. And Culley is aware of his stricture concerning the amount of material available as he begins his examination of the psalms. The number of lines in the psalms is few (about 3,000) compared to such poetry as Homer (about 27,000). Hence Culley realizes that the number of formulas will be comparably minimal. His conclusions will therefore be relative to the total number of lines available and thereupon dependent. The more lines available, the more likely repetition will be found.

The rules of poetic structure in a tradition determine the nature of the formula, if there are any. For Greek verse, these rules of poetry focus upon the meter. The number of syllables to the line, or we should say, the latitude of syllables in the line depends upon the type of meter used. The Greek formula must, therefore, answer to the requirements of the meter[38]. But there does not appear to be —at least not in the classical sense —a "Hebrew meter" for Old Testament verse[39]. We know only that the Hebrew line is divided by the caesura. Thus the Hebrew formula, if it exists, should fit the hemistich or distich. And to add to the difference between Greek and Hebrew verse, the number of syllables in the Greek line, within the given bounds of particular meters, remains fairly regular; the number of syllables in successive lines of Hebrew poetry may vary greatly without disturbing the poetic structure. So a large number of changes may be allowed in the Hebrew line (far more than the Greek line) without altering the verse. Grammatical changes may occur altering suffix, prefix, number, or gender.

---

[38] Parry demonstrates that the formula in Greek poetry must suit the limits of the meter. Studies in the Epic Technique of Oral Verse-Making II: The Homeric Language as the Language of an Oral Poetry, 10.

[39] That the three most respected theories on "Hebrew meter" each go off in different directions, is the case in point. St. Segert's meter of words is explained in his: Vorarbeiten zur hebräischen Metrik I–II, AcOr(L) 21 (1953), 481–542, and 25 (1957), 190–200. Bickell and Hölscher's theory of an alternating meter is explained by Hölscher in: Elemente arabischer, syrischer, und hebräischer Metrik, BZAW 34, 1920, 93–101. And J. Ley's theory of an anapestic meter is found in his classic study: Leitfaden der Metrik der hebräischen Poesie, 1887. But there are other opinions on meter not to be overlooked. See I. Gabor, Der hebräische Urrhythmus, 1929, who believes accentuation to have been originally on the first syllable. Also, J.W. Fück, Bemerkungen zur arabischen Metrik, ZDMG 111 (1962), 464–469; F. Brown, The Measurements of Hebrew Poetry as an Aid to Literary Analysis, JBL 9 (1890), 71–106; E. Sachsse, Untersuchungen zur hebräischen Metrik, ZAW 43 (1925, 173–192; M. Dahood, A New Metrical Pattern in Biblical Poetry, CBQ 29 (1967), 574–579; S. Mowinckel, Zum Problem der hebräischen Metrik, in: Festschrift A. Bertholet, 1950, 379–394.

Since the number of syllables in the line may vary, even the addition of extra words to a line (and so a formula) is permissible. And Culley notes the free substitution of different classes of words, noun for verb, verb for participle. A phrase with a verb may later recur with that verb as a participle. This peculiarity of Hebrew poetry is also due, he thinks, to the freedom of the number of the syllables in the line. And as these changes are allowable in the Hebrew line and formula, so are they permissible in the formulaic system.

Culley next lists those formulas which he has found in the biblical psalms. Again recognizing that his conclusions will be relative to the total amount of material in the psalms, he divides the formulas which he finds into two groups: phrases and lines which recur more than twice, and those which repeat only twice. Those recurring only twice are considered to be too few upon which to base any results. If a phrase repeats just twice, he thinks the repetition may be due simply to accident. In the first group of formulas which repeat more than twice, Culley found seventy-two phrases which are formulas or belong to formulaic systems. Such phrases as the following occur more than once:

I call with my voice unto the Lord (Psalms $3_{5(4)}$ $142_{2a.\ 2b}$ $77_{2a.\ 2b}$)
קולי אל יהוה אקרא

Unto thee I cried, O Lord (Psalms 28_1 $30_{9(8)}$ 61_3 86_3 Joel 1_{19})
אליך והוה אקרא

And in the second group are one hundred and three phrases recurring twice[40].

So it is clear that formulas do exist in the biblical psalms. Their presence there is taken by Culley to be an indication of oral verse-making. They are few, yet they are present nevertheless. But are the characteristics of oral composition found in field studies also present in the biblical psalms[41]?

Culley reports that there are runs (groups of formulas which appear together), but they are not at all substantial[42]. Three formulas recur together only twice; the rest of his examples contain but two formulas recurring together[43]. But the "adding style" so characteristic of oral poetry is very much present in the biblical psalms. This is to say that the lines of the psalms are complete: lines are added to lines with no enjambement. However, as Culley concedes, the absence of enjambement is characteristic of Hebrew poetry in general, and so cannot be

[40] Culley, Oral Formulaic Language, 35–91; but see his description of the way in which he divides the formulas he finds, 32–33.

[41] See page 16 above.

[42] Culley, Oral Formulaic Language, 92–93.

[43] Ibid 93. He lists as runs, verses which have phrases recurring nowhere else. Therefore, these phrases cannot even be considered formulas, let alone runs.

used as a test for oral verse-making[44]. Since the combination of noun-adjective is uncommon in Hebrew, there were found no such stock epithets or combinations which were used inappropriately. There were no contradictions as found in other traditions.

The other characteristics of oral poetry listed above were based upon the fact that formulaic language is traditional language[45]. The first characteristic to indicate that a poetry is oral and traditional was the presence of striking arrangements of sounds by means of similar vowels or consonants. Culley lists two such examples in the biblical psalms. But the recurrence of sounds in Hebrew poetry is really a consequence of grammatical forms and the suffixes used. Furthermore, as Culley points out, such combinations of letters producing assonance and alliteration due to word endings are also found in *written* Hebrew poetry as well. Compared to such poetry as Old French where alliteration is common and artistic, the Hebrew alliteration seems almost nonexistent in comparable amount, and trivial when it occurs. So this cannot be a valid criterion for determining oral composition in Hebrew poetry.

Formulas of oral poetry were also said to contain foreign elements and archaic usages and words[46]. In the first case, Culley refers the reader to standard Ugaritic parallels, but ones which may be found elsewhere in the Old Testament poetry or prose[47]. In the second case, he refers the reader to yet another study of archaic words. And in both cases, Culley admits that neither foreign nor archaic elements are more prevalent in the formulas which he found, than elsewhere in the Old Testament.

And it was noted that in oral composition there is usually a traditional stockpile of phrases passed on from one generation to the next. Culley claims to have found two such bodies of formulas centering around particular forms of the psalms. As we shall discuss shortly, the majority of the biblical psalms containing formulas are either individual complaints or hymns.

We must conclude, therefore, that few of the "field characteristics of oral verse-making" are present in the biblical psalms, certainly too few to convince us that the poems were orally composed. Even the

[44] Ibid 97. But we know of run-on lines, though they are very rare.

[45] See page 18 above.

[46] Culley, Oral Formulaic Language, 99.

[47] M. Tsevat, A Study of the Language of the Biblical Psalms, 1955, 46–55, but also 24ff. J.H. Patton, Canaanite Parallels in the Book of Psalms, 1944. (M. Dahood, however, makes little use of formula. See, Ugaritic-Hebrew Philology, 1965; and his three volumes for the Anchor Bible: Psalms One: One to Fifty; Psalms Two: Fifty-One to One Hundred; Psalms Three: One Hundred One to One Hundred Fifty, 1966, 1968, 1970).

formulas which Culley found, and to which we now turn, do not themselves convince us of that. And considering the formulas and the formulaic systems he located, we must determine their amount, and whether or not a conclusion of oral composition is merited based upon the ones he located.

Culley draws three distribution pictures of the formulas which he has uncovered[48]. First, he sees that the formulas are limited to a few psalms. Only twenty-three psalms have more than 20% formulas. Second, he found that these twenty-three psalms came from a limited number of types: individual complaints and thanksgivings, and hymns only being represented. And last, Culley observed how the formulas were distributed over all the elements of each of the types.

It must be remembered, however, that the use of percentages in determining oral composition is not at all decisive. On the one hand, it is impossible to determine the "normal level" of formulaic diction in an oral poem. On the other, any estimation of percentage is relative to the total material available, which in the case of the psalms is not extensive. But even after articulating these warnings himself, Culley presents his results wholly in terms of percentages. He believes that the psalms which are 40–65% formulaic are significant and most probably orally composed. The psalms which are 20% formulaic, he suggests, but only guesses, may come from a time when oral formulaic language was dying out. Culley concludes that "psalms with a high formula content may be oral formulaic composition, or come from a period when oral formula was practiced"[49]. So his conclusion concerning the characteristics of oral verse-making and the percentage of formulas present is tenuous and not decisive, as tenuous and indecisive as the way in which his above statement is phrased[50].

Culley has attempted to show two things in his study. First, he wished to see if the biblical psalms contained the characteristics of orally composed and transmitted literature. But drawing upon the characteristics taken from field studies of known orally created poetry, Culley has failed to establish concretely the presence of any single characteristic in Hebrew poetry which indicates its oral composition. Second, Culley wished to show that the formula is the major device of composition in Hebrew poetry[51]. While he did find formulas and formulaic systems in the psalms, they were exceedingly limited and confined to but a few types. Their presence proved little as to their origin.

---

[48] Culley, Oral Formulaic Language, 102ff.

[49] Ibid. 114.

[50] What do these percentages mean other than in relation to the total material available? 40%, 95%, etc., are, as he said, all relative.

[51] Culley, Oral Formulaic Language, 118.

But the main weakness of Culley's study lies in his methodology. For at the basis of his research is the assumption that we may learn about obscure things in one literature by looking to parallel examples among peoples about whom more is known. His examples of scholars who have successfully used this methodological approach in the past have all been seriously called into question in recent years, and in the minds of many, soundly disproven[52]. To be specific, he mentions M. Noth's theory of the amphictyony of Israel paralleled to Greek peoples; A. Alt's parallels to biblical texts drawn from Arabian and Aramean peoples; and S. Mowinckel's Babylonian analogies of an enthronement festival. And while Culley believes this comparative approach to be "in principle quite sound"[53], it is the main reason why so many of his observations on peoples far afield from Semitic languages have nothing to do with the biblical psalms[54]. In so framing his work around this principle, Culley failed in *comparatively* discerning relationships between Old Testament formulaic diction and that of, say, Homer. Instead, he sought to carry over the characteristics of Indo-European oral techniques to Hebrew poetry. He failed to examine the Hebrew texts and tradition alone and evaluate their own characteristics[55]. Traditions must first be evaluated independently of other traditions, and especially traditions as diverse as Semitic and Indo-European languages. As Auerbach has noted, "The literary traditions of Greek and Hebrew differ widely and fundamentally."[56] And the

---

[52] M. Noth, Das System der Zwölf Stämme Israels, 1930; A. Alt. Der Gott der Väter, 1929; S. Wowinckel, Psalmenstudien I–IV, 2 vols. 1961 (1933). Each of these theories has been seriously questioned, and has been so, well before the publication of Culley's work. See the summary of G.W. Anderson, Israel: Amphictyony: 'AM, KĀHĀL, 'ĒDÂH, in: Translating and Understanding the Old Testament: Essays in Honor of H.G. May, 1970, 135–151; R. Gordis, Democratic Origins of Ancient Israel: the Biblical 'Ēdāh', in: A. Marx Jubilee Volume, 1950, English section, 369–388; J. Bright, Early Israel in Recent History Writing: A Study in Method, 1956; H. Orlinsky, The Tribal System of Israel and Related Groups in the Period of the Judges, in: Studies and Essays in Honor of A. Neuman, 1962, 375–387; A.R. Johnson, The Psalms, in: The Old Testament and Modern Study: A Generation of Discovery and Research, 1961, 162–207.

[53] Culley, Oral Formulaic Language, 4.

[54] It would be wiser, we think, to seek out a Semitic oral tradition, if one exists, rather than unrelated parallels from diverse literatures. Such studies as J. Shirmann's Hebrew Liturgical Poetry and Christian Hymnology, JOR 44 (1953), 123–161, are a step in that direction.

[55] Culley's book is an expansion and a reinforcement of an earlier article which leads us to suspect that he knew his conclusions before he examined the psalms. An Approach to the Problem of Oral Tradition, VT 13 (1963), 113–125.

[56] E. Auerbach, Mimesis: The Representation of Reality in Western Literature, trans. by W. Trask, 1957, chapter one.

difference between Hebrew and Indo-European languages may be even more complex than even Auerbach, the greatest comparativist of our age, realizes[57]. Yet Culley carries over Parry's entire argument to Hebrew poetry, and expects that Parry's principles should play themselves out there as well. The fact that there still is a looming question among comparativists as to whether or not Serbocroatian literature may be compared to Greek literature, let alone the comparison of Greek to Hebrew, does not trouble Culley in the least[58]. Culley does not function convincingly when engaged in the comparative task. Rather, we believe that the whole study of formula must be adapted to new primary requirements of the poetry to which it is applied.

While he may think otherwise, Culley has failed at every step to show that there is oral verse-making in the biblical psalms[59]. Yet formulaic phrases and words, though exceedingly limited, are present in the psalms. In what is a circular argument, Culley uses formulas to prove the presence of oral tradition in the biblical psalms, and at the same time says that oral tradition proves the presence of the formulas. The oral aspect, for him, is really more important than the formula.

4. *Summary*

We have found from our historical survey that the formula is present, albeit to a limited extent, in the biblical psalms. But the existence of the formula has not been proven to be the result of oral tradition or traditional diction. Culley has lodged a criticism against J. Ross' work in Gaelic poetry which is applicable to himself[60]. Culley says that Ross has studied a now dead tradition of oral composition, namely Gaelic poetry. Thus there is no way to determine how that poetry was created. But certainly, so is Culley's examination of Old Testament poetry a study of a now dead tradition: he cannot, therefore, prove the formula to be the result of oral verse-making, even though they are to some extent present in the psalms.

---

[57] See the facinating account by J. Barr, The Semantics of Biblical Language, 1961, 21–45, and his criticism therein of T. Boman, Hebrew Thought Compared with Greek, trans. by J. Moreau, 1960.

[58] A. Lesky, Die homerische Frage, in his: Geschichte der griechischen Literatur, 1958, 49–58. Also available in English translation, A History of Greek Literature, trans. by J. Willis and C. de Heer, 1966.

[59] Culley, Oral Formulaic Language, 116, says that his work proves the theory of a common heritage of established phraseology for A.R. Johnson, Sacral Kingship in Ancient Israel, 1955, 90 note 6. But it does not.

[60] Culley, Oral Formulaic Language, 20. See J. Ross: Formulaic Composition in Gaelic Oral Literature. MP 57 (1959), 1–12.

C. THE DISCOVERY OF WORD PAIRS FROM NORTHWEST SEMITIC STUDIES

We now turn to a different field of scholarship, a mere infant in comparison to Homeric study, but which has yielded remarkably similar observations in our topic of formula criticism. It has done so, however, by examining a different aspect of the Hebrew poetry.

1. H.L. Ginsberg

Early in the 1930's, Oriental scholarship was rewarded with the decipherment of poetic texts from Ugarit, mainly dating from the fourteenth century B.C.[61]. In the area of Hebrew poetic study, the impact of this was not immediately felt, nor has it been yet to its fullest extent. These texts were found to have been composed in a language closely related to biblical Hebrew[62]. Furthermore, it was determined that the Ugaritic poems exhibited parallelism much like the structure of Old Testament verse. But still more important was the recognition of a poetic diction common to both literatures. "Specific 'pairs' of words in fixed parallel relationship were observed to occur in both Ugaritic and Hebrew literature with such frequency and regularity as to preclude the possibility of coincidence, while the differences in age and locale excluded the possibility of direct borrowing."[63] For example, in the lines:

Like a stranger I have become to my *brothers*,
and a foreigner to my *mother's sons*.
מוזר הייתי לאחי ונכרי ילבני אמי

---

[61] See Stanley Gevirtz's little summary in Patterns in the Early Poetry of Israel, 1963, 2ff.

[62] See F.W. Albright, The Old Testament and Canaanite Language and Literature, CBO 7 (1945), 14–18; Two Little Understood Amarna Letters from the Middle Jordan Valley, BASOR 89 (1943), 7f. Albright accepts Ugaritic as a Canaanite dialect. Writers such as A. Goetze, on the other hand, believe that it is non-Canaanitic. Is Ugaritic a Canaanite Dialect?, Language 17 (1941), 127–138. Many scholars are at work comparing the two languages and literatures: M. Pope, El in the Ugaritic Texts, 1955; A. Bea, Der Zahlenspruch im hebräischen und ugaritischen, Biblica 21 (1940), 196–198; Ras Shamra und das Alte Testament, Biblica 19 (1938), 435–453; Archäologisches und Religionsgeschichtliches aus Ugarit-Ras Shamra, Biblica 20 (1939), 436–453; G. Young, Ugaritic Prosody, JNESt 9 (1950), 124–133; The Present Status of Ugaritic Studies, JKLF 2 (1953), 125–145.

[63] Gevirtz, Patterns in the Early Poetry of Israel, 3.

the pair, "brother/mother's son", ("בני אם/אח") recurs both in Hebrew and in Ugaritic poetry (Psalms 50_{20} $69_{9(8)}$; UM 49 VI 10–11 (14–15); UM Krt 8–9)[64]. (Here and in all other cases, we will list the singular of the words in pair to save space and to establish conformity.)

From results gleaned independently in Classical research, we have said that in the case of Homeric literature a traditional diction of repeatable formulas (words, phrases, lines) was developed for all poets to use. So it seems that in the case of these conventionally fixed pairs of words there was a group of parallel terms from which poets might draw much like the repeated phrases of which Parry and Lord spoke. As we shall later see, some believe that the fixed pair was a device of oral composition equivalent to the formula of the Greek poets. H. L. Ginsberg was the first to note the presence of the word pairs in both Ugaritic and Hebrew texts[65]. Ginsberg suggested that the occurrence of these fixed pairs of words was a common tradition to both cultures; this "stock-in-trade" of the poets he took to represent a stereotyped poetic idiom in both dialects[66].

2. *Umberto Cassuto and Moshe Held*

The task of comparing the pairs of words found first in Ugaritic poetry and then in Hebrew was left to U. (Moshe David) Cassuto and his student M. Held[67]. Together they located some forty word pairs in Ugaritic and Hebrew[68]. And scholars following in their footsteps have

---

[64] On "brother/mother's son", see U. Cassuto, The Seven Wives of King Keret, BASOR 119 (1950), 18 note 1.

[65] H. L. Ginsberg, Rebellion and Death of Ba'lu, Orientalia 5 (1936), 171–172.

[66] The idea of a "stock-in-trade" has been used in the literature. See, for example, A. Guillaume, who speaks of "parallel usages which emanate from the common stock of Hebrew phrase and idiom". Studies in the Book of Job with a New Translation, J. MacDonald ed., 1968, 15.

[67] U. Cassuto, Biblical Literature and Canaanite Literature, Tarbiz 13 (1942), 197–212 (in Hebrew); Biblical Literature and Canaanite Literature (Conclusion), Tarbiz 14 (1942), 1–10 (in Hebrew); Word Pairs in Hebrew and Ugaritic, Leshonenu 15 (1947), 97–102 (in Hebrew); his major work on the subject is The Goddess Anath, trans. by I. Abrahams, 1971 (1953). By M. Held: Studies in Ugaritic Lexicography and Poetic Style, Ph. D. Dissertation, Baltimore, 1957; Still More Word Pairs in the Poetry and the Prose of Ugarit, Leshonenu 18 (1953), 144–160 (in Hebrew).

[68] Cassuto, The Goddess Anath, 25–32. In: The Seven Wives of King Keret, 18 note 1, Cassuto reports that they had found some forty word pairs at that time. And M. Held in Still More Word Pairs in the Poetry and the Prose of Ugarit, 145, makes the same statement.

found many more pairs[69]. Their objective in finding pairs of words in Ugaritic and Hebrew was to show that "despite the differences of their age, locale, and stage of linguistic development", the literatures were not two distinct entities, "but merely represented two branches of a common, Syro-Palestinian tradition"[70]. The scholars seem to have been unaware of the work in Classical studies which we have reviewed, and hence did not carry their discussion over into the subject of Homeric formula[71].

3. Stanley Gevirtz

S. Gevirtz was the first Old Testament scholar to realize the importance of the discovery of word pairs in Ugaritic and Hebrew as an aid to illuminating passages[72]. Gevirtz also recognized in these pairs of words a principle of poetic tradition[73], much like the formulaic phrases which Parry, Lord, and Culley saw as traditional. His small but incisive book, *Patterns in the Early Poetry of Israel*, is an attempt, therefore, at showing how the isolation of word pairs may help in understanding the poetry.

We are not so much interested in the superb individual studies of poetic passages in his book, as we are in his introductory comments and methodology. Nor does our study allow us to be as concerned as he in the Ugaritic-Hebrew relationship[74]. We are more interested in the thinking behind his attempt to use his interpretation of Hebrew poetic diction as a literary critical tool.

The work of Gevirtz predates that of Culley. Also, Gevirtz admits of little familiarity with Parry and Lord[75]. But he prefaces his individual studies of select poems with the following observations on the poet's craft, highly reminiscent of the Homerists.

In antiquity, says Gevirtz, each poet composed verse based upon the examples of a long line of poets before him. Each new versemaker was only the most recent in the line of poets, and he followed the craft

---

[69] R. G. Boling has located about one hundred word pairs in: "Synonymous" Parallelism in the Psalms, JSSt 5 (1960), 223.

[70] Gevirtz, Patterns in the Early Poetry of Israel, 3.

[71] C. Gordon, Ugaritic Textbook, 1965, 108–120 or chapters 13.1–14.4. His work, however, offers little new information.

[72] Other scholars have touched upon it: F. W. Albright, Some Oriental Glosses on the Homeric Problem, 162. He believes that the Ugaritic epics are from oral composition.

[73] Gevirtz, Patterns in the Early Poetry of Israel, 4.

[74] His research on the word pair in Ugaritic and Hebrew may also be seen in: The Ugaritic Parallel to Jeremiah 8 23, JNESt 20 (1961), 41–46, especially 43–45.

[75] Gevirtz, Patterns in the Early Poetry of Israel, 5.

of his predecessors. Gevirtz remarks, "It is not the strikingly original, but the meaningful manipulation of the long familiar which constituted the apex of poetic tradition."[76] In this he sounds very much like Parry.

Gevirtz notes the various types of parallelism found in Hebrew poetry, and made famous with the work of R. Lowth[77]. He points out that each of the types of parallelism have been used in classifying the poetry by viewing entire lines, distichs, and hemistichs. The verse

Does not calamity befall the unrighteous,
and disaster the workers of iniquity? (Job 31₃)
הלא איד לעול ונכר לפעלי און

was classified by Lowth and later scholarship as being synonymous because the entire hemistichs were synonymous. It is Gevirtz's contention, however, that we must begin to look beyond whole lines and phrases and see the component parts of a given verse. In the above example, the hemistichs are synonymous only because the word pairs "calamity/disaster" ("נכר/איד") and "unrighteous/worker of iniquity" ("פלעי און/על" see Job # 135 in Appendix) are synonymous. It is the conclusion of Gevirtz, therefore, that the word pairs are the essential components of the parallelism in both Ugaritic and Hebrew poetry[78]. This conclusion has its implication for the comparative study of Ugaritic and Hebrew literatures. Identical word pairs have been found in both traditions. When a new word pair is located in Ugaritic, it is almost always present in Hebrew. But the amount of Ugaritic literature available is still limited in extent compared to Hebrew. So it is Gevirtz's suggestion that if a word pair is found in Hebrew poetry, but is not found in extant Ugaritic verse, it probably once did exist in Ugaritic. There are many more word pairs in Hebrew because we have more lines of Hebrew verse than we have Ugaritic available to us. As in the previous illustration:

Like a *stranger* I have become to my brothers,
and a *foreigner* to my mother's sons.
מוזר הייתי לאחי ונכר לבוי אמי

The lines contain the word pair "stranger/foreigner" ("נכר/מוזר" Job # 225) which recurs only in Hebrew, not in Ugaritic. But Gevirtz conjectures that the pair would also be found in Ugaritic if more lines were available. In this way, Gevirtz once again affirms, as does Culley,

---

[76] Ibid. 6.

[77] R. Lowth, Isaiah, A New Translation: with a Preliminary Dissertation, 1778, ix.

[78] Gevirtz argues that the word pairs are basic to the poetry, not the phrase. Patterns in the Early Poetry of Israel, 12.

a traditional poetic diction, but for Gevirtz, it resides now within a Syro-Palestinian literature.

Gevirtz poses the question of why creative poets were bound to seemingly trivial clichés of word pairs. Why did master poets resort to word pairs which had been used time and again since their history was recorded? The answer must lie, he believes, in the poet's respect for tradition[79]. And this reliance upon tradition must have come from the need of a period when poetry was still an oral art. Faced with the problem of composing and remembering without writing, poets were forced to rely upon mnemonic devices—a conventional diction with traditional patterns of composition. Armed with a traditional diction of word pairs, after creating one line, the parallel line would come easily to the poet. But this is not to say that new patterns could not be formed by the poet. With his poetic diction—the pairs of words—ready at hand, the poet could adapt to any new situation.

When we reflect upon the results of Homeric scholarship in the area of oral verse-making, Gevirtz's observations sound so familiar that we would do well to return to Parry's insights[80]. To recall, Parry observed fixed phrases in Homeric poetry which represented a fixed traditional diction. These phrases which often were repeated, but were restricted in their position in the line because of Greek meter, were called formulas. These formulas, he argued, were required in a society where men were forced to compose "on their feet", without the aid of writing. Only with such a ready-made diction could a poet create before an audience. So in the Hebrew verse, it appears that it is the repeated word pair which fills the same requirements as the repeated phrase does in Greek literature.

Thus it seems repeated phrases and repeated pairs of words—in two very different literary traditions—function precisely the same way. Repeated words, phrases, and lines in Homer, and repeated words, phrases, and lines in Old Testament poetry differ only insofar as the structural requirements of the poetry differs. While the primary requirement of Greek poetry rests upon meter, the primary requirement of Hebrew poetry is parallelism. The repeated words, phrases, and lines are the materials of the poet with which he fulfills the requirements of the poetry. Hebrew poetry does contain repeated phrases, as Culley has shown, but the presence of the repeated word pair is far more striking and pervasive: as the Greeks used formulaic phrases in metered lines, so the Hebrews used word pairs to produce parallel lines in oral composition.

---

[79] Ibid. 10–11.

[80] Parry, Studies in the Epic Technique of Oral Verse-Making I: Homer and the Homeric Style, 138, and Studies in the Epic Technique of Oral Verse-Making II: The Homeric Language as the Language of an Oral Poetry, 6.

Culley and Gevirtz say as one, though neither allows for the conclusions of the other, that the Old Testament poetry contains formulas: for Culley, repeated phrases, and for Gevirtz, repeated word pairs recur after Parry's definition and so are formulas. Both represent a traditional diction available to the poets composing under the requirements of oral verse-making, as far as these authors are concerned. Both aid the poet in filling out his line or verse, and do so within the structural needs of the poetry. What is more, both types of formulas appear to have been traditional. Both represent large masses of standard tools passed from one poet to the next.

Each literary tradition, Greek or Hebrew, allows for creativity. While the Homeric poet must change his phrases within the limits of the metrical values required, the Hebrew bard may alter the grammatical shape of the word pair at will. But both poets accomplish their task with ease. Creativity, says Gevirtz of the Hebrew poet, is not a modern search for "originality". "Rather, it is the reworking of old themes by means of conventional phraseology, in traditional manner, to reproduce familiar actions uniquely and poetically significant that the poet's genius is to be sought."[81] But so was the same said by Parry regarding the Homeric singer. As the Greek or Hebrew poet combines the traditional diction of phrases or word pairs into a whole, so was he creative.

Culley used formulas to try to prove the oral nature of the biblical psalms. Gevirtz's reason for valuing the formula is not to prove its role in oral verse-making. Nor is he at particular pains to prove that word pairs do recur, for their presence, once attention is called to them, is self-evident. Rather, by pointing to the parallel terms in the Hebrew verse, he hopes to understand better the poetic line: the function of the pairs helps us to understand the poetry.

One example will suffice[82]. In the women's eulogy of Saul and David (I Samuel 18$_7$), the following praise is given the commanders, Saul and David:

Saul has smitten his *thousands*,
and David his *ten thousands*.

הכה שאול באלפו ודוד ברבבתיו

This lyric has been customarily understood as a criticism of Saul's ability as a soldier. By a proper understanding of the use of the word pair "thousand/ten thousand" ("רבבה/אלף") Isaiah # 293; Job # 366), however, Gevirtz is able to show that the increase in the numerical sequence (here "1/10") is but a common method of filling out the parallelism of the line for the ancients. The fixed pair of numerical

[81] Gevirtz, Patterns in the Early Poetry of Israel, 14.
[82] Ibid. 15–24.

increase occurs in both Ugaritic and Hebrew poetry. The verse rings not of insult, but lavish praise for *both* commanders. Gevirtz rightly believes, therefore, that a proper understanding of a parallelism rests upon an understanding of the word pairs involved.

One other innovation is introduced in Gevirtz's use of word pairs, and that is emendation based upon the fixed pair[83]. For instance, in

From the blood of *the slain*,
from the fat of *the heroes*, (II Samuel 1 22)
מדם חללים מחלב גבורים

the word pair "slain/hero" ("גבור/חלל") does not occur elsewhere, and the phrase, "blood of the slain", does not exactly fit the context at hand. But the pair "valiant one/hero" does recur often in the literature (Isaiah 5 22 Jeremiah 48 14 Nahum 2 4). Moreover, the pair better fits the context, and, as is often the case in such formulaic repair work, the words "slain" and "valiant" are not far off in the Hebrew ("חלל" to "חיל"). Emendation to improve parallelism is old in biblical research. But emendation based upon the word pairs is a new and much more convincing technique. The line from II Samuel should therefore read:

From the blood of the valiant,
from the fat of the heroes,
מדם חילים מחלב גבורים

Gevirtz's work is sound, but not without criticism. He fails to prove, as does Culley, that the formula (phrase or word pair) is actually tied to oral verse-making. For him it was only "logical to assume" this. Nevertheless, while he is not alone in the methods he has used[84], he certainly has shown that the word pairs do exist in the poetry, and are useful tools for the scholar. Yet we must add that he fails to see any relationship between the word pair and the phrase which are both repeated in Hebrew poetry. For recognition of this we must turn to the next few sections of our chapter.

4. *Samuel Loewenstamm and Y. Avishur*

Based upon the work begun by Ginsberg and his study of word pairs in Hebrew and Ugaritic poetry, efforts are now under way to create a new catalogue of all word pairs which recur in Hebrew,

---

[83] We cite, for example, ibid. 88–90.

[84] Others have practiced emendation based upon word pairs. G.R. Driver, for one, has been known to correct passages based upon common word pairs: Notes on Isaiah, in: Von Ugarit nach Qumran: Festschrift für Otto Eissfeldt, J. Hempel and L. Rost ed., 1958, 45.

Ugaritic, Akkadian, and Aramaic. The task is being completed by Professor S. Loewenstamm of the Hebrew University with the assistance of his student Y. Avishur[85]. Until the past few years, however, there has been no work done in the area of word pairs and their relationship to many different Near Eastern languages. Loewenstamm himself recognized the importance of the word pairs which were early pointed out in the 1950's. His *Thesaurus of the Language of the Bible* (1957), reveals that he saw the value of Ugaritic-Hebrew comparative studies, especially with regard to Cassuto's efforts in his now classic, *The Goddess Anath*[86]. While this current cataloguing of the word pairs is nearing completion, the publication of a comprehensive lexicon based upon word pairs is some time off. But when such a reference work is made available, the student will quickly be able to see if a particular word pair occurring in say, Hebrew poetry, recurs often among many different literatures, or is simply the only instance wherein that pair so far occurs.

5. *Summary*

So we have seen that scholars working with newly discovered poems from Ugarit have uncovered a principle of Hebrew and Ugaritic poetry which in form and function resembles the formulaic principles of the Homeric epic. But it remained for us to draw attention to the similarity of their conclusions which hitherto has not been perceived. The repeated word pair in Hebrew, as the repeated phrase in Greek, seems to be the parallel tool of the poet's craft. While it has not been proven, the scholars are one in saying that these formulas hail from an oral verse-making society, and have their origin and purpose therein.

We now turn shortly to the first author to recognize the relationship between the Greek and Hebrew formula, and the relationship between the Hebrew repeated phrase and word pair. But before we do so, it will be profitable to compare the views of Culley and Gevirtz.

D. THE DISCOVERY OF REPEATED WORD PAIRS AND PHRASES FROM COMPARATIVE STUDIES

1. *Culley and Gevirtz*

Thus far, we have witnessed the convergence of two different areas of study, Homeric and Ugaritic, and jointly concluded that the Old Testament poetry contains formulaic material. The poetry was said

[85] Personal discussions in June and July, 1971, Jerusalem, Israel.

[86] S. Loewenstamm and J. Blau, eds., Thesaurus of the Language of the Bible, 1957, ix.

to be "formulaic" because in it are found lines repeated word for word, phrase for phrase, often many times over. These repeated words and phrases are characterized by the scholars as a part of a traditional poetic diction employed by poets in a period when oral verse composition was the rule. Be they repeated word pair or phrase, the formulas are seen as a stockpile of useful words or phrases, passed from one generation to the next. By drawing upon this stockpile, poets in any age were assured that their verse would conform to acceptable tradition. As the poet worked among his audiences, the formulas became the tools of his craft.

Scholars agree, then, on a traditional diction stemming from oral verse-making. Within this agreement, however, lies an essential and basic disagreement as to precisely what constitutes the primary formulaic stock-in-trade of Hebrew poets. On the one hand, and growing directly from the work of M. Parry, was R. Culley's attempt at pointing out the formulaic phrases and lines of the biblical psalms, and saying that they were orally created. Because such phrases as

Incline your ear to me (Psalms 31_3 71_2 102_3)
הטה אלי אזנך
Hear my prayer, O Lord (Psalms 54_4 84_9 102_2 143_1)
אלהים שמע תפלתי

repeat, Culley concludes that they are formulas. And however frail his argument, we must agree that, in fact, repeated phrases do occur in the psalms. But Culley was not able to prove that phrases recur because they were created in an oral verse-making society. Nevertheless, he maintains that it is the repeated phrase which is the primary tool of the parallelism of the poetry.

On the other hand, and growing directly from the work of H.L. Ginsberg, S. Gevirtz pointed out fixed pairs of words which repeat in both Hebrew and Ugaritic poetry. Turning to any pericope of poetry, be it prophetic, sapiential, or psalmic, we are immediately struck by the abundance of word pairs which are present. Such common pairs as "dark/light" ("אור/חשך" Job # 10), or "rejoice/glad" ("שיש/שמח" Job # 22) recur thirty times or more in the poetry. Aided then by a suitable lexicon, we shortly find that many word pairs do recur. However, like Culley, Gevirtz was not able to prove that the word pairs are tied to oral verse-making. But opposing Culley, he says that it is the word pairs which are the basis of the poetry.

As to which is the dominant aspect of the Hebrew formula—repeated phrase or word pair—we now must turn. Our decision as to which is the most dominant will be very important for the second half of this study. For it will determine whether we analyze the formulaic phrase or word pair.

2. *William Whallon*

In but one of a brilliant collection of essays on comparative literature, W. Whallon argues that there is something more basic to Old Testament poetry than parallelism or *Gattungen*. That element is the formula expressed as *both* the repeated word pair and the repeated phrase[87]. The thesis of his essay is that the poets of ancient Israel used a traditional diction, a stock of word pairs and phrases which they repeated at will: so much so, in fact, that Whallon maintains that no passage of Hebrew scripture may be said to be an original creation of the author in which it is found. The whole of the literature must be assumed to have been traditional at one time. And to prove his thesis, Whallon attacks his subject from the standpoint of oral literature and oral transmission.

The phrase "oral tradition" to most Old Testament scholars implies a study of oral transmission—in our case, how the poetry was passed on. But Whallon is interested in how the poetry was composed in the first place, not how it was transmitted. "Oral tradition" means for him, therefore, that "because they are often repeated, elements of two types (word pairs and phrases) were developed at least in part without the aid of writing."[88] As we shall see, this is to be a resounding echo of our past scholars who held the formula to be the product of oral verse-making.

a. Word Pairs. Whallon first considers word pairs. Synonyms in parallel cola, that is, the word pairs, are the mark of an oral style created by formulaic composition. This Hebrew synonymy, he says, was a prosodic device analogous to the Homeric epithet and the Anglo-Saxon kenning. Whallon shows that it is the nature of the word pair which determines the different kinds of parallelism made famous by Lowth. Lowth established that the primary requirement of Hebrew poetry is parallelism between hemistichs and distichs. The parallelism is, comparatively, analogous to Homeric meter, Old English alliteration, and Old French assonance.

Now there is an advantage to classifying different kinds of parallelism (or meter, or assonance, etc.), and it is that we become acutely conscious of rarities which occur in the literature. But there is an even greater disadvantage to classification, and that is we are stunned into regarding as regular what is, in fact, irregular. For instance, synthetic parallelism is really not parallelism at all: the sense-rhythm is less evident in synthetic verse than in, say, antithetic parallelism.

---

[87] W. Whallon, Formula, Character, and Context, 138–172.

[88] Ibid. 138.

Therefore, Whallon sees three vitiating limitations on Lowth's classification of parallelism[89]. First, there are "no objective criteria which once and for all define with respect to each other a usefully small number of different kinds of parallelism". Since parallelism in Hebrew verse is determined from meaning, rather than sound, their number is highly questionable. Moreover, all terms for types of parallelism—synthetic, synonymous, emblematic, etc.—will not suffice to answer all instances in the poetry; the criteria are ambiguous at the least.

Second, Whallon judges that "the classification does not observe that certain distichs, though different in kinds of parallelism they exhibit, are nevertheless very much alike in word pairs"[90]. The parallelism of the distich derives from the balance of the word pairs. Or to put it another way, "the synonymy of the hemistichs hangs on the synonymy of the word pairs". (So, of course, the antithesis of the hemistichs is an aftermath of the antithesis of the word pairs.) There can be, therefore, no parallelism without a word pair. Hence, the so-called synthetic parallelism is not parallelism at all for it lacks a word pair. The word pairs discipline the longer clauses or phrases into alignment. The word pairs often show similarities between verses that differ in their kinds of parallelism. Thus an organization of verses based upon their affinity of word pairs and not kinds of parallelism is more meaningful.

And third, Whallon holds that "there is no road from the classification (of Lowth's parallelism) to any further theory concerning the origin of the poetry". He recommends, therefore, that we abandon the categories of parallelism[91]. That parallelism exists, is certainly not the issue; that the categories of parallelism lead us astray, is[92]. This release from the form-critical approach to parallelism allows us to look at the word pairs without worrying about types. But even more important, we gain a deeper understanding of the nature of the poetry because our attention is primarily turned from the end products or large components (the parallelism) toward the basic materials or small components (the word pairs). In seeking to understand the origin and nature of the poetry, it is more important for us to be interested in the word pairs which satisfy the primary requirement of Hebrew poetry than even that primary requirement itself.

Next, with regard to word pairs, Whallon undertakes to describe their purpose. Gevirtz believes that it is the word pair's purpose to aid

---

[89] Ibid. 142. [90] Ibid. 143. [91] Ibid. 168.

[92] While Gevirtz affirms word pairs, he fails to see that they may be divorced from Lowth's classification of parallelism, and so he uses the terminology of parallelism. For example, Gevirtz, Patterns in the Early Poetry of Israel, 24 note 26.

the memory of the poet[93]. In contrast to him, Whallon suggests that their purpose lies in the fact that "word pairs assisted composition rather than memory"[94]. Following Parry's direction with the repeated phrase, Whallon says that repeated word pairs, along with repeated phrases, belonged to a fund of formulas which were national property for poetasters to use. Many word pairs resulted from their everyday character and natural association with each other: these were created by the poets independently and spontaneously. Yet on the other hand, there are a number of words in pairs whose relationship is unknown to us. These pairs are so rare in their relationship suggesting each other that they must have come from common practice at one time. But the pairs do have their purpose in assisting in the creation of the parallelism.

Why then was parallelism established as a requirement of the poetry? Whallon mentions three possible reasons, but elects only one. First, parallelism might have been introduced into the poetry for antiphonal singing by alternating choirs. But responsory hymns (cf. Psalm 136) are few[95]. Second, he suggests that parallelism might have been introduced as an aid to memory for the audience. But as he shows, parallelism does not help us remember how distichs are arranged. The addition of a second hemistich does not insure the survival of the first. And we are not able to recollect the whole of a parallelism more easily than either half alone. In fact, Whallon believes that poets remembered the lines they composed no more easily than if they made them anew at each performance. No, memory is not the answer. It is not the marshalling of distichs which will save the hemistich from oblivion.

These merits of parallelism are all subordinate to its true cause, and that is to satisfy a desire for high style on the part of the poets. For Whallon, this can be the only logical conclusion as to the purpose of the parallelism if we consider, once again, the components (word pairs) of the parallelism[96].

In answering the question of how word pairs came to be established in the first place, Whallon points to the difference between prose and poetry. Related words recur frequently in both, but as we shall later see, in the poetry the key terms stand at an even distance from each

---

[93] Ibid. 10–11.

[94] Whallon, Formula, Character, and Context, 144.

[95] But against his views on antiphonal singing, see I. Slotki who shows the importance of the antiphonal verse: Antiphony in Ancient Hebrew Poetry, JQR 26 (1935–1936), 199–219.

[96] Whallon, Formula, Character, and Context, 148. See also Culley, Oral Formulaic Language in the Biblical Psalms, 16.

other, while in the prose, related words are usually adjacent to each other. In Job 12$_{12}$, for example,

> *Wisdom* is with the aged,
> and *understanding* in the length of days,
> בישישים חכמה וארך ימים תבונה

the word pair "wisdom/understanding" ("תבונה/חכמה" Job # 146) occurs evenly divided in distance. The same words, however, here found in fixed pair, recur in the prose with the words associated adjacently (I Kings 4$_{29}$(5$_{9}$)):

> And God gave Solomon *wisdom and understanding* beyond measure.
> ויתן אלהים חכמה לשלמה ותבונה הרבה מאד

The elements used in series in the prose meet no requirement for their position, while the word pairs used in the poetry meet a crucial requirement—for the poetry consisted of parallelism. So Whallon concludes that the poetry influenced the prose, and not vice versa: the prose did not help to create the poetry.

And as parallelism did little to aid the memory of the audience, so word pairs did little to aid the memory of the poet. Whallon believes that it was no more easy for the poet to remember a line than to compose it anew at each performance[97]. For word pairs became formulaic, and so, frequent, because they assisted the poet in *composing* the parallelism. This body of fixed pairs was a traditional diction created by oral poets as an aid in oral composition. Given a hemistich (that is, an idea), the word pair helped the poet express his idea a second time a bit differently and perhaps more magnificently. The main difficulty for the Hebrew poet was producing parallel cola, and so he resorted to fixed pairs, "synonymous formulas". Thus even the most complicated pairs seem to have been composed with little difficulty. As the poet needed to fulfill ornately the requirements of the parallelism, he resorted to word pairs.

To summarize: Whallon says that parallelism was developed not for antiphonal singing by opposed choirs, nor as an aid to memory for the audiences, but only for its own impressive elegance. The word pairs of the poetry were established not from the influence of the prose convention, nor as an aid to the memory of the poet, but to assist him in creating the parallelism, and to do it artistically.

---

[97] Oppositely, as we have said, Gevirtz believes the word pairs were created to aid the memory of the poet and the audience. Patterns in the Early Poetry of Israel, 10–11.

In his third section dealing with word pairs, Whallon notes that word pairs raise the question of economy[98]. By this he means a number of things. First, often passages in the poetry have many words paired together meaning the same thing. And while translators are at fault in translating a number of similar words interchangeably, these strings of words do not refute the theory of a traditional diction. Where usually one pair is good enough to handle a particular description, poets often seem to enjoy using more pairs for impressiveness. In Isaiah 24 2 (# 238), to cite an example, we find the word pairs "people-priest / slave-master / maid-mistress / buyer-seller / lender-borrower / creditor-debtor." Or in Isaiah 41 19, the word pairs are "cedar/acacia / myrtle/olive / cypress/ plane/pine." The economy of using one word pair is, in these and other instances, broken.

But the violation of poetic economy in Hebrew verse may occur in another way. The poets may move from a standard word pair to a variation of one of its members. The word pair "poor/needy" ("עני/אביון" Job # 278) is commonplace. Yet careful examination of the poetry reveals that one member may be substituted for another synonym such as "דל". And "iniquity/sin" ("פשע/עון" Job # 93) is another very common word pair. Yet the pair recurs time and again with various synonyms for "sin" or "iniquity" such as "חטא, רע, עון, אשם." The author here violates the standard economy of the word pair.

Whallon observes that this violation of economy is done consciously by the poet and for a purpose. Poets violate their normal economy (the use of only one word pair for an idea) in order to retain and repolish words which would otherwise die from disuse. These long passages, therefore, constitute a safeguard for a great number of synonyms in the poetic vocabulary of the people. And since Old Testament parallelism depends upon sense alone and not sound, Hebrew poets had far more freedom when choosing terms to suit their verse than, say, Old French poets who were restricted by the requirements of assonance.

In his fourth section on word pairs, Whallon argues that they may have been traditional. In this he sounds much like Gevirtz. And since the Old Testament formula can occur anywhere in the poetry where the meaning is right—sounds and meter being of little importance—single word pairs are found more often than any of the comparative analogues of Homeric, Old English, or Old French poetry.

Whallon believes that Hebrew poetic diction was traditional. The diction was formulaic because it was developed by oral poets who composed on the instant. Literary poets would not have had the *incentive* to create such a diction. And since Hebrew formulaic poetic diction

---

[98] Whallon, Formula, Character, and Context, 154.

is so pervasive in the literature, there must have been many more poets than we now know about. A few poets would not have expressed themselves in the same manner.

Culley has said that the word pairs come from oral verse-making alone, and are not the work of literate poets. Whallon points out, however, that we cannot be sure Hebrew poetic diction, after it developed as a national property, was not also used by literates. We cannot, for instance, assert that Job was in every sense, or not in any sense, made up of oral poems retold from the past. We just cannot be sure that the text was written, oral, or possibly a combination of both. Whallon therefore concludes that when a word pair occurs only once in the poetry, it probably was a commonplace at one time[99].

b. Phrases. Whallon next turns his attention to the formulaic phrase (the titles hemistich and distich having only to do with length)[100]. Using the same argument against form criticism which he employed against Lowth's parallelism, he turns to Gunkel's *Gattungen*. Gunkel classified passages from the biblical psalms categories[101]. Taking into account cult worship in Mesopotamia and Egypt, Gunkel sought to define a "situation in life" for each category. But like Lowth's categorizing of parallelism, Gunkel's categorizing of *Gattungen* too had disadvantages: he postulated the existence of a uniform culture; he associated the literature we possess with the religious life of the community; and he forced the psalms to be liturgical from the first, and the source of all *Gattungen*. With these thoughts in mind, Whallon levels the same three criticisms against the form criticism of Gunkel as he used on the parallelism of Lowth[102].

First, there are no objective criteria which, once and for all, define with respect to each other, a usefully small number of different *Gattungen*. The classification of a poem can seldom be made with certainty, and we cannot break up books into meaningful units. Second, Gunkel's classification does not observe that certain poems or passages, though different in the *Gattungen* to which they may be assigned, have nevertheless a hemistich or distich in common. Once again, Whallon calls us to look at the components (the repeated phrase) and not the composite (the *Gattung*). And third, there is no road from the classification to any further theory concerning the origin of the poetry. The whole (the *Gattung*) has once again, as in the case of the parallelism,

[99] Likewise, Gevirtz says that a word pair found only in Hebrew poetry was probably once a commonplace in both Hebrew and Ugaritic verse. Patterns in the Early Poetry of Israel, 8.

[100] Whallon, Formula, Character, and Context, 161 ff.

[101] H. Gunkel and J. Begrich, Einleitung in die Psalmen: Die Gattungen der religiösen Lyrik Israels, 1928.

[102] Whallon, Formula, Character, and Context, 162.

prevented us from getting at the components (repeated phrases) as in the case of the word pairs. The form criticism of Gunkel has prevented us from getting at the origin of the poetry.

Hemistichs and distichs recur as formulas, just as word pairs do. Whallon reasons that this is the case because Old Testament poetry is paratactic to a high degree. The verse tends to repeat itself in full assertions, that is to say, complete statements without much unity in between. As we have noted, enjambement is rare in the poetry. This discontinuity of the lines in itself would cause suspicion that distichs and hemistichs would repeat themselves because they can be so completely removed from one setting and placed in another. And if the shorter elements (the word pairs) of the poetry are repeated, it is likely that so will be the larger elements (hemistichs and distichs)[103].

Whallon suggests criteria for selecting formulas above and beyond the fact that they repeat themselves, and above and beyond the grammatical changes allowed by Culley. For Whallon, the phrases must be substantial and impressive. They must recur in more than one book. Verses or half verses are allowed if found in different passages. Small variations in the passages are disregarded.

They conceive mischief and bring forth vanity (Isaiah 59_4 Job 15_{35} Job # 30)

הרו עמל והוליד און

He turns the wilderness into standing water;
and the dry ground into water springs (Isaiah 41_{18} Psalm 107_{35} Job # 279; 404; Isaiah # 490)

ישם מדבר לאגם מים וארץ ציה למצאי מים

Phrases and lines such as these would be acceptable to Whallon because they recur in more than one text and are certainly substantial.

Whallon concludes, therefore, that the Old Testament poetry has formulaic phrases and word pairs. The phrases transcend in importance the passages of special nature (the *Gattungen*), and the word pairs transcend in importance the lines of special nature (the parallelisms). And both repeat anywhere. While the phenomena of parallelism surely exist in the verse, the categories of parallelism and *Gattung* should be abandoned since they prevent us from seeing the essence of the poetry and its component parts.

Hemistichs and distichs, like word pairs, may all have been traditional. That a phrase or word pair is repeated, however, cannot show us which is the original phrase or word pair: we cannot show dependency with recurring formulas. Whallon points out that since we

---

103 Ibid. 163.

cannot prove that a formula which recurs is earlier in one place than another, then we cannot use such phrases to date a passage or book. Rather, neither instance of a repeated phrase or word pair need have been taken one from the other, if a traditional, stereotyped diction is maintained. Since the phrase or word pair is within the stock-in-trade of poets, it could be used at any time, the poet perhaps being unaware of any previous uses[104].

Whallon concludes by saying that these long (phrases) and short (word pairs) formulas must have come from an oral period when all poets aimed at the finest poetry possible created from all available diction. Priest, prophet, and wise man all drew upon the same tradition of word pairs and phrases. It is even possible, he thinks, that repeated word pairs and phrases had a source which was never written down. The introduction of categories of parallelism and *Gattungen* have led us away from this traditional treasury of formulas.

Because poetic diction could not have become so commonplace without much more material than we now have, distichs which do not recur were probably once commonplace. A verse found in Isaiah, for example, is to be considered Isaianic only because it was found in Isaiah. But we must doubt that it was first created for Isaiah by the author. No element of Old Testament poetry is more likely than not to have been created for the passage in which it now appears.

Given Parry's work on the Homeric formula, Whallon's advances are superb and astonishing. Nevertheless, his chapter is not without a number of criticisms which we shall deal with later. Let it suffice here only to say that his principle argument, namely, that no element of the poetry was created for the passage in which it now appears, is extreme to say the least. While such caution in viewing a phrase of word pair is commendable, it assumes that Old Testament poets, like Homeric poets, spoke *entirely* in formulas. Such cannot be the case if we are to allow poets their due as creative artists and individualists. And that his theory completely overlooks the pairs which do not repeat, will be shown later.

3. Summary

In this section, we have witnessed the convergence of hitherto unrelated material. The work of Parry and Lord which led to Culley's research in the repeated phrases was united with the word pair of Ginsberg, Cassuto, and Gevirtz. Both were seen to be but one aspect of a single phenomenon, the Hebrew poetic formula.

---

[104] Culley claims that because formulas are timeless, they cannot be used to date the passage in which they are found.

Whallon has maintained, as have those considered before him, that the formula hails from an oral verse-making society. But in this he is not so sure as were Culley and Gevirtz. Yet in the final analysis, the relationship between oral verse-making and the formula in Hebrew poetry remains unestablished.

E. CONCLUSION AND ANTICIPATION

We have now finished tracing the short but exciting history of formula criticism from its varied roots in Homeric, Ugaritic, and comparative studies. In the first case, we have seen how the formulaic phrase was noted by Parry and Lord in Homer and in other oral literature. Living oral literatures were examined for their own characteristics, and these in turn located in the Iliad and the Odyssey. This same methodology was then used by an Old Testament scholar, Robert Culley, with the result that repeated phrases were located in the biblical psalms. Here it was argued that the repeated phrase was the major device of Hebrew composition, and that these repeated phrases were the result of oral verse-making. But neither one of these theories was proven to our satisfaction.

In this second case of Ugaritic studies, in the work of Ginsberg and Gevirtz, we were introduced to the phenomenon of word pairs along with some compelling evidence that they were in fact the major device of Hebrew poetic composition. It was also assumed, but not in any way proven, that the word pairs come from an oral verse-making atmosphere.

Finally, in the hands of a skilled comparativist, W. Whallon, we considered both the formulaic phrase and word pair as but two aspects of one phenomenon in the poetry. But the word pair was found to be far more dominant, pervasive, and basic to the verse. That both come from oral verse-making was again proposed, but not in any way proven.

In the following chapters, our task will be to weigh with textual examinations the assertions of the above scholarship in the field of formula criticism. And in dealing with the major observations and theories of the scholars, our test in every case will be the results which we have gathered from our examination of whole poetic texts. The very fact that we shall raise issue with the statements of other writers will be the result of our application of those statements to the poetic texts. The issues raised at each point will indicate the places at which our results were at odds with the hypotheses. But in all cases, our research shall yield our results, and not vice versa. For example, we shall ask whether or not the word pair is actually the dominating element of the poetry; and we shall tackle the problem of whether or not the formula stems from an oral verse-making society. It has been said throughout this chapter that the formulas have their locus in a traditional diction made to assist the poet in creating the verse. But this actually has never been proven. And we must test the theory that the formulas recur only in certain types of poetry. Our immediate focus, however, will fall upon the question as to whether or not the word pair or the phrase is the dominant element of the poetry.

Chapter II

The Nature and Occurrence of Word Pairs

A. INTRODUCTION

It now remains for us to compare the results of our own research with the theories we have discussed. Our aim is to place the methodology of formula criticism in proper perspective. We seek to discuss the foregoing theories of the scholars by applying them to biblical texts, and, if found valid, to action. We have summarized the various ideas in the field of formula in Chapter I with only minimal criticism. Now we shall use our own research to answer these theories of the writers in a number of ways, sometimes agreeing, sometimes disagreeing with them. But however qualified, we shall always seek to ascertain the value and usefulness of the formula critical method.

Of the studies on formula described in Chapter I, with the exception of that by S. Gevirtz, all constitute expositional proofs of the presence of formulas in the literature, or the influence of oral verse-making on the formula. The theories on formula stem from logic and the results obtained in related fields of research, however, and none of the ideas has been expressed in terms of Hebrew texts as a whole. To accomplish their task, the scholars have been at liberty to pick and choose formulas from anywhere in the Old Testament poetry to prove a point here or there in their arguments. We shall not enjoy that luxury. Rather, we shall exhaust whole individual texts of their word pairs, and then evaluate the theories in light of our results. It is not difficult, as Whallon and Gevirtz have shown, to select passages and word pairs to illustrate an aspect of their argument. It is quite another matter to assemble all word pairs and phrases in a given poem and evaluate them in their entirety. Gevirtz, for example, deals with about one hundred occurrences of word pairs. We have listed and examined thousands. We wish, in other words, to see what the practicalities of cataloguing word pairs tell us about composition, authorship, and traditional diction. We have no interest in field studies of living oral verse-making be they taken from the South Seas or the Ukraine. Theories are fine to propose and thereon cite a few supporting examples. But do the theories hold up under the scrutiny of many thousands of examples? This, then, will be our approach to the ideas on formula which have thus far been proposed.

Four Old Testament texts have been selected for examination: Isaiah, because it is the longest and best of the poetic prophecy; Lamentations, for its peculiar poetic structure in four out of five poems; Ruth, because it is the best short story with, what some believe, are indications of a poetic origin and transmission; and Job, since it is the longest and most coherent example of the wisdom literature. Each text has been exhausted of its word pairs, and our results appear in the Appendix lists. Since these lists represent the bulk of our investigation and the basis of our results, they need to be taken very seriously.

The use of these four biblical texts will cause us to come into direct contact with a few giants of scholarship who have dealt extensively with the books in question: N. Gottwald on Lamentations, R. Gordis and A. Guillaume on Job, and J. Myers on Ruth. But by and large, we shall not mention most of the work which has been done on these texts, unless it directly relates to our own observations.

B. THE WORD PAIRS AS THE DOMINATING ELEMENT OF FORMULAIC HEBREW POETRY

That biblical Hebrew poetry contains formulaic elements is undeniable. An examination of the Appendix lists reveals that there are both repeated phrases and word pairs in each of the four texts. In prophecy, in wisdom literature, in poetry, yes, even in what is often printed as prose in the Hebrew texts, we find repeated phrases and word pairs[1]. Only which is the dominating formulaic element of the poetry—phrase or word pair—is here to be considered.

R. Culley has been able to show that there are repeated phrases in the biblical psalms, and as a result, maintains that these constitute the main element in the oral technique of Hebrew poetry, and are for him the only true formula[2]. Moreover, he is aware of some of the earlier essays of W. Whallon, as well as the work of S. Gevirtz, who together proclaim the word pair, and not the repeated phrase, to be the major device of Hebrew poetic composition[3]. Culley, therefore, sets himself against Gevirtz and Whallon as defender of the repeated phrase. Both sides voice their opinions with discernible vigor: Gevirtz holds that

[1] Our Hebrew text is Biblia Hebraica, R. Kittel, ed., 1962, R. Kittel – Isaiah; G. Beer – Job; Th. Robinson – Lamentations and Ruth.

[2] Culley, Oral Formulaic Language in the Biblical Psalms, 1967, 118.

[3] Whallon wrote two early articles which were altered somewhat for the publication of his book: Formula, Character, and Context: Studies in Homeric, Old English, and Old Testament Poetry, 1969. The two articles are: Formulaic Poetry in the Old Testament, CL 15 (1963), 1–14, and Old Testament Poetry and Homeric Epic, CL 18 (1966), 113–131.

the repeated word pair is the major device of Hebrew poetry, Culley claims it to be the repeated phrase, and Whallon, in his later work, defends both the repeated phrase and the word pair.

Culley speaks at length about word pairs. He does not doubt that the phenomenon of fixed pairs goes back to an early time when oral composition likely existed. And he believes that fixed pairs appear to have been a convention, and that conventional language plays a part in oral composition. In addition, the need to produce parallel cola is central to the Hebrew poets, so that the poet requires the word pair device to assist him.

But on the other hand, Culley claims on the basis of research, that repeated phrases have turned up in the biblical psalms, and that these are equivalent to the formulas in other extrabiblical poetic traditions. Their presence, as we have also said, cannot be doubted. Therefore, Culley concludes, the major device in Hebrew oral composition, as in other literatures, is the formulaic phrase, and not the word pair.

In other words, Culley's argument rests upon the assumption that since all other oral languages have formulaic phrases, so should the formulaic phrase likewise be the major device in Hebrew oral literature. But his assumption is based upon research in only a few oral verse-making societies, none of which are in the Near East[4]. And the argument seems to us to be circular: formulas are used to prove oral verse-making in the psalms (which alone they do not); and oral verse-making in other literatures is used to provide the reason for the appearance of formulas in the psalms[5]. Yet once again, as we have noted in Chapter I, Culley has failed to look comparatively at his evidence from other literatures and peoples, and has tried to force their devices and techniques onto the Hebrew poet. He has not allowed the Hebrew poet his due. Nevertheless, his argument does not end here.

Second, Culley argues that Hebrew poetic structure does not suggest that the poet would favor repeated fixed pairs of words over repeated phrases as the major device of composition. The freedom of meter in the Hebrew poetry does not negate the use of phrase. But in so saying, Culley again forces his own theories upon the literature. While both the phrase and the word pair are used in the poetry, Culley cares little about which of the two predominates. And it is no concern of his as to which tool (word pair or phrase) satisfies the primary

---

4 To name them: Homeric, Anglo-Saxon, Middle English, Gaelic, the Todas of South India, and Russian.

5 Even the Septuagint is difficult to compare to the Hebrew poetry for the Greek translation required radical alteration of the Hebrew parallelism. See the poetic form changes in G. Gerleman, Studies in the Septuagint, LUÅ NS Aud. I, 52,3 (1956), 18.

requirement of the poetry (the parallelism). Yet a simple check of the quantity of repeated word pairs and phrases in Isaiah, for example, tells us that there are well over 500 repeated word pairs in the text, and just 80 repeated phrases in the text. And in Job, there are 386 pairs which repeat in the text and elsewhere, and just 57 phrases which repeat. Likewise, we would guess that repeated word pairs outnumber repeated phrases 50 : 1 in the biblical psalms or any other Hebrew poetry. There are simply far more repeated word pairs than there are repeated phrases. As Whallon has observed, it is the word pairs which are the very basis of the parallelism, and it is the word pairs which are so easily and quickly made because of the freedom of the poetic line. The parallelism of the line is dependent upon the terms of that line which are themselves held in parallel. There can be no parallelism without a word pair. The repeated phrase rarely contributes to the structural requirements of Hebrew poetry, that is, the parallelism; the word pair always does. In fact, quite often, phrases which recur as runs are found to be merely repeated word pairs with the excess baggage of other words along for the ride.

Finally, Culley argues that not every line of Hebrew poetry has parallelism and hence, word pairs. "So there is something more fundamental to Hebrew poetry than the parallelism, and this probably has to do with meter, which, although we cannot as yet say precisely how, restricts the cola within certain limits."[6] To this we reply: while many lines of Hebrew poetry may lack parallelism and hence, word pairs, many, many more lines lack repeated phrases. Parallelism is the rule, and lines without parallelism are more often than not poor examples of Hebrew poetry. The parallelism as well as the sense of the line is based upon the word pair. But we agree with Culley that there is something more fundamental to the poetry than the parallelism and even the word pairs, and that is the standardized patterns ruling the pairs, which we shall turn to later. Yet we must point out that Culley's entire study has avoided any attempt at examining meter or relating formulaic phrases to meter. We maintain, therefore, that if either word pairs or phrases are the dominating element of the poetry, it is the word pair, not the phrase. What will hold for the word pair will also hold for the phrase, but it is the word pair which clearly dominates and regiments the line into an artistic and intelligible unity. And we shall demonstrate that it is the word pair which may better help us to understand the meter[7].

---

[6] Culley, Oral Formulaic Language, 119.

[7] Culley's criticism of Gevirtz, Whallon, and word pairs suffers from the fact that Whallon published his fullest discussion on the subject of formula after Culley's work was completed. Culley knew only about Whallon's first article: Formulaic

C. THE NATURE OF THE WORD PAIR

As Whallon has shown, Culley denied, and Gevirtz ignored, repeated phrases and word pairs are simply two aspects of one principle of Hebrew poetry, the formula. What appear to be formulaic phrases may often in reality be word pairs united into phrases. For example:

GOD looked up to *the heavens*;
THE LORD saw *on high*
צפה אלהים לשמימה ראה יהוה מרומה

if found repeated as two phrases, is no more than two hemistichs with three word pairs. The word pairs often rule the phrases and bring them into line. We have just mentioned, however, that word pairs are by far the dominating device of the two. And while we have encountered many repeated phrases in our research (see Appendix lists), they are infrequent in comparison to word pairs. Therefore, it will be the word pair we are led to study, not the repeated phrase. But before we proceed with an analysis of word pairs, it is best to clarify our terminology.

The terminology in the above historical survey of formula criticism has been confusing. Culley terms the repeated phrase a formula; Gevirtz calls the repeated word pair a formula; and Whallon deals with repeated word pairs and repeated hemistichs and distichs, both of which he calls formulas. We shall try to simplify matters by saying that a word pair or phrase is a formula if it is repeated. (The titles hemistich and distich, cola and line, have only to do with the length of the phrase or position of the word pair.) The key to the formula is its necessary repetition.

It must be noted, however, that in this classification of formulas, there is an essential and fundamental difference regarding the word pair and the phrase, hitherto unseen. This difference lies hidden and must be recognized, but not allowed in our definition of formulas. The difference is that a word pair need not be repeated to be discovered in the text; a phrase always must be repeated to be discovered. As we shall point out in Chapter V, Lowth, who was the first formally to note the word pair, did not himself require that they be repeated to be identified[8].

Poetry in the Old Testament, and not about the second: Old Testament Poetry and Homeric Epic. In these early essays, Whallon concentrated his attention on word pairs and not phrases. But in his latest work (Formula, Character, and Context), as we have seen, he supports both word pairs and phrases as repeated formulas. But as to the question of which is the dominating element of the poetry, the essential difference remains between Culley and Whallon.

[8] R. Lowth, Isaiah, A New Translation: with a Preliminary Dissertation, 1778, ix. See also his: Lectures on the Sacred Poetry of the Hebrews, trans. by G. Gregory, 1829 (1753).

For example, whether or not the verbal word pair "look up/see" ("ראה/צפה" Job # 231, 321) ever recurs elsewhere is of no consequence to the primary fact that it is a word pair in the following line:

God *looked up* to the heavens;
the Lord *saw* on high.
צפה אלהים לשמימה ראה יהוה מרומה

Word pairs may be determined, then, with little degree of speculation. Phrases, however, are a different matter, for if a particular phrase is not repeated elsewhere, though we may have a "feeling" that it was a common expression, we can never be sure whether it was a formula or not. We cannot tell, for instance, whether the following phrases are formulaic (although they are) by seeing them only once:

Spread forth your hand, (Isaiah 1_{15} 19_{8} 25_{11} 65_{2}; Isaiah # 5)
פרשכם כפיכם
Breath of the Lord (Isaiah 11_{2} $40_{7.\ 13}$ 59_{19} 61_{1} 63_{14} Isaiah # 54)
רוח יהוה

Nevertheless, we must require that word pairs, like phrases be repeated to be considered formulaic. In terms of determining a diction, therefore, in texts it will be necessary to require both to repeat, but also to be aware that word pairs can be seen irrespective of repetition. Word pairs are a poetic construction easily recognizable, while phrases by their primary nature are merely a series of words.

All this is by way of saying that we disagree entirely with Whallon who says that "since word pairs are determined in Hebrew verse from meaning, rather than sound, their number is highly questionable"[9]. While fixed pairs are certainly determined by meaning, the pairs stand out very easily in the texts. Proof of this lies in the fact that after all word pairs in each of our texts were listed on note cards, we found, when uniting the repeated ones with the aid of a Hebrew lexicon, that we had failed to note originally less than 2% of 3168 word pairs. We can see a word pair in a line from its association and meaning, repeated or not. Repetition alone makes them formulaic.

We shall define a formula as a repeated phrase, a distich or hemistich in length, or a repeated pair of words fixed in parallel relationship in one or more distichs of poetry. We are singularly interested in the word pair, but to the Hebrew formula in general we have found that we may allow a degree of modification and still permit it to be considered repeated[10]. Grammatical changes in the formula are allowed.

[9] Whallon, Formula, Character, and Context, 147.

[10] M. Parry, Studies in the Epic Technique of Oral Verse-Making II: Homeric Language as the Language of an Oral Poetry, HSCP 43 (1932), 10. In Greek, the formulas are more restricted to the meter.

Hebrew poetry lacks strict metrical regularity. Therefore, an increase or decrease in the number of syllables in a line does not necessarily destroy the poetic structure, nor does it render the formula useless as an aid to composition. The addition or omission of the definite article, final pronominal suffixes and the -ā ending on the imperative and the first person of the imperfect are permissible. Changes of aspect, person, gender, and number are also allowed[11]. When considering formulaic phrases, because of the freedom of the number of syllables in the line, we have found that we may allow the addition of extra words to the phrase; but phrases in general do not concern us. We have found from our research what Culley calls "free substitution" of different classes of words, noun for verb, participle for verb, etc. If, for instance, the two lexical roots of a verbal word pair recur in different classes, we shall include them together as formulaic. As an example, the word pair "to judge/to be righteous" ("צדק/שפט" Isaiah # 36; Job # 95) is included with the word pair "judgment/righteousness" ("צדקה/משפט"). But we have found, of course, that the words in pair are usually of the same class. And certainly we must permit word pairs to reverse themselves in different contexts. "Slay/kill" and "kill/slay" are but two examples of one repeated word pair (cf., Isaiah 31$_{1}$). And in keeping with these changes which are allowed, we have listed, wherever practical, the verbal roots of the word pairs for ease of identification. Finally, we list the pairs in the singular, even if the words occur only in the plural, to save space in our lists, and for the sake of consistency.

These observations on what is permitted and not permitted regarding the Hebrew formula are made based upon the results of our own research. But in addition to the above, a few words need to be said on how the pairs may occur in the poetic line. We have found word pairs to occur internally within hemistichs, and between hemistichs in a line. And they may occur externally between hemistichs of different lines, the hemistichs not necessarily adjacent to one another. We submit the following examples:

Hear, O heavens, and *give ear*, O earth;
for the Lord has spoken: (Isaiah 1$_{2}$; cf. 28$_{23}$)

שמעו שמים והאזיני ארץ כי יהוה דבר

Who among you will *give ear* to this,
who will *hear* for the time to come. (Isaiah 42$_{23}$)

מי בכם יאזין זאת יקשב וישמע לאחור

Hear the word of the Lord,
you rulers of Sodom! (Isaiah 1$_{10}$; cf. 32$_{9}$)

[11] Culley, Oral Formulaic Language, 31. Of course, his rules for repeated phrases also apply to repeated word pairs.

Give ear to the teaching of our God,
you people of Gomorrah!
שמעו דבר יהוה קציני סדם
האזינו תורת אלהינו עם עמרה

Is it by your wisdom that the *hawk* soars,
and spreads his wings toward the south? (Job 39 26-27)
Is it at your command that the *eagle* mounts up
and makes his nest on high?
המבינתך יאבר נץ יפרש כנפו לתימן
אם על פיך יגביה נשר וכי ירים קנו

In the first example, the pair "hear/give ear" ("אזן/שמע" Isaiah # 1) occurs within the hemistich; in the second, the pair occurs within the distich between the hemistichs; the third example pairs the words between two hemistichs of different lines; and the fourth example does the same thing as the third with the pair "hawk/eagle" ("נשר/נץ"), but at a greater distance and between two lines and verses.

Unlike the repeated phrase, the word pair is always shorter than the hemistich, and so, not directly dependent upon the caesura: the word pair may occur in two hemistichs or in two lines. We have found broken chains of word pairs where one word might relate with another even after many hemistichs or lines have intervened. For example, the word pair "daughter/maiden" ("בתולה/בת") in Lamentations 2 10 is separated by a whole line, but is still clearly a word pair:

The elders of the *daughter* of Zion
sit on the ground in silence;
they have cast dust on their heads
and put on sackcloth;
the *maidens* of Jerusalem
have bowed their heads to the ground.
ישבו לארץ ידמו זקני בת ציון
העלו עפר על ראשם חגרו שקים
הורידו לארץ ראשן בתולת ירושלם

(See also Lamentations 2 14, "deceptive/misleading" ("מדוח/תפל").) All variations in a line or in two lines, first hemistich to first hemistich, second to fourth, etc., occur in the literature (cf. Isaiah 57 18).

We have described what we have found so far in examining the biblical texts in terms of quantity and statistics. But we can also speak in terms of quality when we look at the diction of the poetry.

So far as we know, no author dealing with the subject of formula has taken note of the relationship between words found in fixed pairs in the poetry and the same words which are also found as words adjacent to each other in the poetry. Since the use of the formula implies a conscious association of two or more words on the part of the poet, adjacent words also recurring as related pairs need be considered.

The *ox* knows its owner,
and the *ass* its master's crib. (Isaiah 1_{3})
ידע שור קנהו וחמור אבוס בעלין

. . . let the feet of *the ox and the ass*
range free. (Isaiah 32_{20})
משלחי רגל השור והחמור

Here the two words, "ox" and "ass" are found as a word pair ("שור/חמור" Isaiah # 5, Job # 277), and as adjacent words related to one another. (And there are hundreds more of such pairs. See, for example, "distress/anguish" in Job 15_{24}; Job # 191.) It is for this reason, therefore, if for no other, that we must allow words in pair the benefit of the doubt if the pair recurs elsewhere in proven formulaic fashion. If by formula, we mean repetition, then we must allow words, phrases, and lines to recur in more than one way.

Qualitatively, we must also set down a working principle concerning the nearness of repeated word pairs to each other to still be considered formulaic. We cannot, for example, accept a word pair which recurs two or three times within a few verses of each other, but nowhere else. We must doubt the value of such word pairs as "lamb/kid" ("גדי/כבש" Isaiah $11_{6a.\ 6b}$ Isaiah # 110), "fear/dread" ("ערץ/ירא" Isaiah $8_{12.\ 13}$ Isaiah # 155), "be jealous/harass" ("צרר/קנא" Isaiah $11_{13a.\ 13b}$ Isaiah # 228), which recur only within one verse or two, unless they occur elsewhere. In fact, we are even suspicious of pairs which recur as close as a few verses, but are found nowhere else. For example, we question: "terror of the Lord/glory of his majesty" ("גאון/פחד יהוה הדר" Isaiah # 67) in Isaiah $2_{10.\ 19.\ 21}$, because it occurs there only. The repeated pairs must stand at least some distance from each other when they repeat to be acceptable.

Whallon also looks for adequately complex formulas as he examines texts[12]. He establishes his criterion for determining repeated formulas in terms of the whole literature. A phrase or word pair must be repeated for him in more than one book to be acceptable as formulaic[13]. But the use or disuse of a formula within the confines of a given text, as we will show, is a valuable means of determining and establishing a diction for one author or one book. M. Tsevat, for instance, has statistically checked word usages in the biblical psalms alone to determine any unity within, and then compared his psalmic findings with the rest of the

---

[12] Whallon, Formula, Character, and Context, 163–164.

[13] R. Gordis lists many of the full phrases and lines in the book of Job which repeat elsewhere. But we have noted that often these repeated phrases contain recurring word pairs within them. The Book of God and Man: A Study of Job, 1965, 175–189.

poetry as a whole[14]. Therefore, we believe the study of the formula in any one book may go far to helping us understand that text alone.

Qualitatively, simple pairs, such as "day/year" ("שנה/יום" Job # 115) or "see/hear" ("שמע/ראה" Isaiah # 132; Job # 153) are not elaborate enough to be considered important to Whallon. We disagree. In every instance, we seek to establish the poetic diction of the author or transmitter of a text. Therefore, every repeated word pair will be allowed, no matter how trivial or basic. All repeated word pairs (with the exception of those which occur close to each other) are important, if our task involves the gathering of every sample. So such pairs as "say/speak" will not only be allowed, but will be considered just as important as any other pair in seeing poetic diction at work. And as we shall demonstrate at a later point, poetic diction involves habit and common traits of speech. It will follow, then, that all word pairs are important, but especially the most common ones which a poet might use frequently.

And last, we must acknowledge that percentages *per se* will be of little use or interest to us. We have seen how at least one attempt (Culley's) at mathematically attacking the problem of formula was found wanting. For all such studies are relative to the total amount of material available. Yet the importance of statistical examination is affirmed as evidenced by the research of Sperber, Schlesinger, and Tsevat[15]. Following in their footsteps, we shall present our findings in the Appendix numerically in terms of tens versus hundreds, hundreds versus thousands. Yet we shall always be interested in the total weight of our results, and not in the percentages they imply. The statistical method is valuable, and however related to the total material available, certainly indicates trends.

D. THE PRESENCE OF WORD PAIRS IN BOTH ORAL AND WRITTEN POETRY

Do word pairs stem from a literate verse-making society, an oral verse-making society, or do they occur in perhaps both situations? As we have said above, from Parry's impetus, scholars have spent con-

[14] M. Tsevat, A Study of the Language of the Biblical Psalms, 1955.

[15] A. Sperber disproved the alleged rarity of the assimilation of the נ of the preposition מן to the article מה, by statistical analysis. Hebrew Grammar: A New Approach, JBL 42 (1943), 140–143. K. Schlesinger challenged the supposed normalcy of the word order predicate-subject in the verbal clause by statistical analysis. Zur Wortfolge im hebräischen Verbalsatz, VT 3 (1953), 381–390. And Tsevat statistically examined the biblical psalms and their words in: A Study of the Language of the Biblical Psalms, 10–11. His cautions, however, concerning the statistical method are not to be overlooked.

siderable time yoking the formula, repeated phrase or word pair, to a period in which the poetry was created orally. In fact, the discussion of a traditional diction available to poets creating in performance, is central to the arguments of Culley and Whallon[16]. They are at least able to agree that formula is the consequence of an oral verse-making society. It is not our purpose here to question why or how the pairs are used in the poetry. We leave those questions for later chapters. Rather, we seek only to determine where the pairs are used, in oral poetry, in literate poetry, or in both; and if in both, to what extent.

Culley's correlation of the results of field studies on Indo-European languages with Hebrew poetry is, as we have noted, without much basis. Nor is his study in the main, comparative. Had Culley been more successful in imposing his "field characteristics of oral verse-making" upon the biblical psalms, he might have claimed our attention and respect. But he fails to show his "oral characteristics" to be present in the biblical psalms, and so is unable to prove that the formulas he did find, stem from oral verse-making. Even if his "oral characteristics" *were* present in the text of scripture, we doubt that they would necessarily prove oral verse-making to be the mother of the invention (the formula). As examples of what we are saying, we mention but two of Culley's characteristics found in the poetry, and which he says point to oral verse-making: the lack of enjambement, and the presence of archaic and foreign words.

First, there is a characteristic lack of run-on lines in oral poetry which has been gathered in the field, as we have noted. We find no such lines in Hebrew verse wherein lines are interdependent:

Ham. Whither wilt thou lead me? Speak; I'll go no further.
Ghst. Mark me.
Ham. I will.
Ghst. My hour is almost come,
when I to sulphurous and tormenting flames
must render up myself.
Ham. Alas, poor Ghost!

(Hamlet I 1.1–15)

The obvious enjambement of these Shakespearean lines is not to be found in the Hebrew poetry. The Hebrew lines are usually complete in themselves. But the absence of enjambement is a characteristic of Hebrew poetry as a whole. The fact that all Hebrew poetry completes its lines may therefore not be taken as an indication that the poetry was orally created. The wisdom literature of the Old Testament, for

[16] Gevirtz believes that formulas came from an oral verse-making society also, but he does not labor the point. Patterns in the Early Poetry of Israel, 1963, 11f.

instance, is highly paratactic so that the poet had the greatest tendency to complete his wise sayings in whole lines.

Another of Culley's "characteristics of oral literature" is the presence of archaic or foreign words in the oral text. For his "archaic words" in the biblical psalms, Culley points to many Canaanite loan words and particles[17]. These are said to come from a period early in time when the Hebrew incorporated the loan words into their own vocabulary. In our textual studies, such words and constructions as בל in Isaiah 26 14, or -שׁ in Lamentations 2 15. 16, and יה in Isaiah 38 11, would likely be included by Culley[18]. But it has been shown that these "Canaanite words" and constructions are found just as often in the prose and other poetic pericopes which were not orally created. And it is simpler to assume that these Canaanite words and phrases were common to the Syro-Palestinian languages, irrespective of any difference of peoples[19]. No, the presence of such "foreign or archaic words" most certainly cannot be taken as an indication of an oral verse-making society[20]. These words occur throughout the poetic texts, and originate whenever and wherever the Hebrews had relations with other peoples: Greekisms, Aramaisms, Arabisms abound in the literature and reflect the intermingling of peoples[21].

---

[17] Some of the better studies on Canaanite-Hebrew interaction are: R. T. O'Callaghan, Echoes of Canaanite Literature in the Psalms, VT 4 (1954), 164–176; R. de Langhe, Le Bible et la Literature ugaritique, OBL 1 (1957), 67–87; N.H. Tur-Sinai, Some Ideas on the Place of Ugaritic among the Semitic Languages, Tarbiz 23 (1952), 143–145 (in Hebrew); G.D. Young, Ugaritic Prosody, JNESt 9 (1950), 124–133; and M. Dahood, Ugaritic-Hebrew Philology, 1965.

[18] Gevirtz believes that many of the archaic words and forms were kept in the poetry for the sake of the meter. Patterns in the Early Poetry of Israel, 13.

[19] On the ancient Near Eastern influence upon words which we classify as "archaic or foreign", see: for Arabic words, J.L. Palache, Semantic Notes on the Hebrew Lexicon, 1959; for Canaanite words, R. Dussaud, La Poesie phenicienne et son rhythme, RP 44 (1937), 208–216; for Akkadian words, E.P. Dhorme, L'Emploi Metaphorique des Noms de Parties du Corps en Hebreu et en Akkadien, 1963 (1923); for Aramaic words, Z. Ben-Hayyim, The Literary and Oral Tradition of Hebrew and Aramaic Amongst the Samaritans, vol. I–II, 1957.

[20] See Sperber's argument that what many call archaic words are really simply infrequent words. He suggests that it is better to see Hebrew and its sister languages as all coming from one Proto-Semitic tongue. In this view, what might seem to be a rare word in Hebrew, may well be a common word elsewhere. A Historical Grammar of Biblical Hebrew: A Presentation of Problems with Suggestions to their Solutions, 1966, 105–297.

[21] For discussions of how words are easily taken over from one language to another, see R. Marcus, Jewish and Greek Elements in the Septuagint, in: Louis Ginzberg Jubilee Volume, I, 1945, 227–245, English section; A. Sperber, Hebrew Based upon Greek and Latin Translations, HUCA 12–13 (1937–1938), 205–297. The

Thus Culley's inability properly to compare literatures has told against him once again. His "characteristics of oral composition" taken from field studies do not instruct us about the relation of oral composition to biblical texts. Rather, we must analyze the characteristics of Hebrew poetry on its own ground[22].

Like Culley, Whallon also fails to relate oral composition and the formula adequately, and to ground the phenomenon of the formula in oral verse-making. While he believes otherwise, he fails to prove that the formulas are orally engendered. Whallon is admittedly more cautious on the matter than Culley when he says, "Because they are often repeated, elements of two types (word pairs and phrases) were developed, *at least in part without the aid of writing.*"[23] (The italics are ours.) He argues that men of letters would not have had the *incentive* to develop such a traditional diction[24]. Yet somewhat later he says that we cannot infer that the dialogues of the book of Job are in every sense, or not in any sense, oral poems which were retold from the past[25]. That is, Job could at once be both written and oral in form in different passages. Whallon seems to be saying that the formula hails from an oral verse-making society because it was needed for composition. But we cannot say for certain that the received texts contain amounts of both oral and literate composition. For Whallon, the formulas of the poetry may have been used in both.

No matter how weighty the arguments of these writers may appear, we are not at all convinced *from their reasoning* that the Hebrew poetic formula has its origin in and its dependence upon oral composition alone, nor are we certain that the pairs occur only in oral poetry. We must resort to the development of our own proof relating or dis-relating oral composition and Hebrew formulas. There is little doubt in our minds that formulas occur in the oral poetry of the Old Testament. If we are to understand more about their occurrences, however, we must compare those orally used word pairs to pairs which are found in written poetry.

Our problem at the outset will be finding a passage or entire poem which we can be fairly sure was composed in writing, and not orally.

---

book of Job is thought to have many foreign words, especially Arabisms and Aramaisms. See R. Gordis, The Book of God and Man: A Study of Job, 161–163, and A. Guillaume, Studies in the Book of Job with a New Translation, 1968, 1–15.

22 See note 5 above.

23 Whallon, Formula, Character, and Context, 140.

24 Ibid. 160.

25 Ibid. 160.

For this we turn to Lamentations[26]. In the first four chapters of Lamentations, the acrostic format is used by the poet extensively and in a number of ways[27]. In contrast to these first four chapters, chapter five of Lamentations is a poem without acrostic form[28].

Let us return to Culley for a moment. His comments concerning the nature of orally composed poems are valuable here. He says that when an oral poet creates a poem in an unfixed fashion, he reconstructs the poem around certain basic themes and motifs as he goes, filling in the lines with stock formulas. Field study reports show that a single poet giving the same poem over and over again will vary its presentation as he goes[29]. Thus, each oral poem must be considered a one shot example of a given poem known to the poet only in general outline, not in fixed form, and the outline being filled out with appropriate formula. The singer recreates at each performance, a little differently each time. He needs store in his memory no more than the poem's outline. In poems of the Old Testament where formulas are common, oral verse-making then should be the origin of the poem.

---

[26] In our examination of Lamentations, we have consulted: W. Rudolph, Die Klagelieder, 1939; H. Gunkel, Die Klagelieder Jeremiae, RGG 3, 1913, 1499–1504. A.W. Streane, Jeremiah and Lamentations, 1913; W. Beyerlin, Die *tôdā* der Heilsvergegenwärtigung in den Klageliedern des Einzelnen, ZAW 79 (1967), 208–224; K. Budde, Das hebräische Klagelied, ZAW 2 (1882), 1–52; A. Condamin, Symmetrical Repetitions in Lamentations Chapters I and II, JTS 7 (1906), 137–140. The best bibliography on the work done on Lamentations is found in B. Albrektson Studies in the Text and Theology of the Book of Lamentations: with a Critical Edition of the Peshitta Text, 1963, 240–250.

[27] On the nature and use of the acrostic, we have considered: P.T. Piatti, I carmi alfabetici della Bibbia chiave della metrica ebraica, Biblica 31 (1950), 281–315. 427–458; S. Oettli, Die Klagelieder, 1889, 199; T.K. Cheyne, Lamentations of Jeremiah, 1885, 1; H.B. Swete, Introduction to the Old Testament in Greek, 1902, 360f.; R. Marcus, Alphabetic Acrostics in the Hellenistic and Roman Periods, JNESt 6 (1947), 113; M. Löhr, Der Sprachgebrauch des Buches der Klagelieder, ZAW 14 (1894), 31–50; Threni III und die jeremianische Autorschaft des Buches der Klagelieder, ZAW 24 (1904), 1–16; Alphabetische und alphabetisierende Lieder im alten Testament, ZAW 25 (1905), 173–198; H. Jahnow, Das hebräische Leichenlied im Rahmen der Völkerdichtung, 1923, 169; C.D. Ginsburg, Introduction to the Massoretico-Critical Edition of the Hebrew Bible, 1966 (1894), 20; D. Hillers, Lamentations, 1968, xxiv–xxvii.

[28] Chapter 5 is not an acrostic. Some have argued that it is an acrostic based upon the fact that the poem has the same number of lines as there are letters in the Hebrew alphabet. But this begs the question. For the full argument, see G. Fohrer, Introduction to the Old Testament, trans. by D.E. Green, 1968, 297. As we will show later, there are clear differences in the use of word pairs in chapters 1–4 in comparison to chapter 5.

[29] A.B. Lord, The Singer of Tales, 1954, 100.

Now Lamentations contains in its chapters, as the Appendix lists show, a great deal of formulaic language, and by this we mean repeated word pairs. In our study of Lamentations, we have sought a diversity of examples attesting to the wide use of word pairs throughout the whole of the poetic texts. So rightly, based on Culley's observations above, these poems must hail from an oral verse-making society.

To reinforce Culley, we call upon W. Whallon. Whallon has made plain in his examination of oral literature that the traditional diction of the poetry was developed to aid in freely composing poems where memorization of vast amounts of material was impossible. He avers that it was easier for the poet to recreate around the poem's general theme, than to commit a poem to memory in its entirety. But if it was difficult for the oral poet to memorize the *narrative poem* in oral verse-making, how much more difficult would it have been for him to memorize poems in the acrostic form. Recalling of the acrostic form requires strict memorization of the lines, the first few words of which cannot vary. No, the acrostic form of Lamentation which must have been written (as we shall show), also contains formulas. And here will be the crux of our argument: If oral poetry is typified by the presence of formulas, and the written acrostic contains formulas, then we shall conclude that oral verse-making is not the exclusive domain of the formula. That the acrostic contains formulas, is self-evident. Thus we need only work up a few arguments in support of the fact that the acrostic was written.

In his monograph, *Studies in the Book of Lamentations*, N. Gottwald notes in passing how very difficult memorization of four separate acrostics would be for the poet and for the audience hearing the poem, both in terms of content and in terms of the alphabetized first words of the lines[30]. While memory may play a limited role in the use of the acrostic form, for Gottwald, it is not a primary one[31]. One particular characteristic of the acrostic form which would make memorization very difficult is the dis-

---

[30] N.K. Gottwald, Studies in the Book of Lamentations, 1962.

[31] The value of the acrostic form in terms of memory is still under great debate. For the view that the acrostic does not aid the memory, see R.K. Harrison, Introduction to the Old Testament, 1969, 1068. For the view that the acrostic is a mnemonic aid, but without proof, see R. Gordis, Poets, Prophets, and Sages: Essays in Biblical Interpretation, 1971, 83; and R. Lowth, Lectures on the Sacred Poetry of the Hebrews, 39. 318. The most balanced views are to be found in W.F. Albright, From the Stone Age to Christianity, 1957, 31f.; A.W. Streane, Jeremiah and Lamentations, 355. The entire argument hangs on the proposition that there were one or more authors of chapters 1–5. Gottwald, Studies in the Book of Lamentations, 21, believes that there was one author, while R.H. Pfeiffer, Introduction to the Old Testament, 1963, 722–723 believes that one author did not write all five poems.

association of the lines in such a poem: one line or lines united by a letter of the alphabet does not often have any relationship, as far as content, to what comes before or after it. This, of course, is a result of the lack of enjambement between lines. That the line beginning with *gimmel*, for example, belonged to one acrostic poem and not another, would be very difficult to remember. The first words of the lines, with the letters and structure they represent, simply do not help in the task of memorization. For instance, some of the words which begin lines are even repeated at the beginning of the same alphabetical line in another acrostic poem. איכה is used in three of the Lamentations poems, and ו־ is used in four of them. In such instances, the first words of the line would only assist in confusing the memorization process, and not help it.

And there are even more weighty arguments telling against the use of the acrostic format in Lamentations as a mnemonic aid and oral form. P. Munch notes rightly that the acrostic form in Lamentations appeals secondarily to the ear, and primarily to the eye[32]. Munch points out that the more complex the acrostic becomes, the more difficult it would be for the oral poet to sing, and the audience to perceive that the acrostic form was actually being used. The form, says Munch, is not compatible with the needs and practicalities of oral poetry.

We must conclude that the acrostic form was not resorted to as an aid to memory for either the poet or audience. On the contrary, this form of verse would only complicate matters for the oral poet to retell, and for the audience hearing the poem to remember. Moreover, if we allow the acrostic to be recomposed at each setting, we would have to agree that we would have nothing more in our received text than a one-shot example of how one poet thought an acrostic should go. Rather, and as far as we can tell, the form of the acrostic seems to have been resorted to for its own impressive high style and distinctiveness of construction as a literary form. As Gottwald put it in terms of the acrostics of Lamentations, the form represents the fullness of grief on the part of the author expressing the loss of Jerusalem in a highly dramatic way[33]. And Gottwald's opinion conforms exactly to the thoughts of Whallon on the use of the word pair in Hebrew poetry: the word pairs were not used as an aid to memory, as Gevirtz holds[34], but were used for their

---

[32] P. A. Munch, Die alphabetische Akrostische in der jüdischen Psalmendichtung, ZDMG 90 (1936), 704f.

[33] Gottwald, Studies in the Book of Lamentations, 23–32, believes that the author of Lamentations resorted to the acrostic format to convey to his audience the fullness of grief, as if he were saying everything from "A to Z", as it were, on the subject of the loss of Jerusalem.

[34] Ibid. 10–11.

own impressive high style[35]. The form in Lamentations could only have been created by the seated, literate poet, not by the standing, oral one.

And our research shows that there are some remarkable differences between the word pair located in the acrostic form, and those found in other poems, as we shall shortly see. But the acrostic's difficulty of construction, memorization, and retelling can only be properly accounted for if we conclude that the acrostic form must be a literary one, written, not orally composed or retold. And we speak here of all the ornate biblical acrostics in general, not just Lamentations. They were constructed in a literate format, and as we shall indicate, contain fewer word pairs than the oral poetry. Even the psalms acrostics, as simple as some of them may be, contain fewer word pairs than the rest of the poetry[36]. When the acrostic form is used, it seems the word pairs and the parallelism of the line become of secondary interest to the poet.

The Appendix list of our work on Lamentations shows us that both in the acrostic (we use Lamentations 1–4) and in the non-acrostic (we use Isaiah) poetry, the verse contains formulas. And now we see where we are going: if the acrostics of Lamentations contain formulas and were written, then the formula is not the exclusive domain of oral verse-making, nor must it be considered to be strictly a party to the so-called oral verse-making period of Hebrew poetry. Rather, the formula occurs in both oral and written verse-making, and the word pair recurs in non-orally created poems. Our research in Lamentations has led us directly to this conclusion. But our argument is not finished.

A closer examination of the formula in Lamentations, more specifically, the word pair, convinces us that the acrostic was written. But at the same time there is a distinct difference between the word pairs found in the acrostics and those of other poems, but at the same time a certain sameness. In terms of difference, it is not so much the lack of word pairs in the acrostics compared to other poetry that strikes us, as it is the oddity of the ones which are present. On the one hand, and as will be seen below, the word pairs of Lamentations 1–4 are very choppy and erratic, but at the same time, very elaborate. Rarely do we encounter three, four, and five pairs of words per line as we do in other biblical poetry. Yet how elaborate and extended a poetic creation they are, may be seen in Lamentations 1 6:

> From *the daughters of Zion* has departed all her majesty.
> *Her princes* have become like harts that find no pasture;
> they fled without strength before the pursuer.

[35] Whallon, Formula, Character, and Context, 148.

[36] Culley's comments on the fixing of oral poetry just prior to writing has no bearing on the matter here since we are holding that the acrostic is written from the moment of its inception. Oral Formulaic Language, 15.

And the same ornate structure is seen in Lamentations 2_{10} (Lamentations # 38):

> *The elders of the daughter of Zion* sit on the ground
> in silence;
> they have cast dust on their heads and put on sackcloth;
> *the maidens of Jerusalem* have bowed their heads to the
> ground.

The word pairs move from one line to the next uniting the whole with few internal word pairs between the hemistichs of one line.

And often the pairs are separated at such a distance, that we can only conclude that the author needed to have "seen on paper" the poetic construction he was creating. Lamentations 2_{3} (Lamentations # 20):

> He has cast down in fierce anger all the mighty of
> *Israel*;
> he has drawn from them his right hand in the face
> of the enemy;
> he has burned like a flaming fire in *Jacob*,
> consuming all around.

The characteristic shortness and didactic nature of most of Hebrew poetry is wanting here. When these lines are compared to the abundant word pairs of paratactic Job, it is clear what we mean. And there is, as a matter of fact, even some enjambement found in Lamentations, unheard of in other Hebrew verse (cf. Lamentations $2_{4a.b}$):

דרך קשתו כאויב נצב ימינו
כצר

Long and elaborate lines exist in which there are no word pairs to be found at all. Lamentations 3_{55-57} reads:

> I call on thy name, O Lord, from the depths of the pit;
> thou heard my plea, "Do not close thine ear to my
> cry for help!"
> thou didst come near when I called on thee;
> thou didst say, "Do not fear!"

קראתי שמך יהוה מבור תחתיות
קולי שמעת אל תעלם אזנך לרוחתי לשועתי
קרבת ביום אקראך אמרת אל תירא

But in contrast, chapter 5 of Lamentations, which is not an acrostic, reads much more smoothly and easily in terms of word pairs. G.B. Gray was the first to note the "ordinary parallelism" of chapter 5 compared to the "peculiarities of parallelism in chapters one through four"[37]. However, Gray never bothered to reckon why there was such a difference in chapters, but was interested only in demonstrating his *kinah* verse. The difference between chapters 1–4 and 5 indicated to us that probably, unlike chapters 1–4, chapter 5 was created or passed on orally, or at least has far less written influence in its freedom of construction. For the smaller number of lines in chapter 5 compared to the first four chapters, the last has a large number of word pairs in its twenty-two distichs. After reading chapters 1–4, the pairs in chapter 5 literally jump out at the reader who is looking for them. Lamentations 5 4 (Lamentations # 93) offers us three pairs:

We must pay for the water WE DRINK,
the wood WE GET *must be bought.*

The first four chapters strike us as being more selective, more elaborate, indeed more bizarre in its use of formulas, as if someone *took the time* to sift and choose the pairs and phrases which suited his poem best. We notice, also, that more of the word pairs which were found in chapters 1–4 are external, between the lines. This is characteristically not the case to such a great degree in oral Hebrew poems. We suggest that this is due to the ability of the writing poet to see through his composition, and parallel in later lines what he had earlier said. This we take as yet another indication of the writing poet, for oral composition would preclude great distance between words in pair: pairs are simply too hard to maintain or remember beyond two or three lines of poetry.

Finally, it must be noted in passing that our position, namely, that the complexity of elaborate acrostic construction requires writing, is upheld by the later trends in Hebrew verse from the post-biblical period onward. During the Middle Ages, the acrostic became something of a Hebrew poetic art in which many of the most outstanding poets of the age took part. That the power of the Hebrew alphabet was best shown by the acrostic construction was the belief of the poets[38]. The mysterious powers inherent in the letters were manipulated by these poets in a variety of ways. The point to be taken here is that the acrostic form grew in stature in post-biblical times, was a part of the writing poets, and if anything, gained in complexity of construction.

---

[37] G.B. Gray, The Forms of Hebrew Poetry, 1915, 87–120, especially 93ff.

[38] J. Trachtenberg, Jewish Magic and Superstition: A Study in Folk Religion, 1970 (1939), has the best discussions on the importance of the acrostic in post-biblical times. He discusses the mysterious powers inherent in letters, 82f., the complexity of gematria, 152. 262–263, and the creation of acrostics for mystical reasons. His chapters on the potency of letters, 78–103, and the use of amulets, 132–152, are also very instructive concerning acrostics.

It may be objected that our observations on the formula found in Lamentations and in other Hebrew poetry are subjective, and they may well be, to some degree. Yet there is an undeniable difference in the use of formula in the acrostic format which we can account for in no other way than to say that Lamentations 1–4 were originally written. The word pairs occur mainly in oral poetry, but also are found in literate verse.

Earlier, we said that in addition to the differences in the word pairs used in Lamentations 1–4 and other Hebrew poetry, there was also a certain sameness throughout the poems of Lamentations regarding the pairs used. For those pairs commonly used elsewhere, were also used in Lamentations. This we must take to indicate what we shall later demonstrate: that the vast number of words in fixed pairs are no more than everyday common associations easily created by anyone. As we shall show, most word pairs are little more than commonplace associations accompanied by infrequent flashes of brilliant usage on the part of the poet. This fact, if later proven, will therefore hold true for both oral and written verse-making. But here we have maintained that if the pairs recur in complex and ornate poetry (Lamentations) and in simpler, more direct poetry (Isaiah), then the focus of the formulas may not be considered to be an aspect of oral poetry alone. To be sure, the word pairs are far more numerous in orally created verse. The presence of more frequent and better word pairs in the oral poetry suggests that they have their locus and origin in oral versemaking. And their less frequent presence in literate poetry suggests that they continued as a stylistic device in written poetry as well. Thus the formula occurs in oral and written poetry alike. Only the form of the poetry differs; the content of the formulas remains largely the same.

E. CONCLUSION AND ANTICIPATION

In this chapter, we have first observed that while both the repeated phrase and the repeated word pair are formulaic in Hebrew poetry, it is the word pair which dominates Hebrew verse-making even to the point of being the basis of the parallelism. Repeated phrases are almost insignificant in amount when compared to the proliferation of the word pairs. And we indicated that our research has shown that the word pairs are not placed carelessly in the poetic line, but instead follow somewhat standardized procedures. But this must be discussed later.

Secondly, we have said that the formula—and we have maintained this for Hebrew poetry alone—is found both in oral and written verse, but is certainly more frequent and dominant in the oral poetry. We can conceive of—but have only Lamentations as proof—*literate* poets armed with just as weighty examples of formulaic diction as we have found in texts which we ascribe to oral composition. Word pairs certainly have their locus in orally created poetry. But they are also found in written poetry, even though there they are something of secondary importance. The difference between word pairs in written and oral poetry indicates this.

To our knowledge, none of the authors has so far recognized the fact that sacred literature in general is formulaic by nature, and that piety, a test of tradition, would require both an oral *and* written diction[39]. And we need not study the Todas of South India as Culley does to reach this conclusion[40]. We can note formula, both written and oral, in sermons, hymns, and prayers of either Jewish or Christian tradition. The pious Jew or Christian can easily compose sacred prayer and poetry both orally and in writing, and complete with formulas, more often than not without thinking about what he is doing[41]. The parts (oral and written poetry) will conform to the piety of the whole (the tradition).

We have seriously disagreed with Culley and Whallon in our conclusions, for we have shunned the general assumption that the formula has its livelihood in oral verse-making alone: they are found in both written and oral poetry. And our difference of opinion is not yet at an end. Next we must consider *why* the word pairs are used. The matter of oral verse-making will have to be pursued, therefore, because these scholars have held that formulas exist in the poetry for the sole purpose of aiding the oral poet as he composes before audiences. The presence of word pairs in the written poetry even as a secondary poetic device forces us to consider the composition and the transmission of the poetry further.

We have frequently alluded to the judgment among the scholars that the formula is made available to the poet by means of a traditional diction, a stockpile of pairs and phrases available for him to draw upon. And this traditional diction has been said to be passed on from one generation to the next as an aid to the poet's craft. But to this point in our study, we have only tacitly allowed this belief in a stock diction to go unchallenged. In the next chapter we must directly reckon with it. Formulas exist in both oral and written poetry. But now we must ask: Does this fact require us to postulate a traditional diction to answer for the formula's use and locus? The theory that a traditional diction is the locus of the word pairs used in Hebrew poetry is at the foundation of the work of all three scholars—Culley, Whallon, and Gevirtz. Formulas exist. That is certain. But does their presence in the poetry require the existence of a traditional diction?

---

[39] That piety is equated with tradition may be seen in M. Tsevat, A Study in the Language of the Biblical Psalms, 46.

[40] Culley, Oral Formulaic Language, 8–9. 128–129.

[41] See J. Schirmann, Hebrew Liturgical Poetry and Christian Hymnology, JQR 44 (1953), 123–161.

Chapter III

Word Pairs in the Transmission and Composition of the Poetry

A. THE ORIGIN OF WORD PAIRS IN THE ORAL AND WRITTEN COMPOSITION OF POEMS

Whallon says that formulas are traditional[1]. By this he means that no formula found in a text can be considered the creation or possession of the author of the book in which it is located. Formulas assist the poet in the creation of this verse, but being traditional, are assumed to have been taken from the stockpile of poetic diction available to each poet, and then passed on in time. For example, the common word pair "born/conceive" ("הרה/ילד" Job # 9) found in Job 3_{3} 15_{35}, recurs also in Numbers 11_{12} Psalm $7_{14(15)}$ Isaiah 26_{8} 33_{11} 59_{4}. Or as another instance, the word pair "hear/listen" ("קשב/שמע" Job # 157) in Job 13_{6}, also is found in I Samuel 15_{22} Psalms 17_{1} 61_{1} Proverbs 4_{1} 7_{24} Isaiah 28_{23} 49_{1} Jeremiah 18_{19} Hosea 5_{1} Micah 1_{2}. And on the list goes. Whallon says that these recurrences tell us that we cannot ascribe authorship of the line in which these pairs occur to any one of these poets, for the pairs are traditional. We can neither tell which poet created the pair first, nor can we identify the first example of the pair's use. And the same holds true for phrases. "Bitter in soul" ("מר נפש" Job # 3) in Job 3_{20} 7_{11} 10_{1} 21_{25} 27_{2}, is also found in Proverbs 31_{6} Judges 18_{25} Isaiah 38_{15}. "Words of my mouth" ("אמרי פה" Job # 8) is repeated in Job 8_{2} 23_{12} Deuteronomy 32_{1} Psalms $19_{14(15)}$ $54_{2(4)}$ 138_{4}. Since these phrases repeat, their authorship cannot be proven.

But this view that such word pairs and phrases are traditional allows for little creativity on the part of the poets themselves, and relegates all creativity to a reworking of tradition. If, for example, "born/conceive" recurs in Job, Numbers, Psalms, and Isaiah, this view does not allow

---

[1] This is his thesis in: No element of Old Testament poetry is more likely than not to have been created for the passage in which it now appears; Formula Character, and Context: Studies in Homeric, Old English, and Old Testament Poetry, 1969, 139–173.

the pair to be original with any one of these authors. The Hebrew poet is seen as an artist bound to the fixed stockpile of traditional diction, unable to create his formula at will: he is restricted to the formulas handed down from the past.

Whether or not word pairs assist in composition and in the creation of the poetry is of present concern. Whallon says that they do, for in the formula he believes that we can see the origin of the poetry at hand. Poets are creative only insofar as they selectively pick and choose formulas to fit their poetic subject. He sees the truly creative poet as one who skillfully employs traditional word pairs in the creation of his text. And all will be well with Whallon's theory if we find that all formulas obtain their existence at the creation of the verse. But if our research indicates that all the formulas which are present in the poetry did not get there via the *creation* of the verse, then we shall be forced to consider whether or not formulas were acquired in the poetry *after* it was first created, that is, in the transmission of the verse. Our own research, then, will allow us to decide whether formulas obtain in the poetry in the composition of the verse, or its transmission, or perhaps in both occasions. Are formulas the exclusive domain of poetic composition or not?

Since J.C. Döderlein published his theory in 1775 that the book of Isaiah is made up of more than one part, scholars have suggested, with various degrees of acumen, that the book is sectionally divided[2]. After Döderlein, the scholarship has fallen into two camps: those stressing the unity of Isaiah, more recently this view being expressed in terms of an Isaianic anthology[3]; and those advocating the divisions and multiple authorship of the text, principally into the sections 1–39, 40–55. 56–66[4].

Now it is not for us here to enter into the history of the scholarship nor the approaches the writers have taken. Let it suffice to say that the research has followed, at different times, criticism of either the historical content of the book, or its literary character. The former, historical camp, has largely held sway in recent times, and most have accepted the threefold division of the book. With this view, we also concur.

---

[2] J.C. Döderlein, Esaias, 1775, ix.

[3] For the views of conservative, yet responsible, scholarship along the lines of Isaiah's unity, and in terms of an anthology, see R.K. Harrison, Introduction to the Old Testament, 1969, 764–795, but especially 780–785. Also, J.J. Lias, The Unity of Isaiah, BS 72 (1915), 560–591; BS 75 (1918), 267–274.

[4] The history of Isaianic criticism with an eye for dividing the book is best seen in O. Eissfeldt, The Old Testament: An Introduction, trans. by P.R. Ackroyd, 1961, 303–330. 330–341. 341–346. Eissfeldt divides the book, 1–39, 40–55, 56–66, as does C. Westermann, Isaiah 40–66: A Commentary, 1969, 3–30. 295–308. But the book has been divided in almost an endless number of ways. See R.H. Pfeiffer, Introduction to the Old Testament, 1963, 415–448. 449–481.

So far as we know, however, no scholar has approached the *whole* of Isaiah by seeking a uniform diction throughout[5]. A careful examination of the word pairs of the book should indicate something of significance about its composition. Since there are three separate sections of Isaiah, written by different "authors", we should be able to see this fact clearly in three distinctive poetic dictions[6]. Each section should have its own word pairs and phrases peculiar unto itself, and for the most part not found anywhere else in Isaiah. Of course this will be the case if Whallon's theory holds true, namely, that the formula assisted the poet in the creation of his verse. In other words, each one of the three poets should exhibit his own peculiarities and repetitions in his use of the "traditional stockpile of formula" available to him.

But if, on the other hand, we find from our research that many of the formulaic word pairs and phrases occur evenly and uniformly throughout Isaiah 1–66 without respect to the historical divisions, then we must re-examine Whallon's thesis that the word pairs assisted in the creation of the poetry alone. If the formulas do not obtain directly from the authors creating their sections, then we will have to reckon with at least four possibilities as to the origin of those formulas. First, we might conclude that since the pairs were not created by the sectional "author", that they came about in the later transmission of the text. Going one step further, if we find that the vast majority of word pairs in Isaiah recur without regard for the three historically different sections, then we will be able to say with some certainty that the formula has to do with transmission of given texts and not with composition alone.

And the possibility of the word pairs recurring evenly throughout Isaiah might be understood in other ways. Second, it may mean that there was one author for the whole of Isaiah. But this option has been largely disproven by historical means. Or third, it may indicate that there was one or even a number of organizers and transmitters of the three complete sections who, in their own way, gave the sections a sense of formulaic unity. And fourth, formulas recurring evenly throughout Isaiah may imply that most formulas are no more than commonplace associations occurring naturally and spontaneously in the mind of any author.

Our options in the study of Isaianic formulas may be organized as follows: if particular pairs recur in one section alone, and not in the

[5] There are instances, when literary criticism was in vogue, in which the unity of Isaiah was examined in terms of a few repeated lines. See R. Rückert, Hebräische Propheten, 1831, who divided up Isaiah based upon the repeated lines 48_{22}, 57_{21}, and 66_{24}.

[6] For ease of discussion, we shall continue to refer to three different "authors" of Isaiah 1–39, 40–55, and 56–66, even while this is literally not the case, especially with regard to 56–66. See O. Eissfeldt, The Old Testament: An Introduction, 341–346.

other two sections, then we shall conclude that the pairs obtain in the creation of the poetry. But if formulas are found uniformly recorded throughout the whole of Isaiah, then we shall have to reckon with one of two possibilities: either these formulas were created in the transmission of the poetry, or they uniformly occur simply because of their common association by all poets.

Our first interest is in determining if the cataloguing of the word pairs in Isaiah indicate that the book is a unity or not. And for the answer, we must now consult the results of our study of Isaiah in the Appendix lists. In the case of Isaiah, unlike Lamentations or Job, we concerned ourselves with all the recurrences of word pairs within the book alone, and did not seek recurrences of the pairs elsewhere. We wish to check the diction of that book alone. And a close look at the results of our work shows that only 45 word pairs out of 543 individual ones, repeat in all three of the historically different sections 1–39, 40–55, 56–66. However,

TABLE 1

ISAIAH I, II, III

Total Word Pairs Found	3168
Pairs Found Only Once	1278
Individual Pairs which Recur	543
Total Repetitions in Text	1890
Repeat in I-II-III	45 of 543
Repeat in I-II	111 of 543
Repeat in II-III	61 of 543
Repeat in I-III	62 of 543
Total	279 of 543

279 of the 543 word pairs which recur, repeat in more *than one* of these three sections; the rest recur in but one of the three sections. And there is a clear distinction between the three historically different sections of the book with respect to the word pairs which recur: pairs which recur in one section often do not recur in another; pairs unique in one section often do not recur in others.

These observations alone strongly suggest two things: first, the restrictions of about half the repeated word pairs to one of the three sections indicates that there are indeed three separate "authors" at work in Isaiah: half of the frequent pairs found in 1–39 simply do not recur in 56–66, for example. But second, we have noted that there are an equally large number of the repeated pairs which recur at will in more than one section of the book. If our first observations are correct, that there are three divisions in the text of Isaiah, then we must assert with respect to our second result that there are a great number of pairs which seem not to care for these sectional divisions. We have said above that if we find the pairs recurring irrespective of the sections, these could be explained in a number of ways. First, these word pairs which repeat irrespective of the divisions could hail from the influence of those who transmitted the text. This is to say, as the parts of Isaiah were passed on, their diction developed more of a unity under the influence of those who transmitted it. Or second, the recurrence of these pairs across the sections may reflect the fact that many of the word pairs are nothing more than common association of everyday ideas and things which any poet would create irrespective of age and locale. Or the option was suggested that there might have been one organizer and transmitter of the three sections who alone supplied the unity of diction which we have discovered. Or last, we suggested that there might actually have been one author of the whole of Isaiah. But this solution to our dilemma is precluded by the fact that we have unquestionably found three distinct dictions in the book.

While it is clear that half of the repeated word pairs used in Isaiah come from the composition of the verse originally, because they recur only within the section they are found, the other half of the repeated word pairs recur anywhere in the text, in two or more of the sections. Does this latter observation result from the transmission of the text, or from the commonplace nature of the pairs? Do the pairs have to do with both the composition *and* the transmission of the poetry? Whatever the answers, and we shall try to resolve these questions on transmission and common association in this chapter, we must relate our results to Whallon's argument which held that all word pairs coming from a fixed traditional diction assisted the author of the poetry as he composed. But let us hold off our judgment for a moment on these word pairs in Isaiah which recur irrespective of the sections.

Let us return again to that half of the pairs which repeat within their own part of the book, and so are themselves significant. We notice, for example, a particular tapering off the use of word pairs in the three sections: "nation/people" ("עם/גוים" Isaiah # 8) recurs in sections I–II–III in the following frequency: 14–2–2; "Zion/Jerusalem" ("ציון/ירושלים" Isaiah # 52) 9–4–2; "nation/land" ("ארץ/גוים" Isaiah # 225) 9–2–1; "Jacob/Israel" ("ישראל/יעקב" Isaiah # 179) 5–16–9; "justice/righteousness" ("צדקה/משפט" Isaiah # 36) 11–4–4; "land/people" ("עם/ארץ" Isaiah # 190) 11–4–2. Clearly then, there are some pairs which are favorite to one section and author, and probably just accidental associations in others. And there are many pairs and phrases which recur in one section, and not at all in another: the pairs: "thorns/briars" ("שית/שמיר" Isaiah # 95) 8–0–0; "mouth/lips" ("שפה/פה" Isaiah # 219) 3–0–0; "graze/lie down" ("רבץ/רעה" Isaiah # 264) 3–0–0; and the phrases: "fall by the sword" ("חרב נפל" Isaiah # 31) 4–0–0; "raise a signal" ("נס נשא" Isaiah # 21) 4–0–0. Significantly, if there were much borrowing between the sections of Isaiah, the number of recurrences should recur in ascending fashion, 2–6–18, for example, and not 10–2–0, etc., as is often the case. We therefore surmise that there were three separate "poets" at work in Isaiah, and the latter two were greatly unaffected by the work of their predecessors. Our results indicate that even though a later poet might consciously copy whole lines and ideas from previous poets, it is difficult for one poet to hide or even mask his own diction.

These pairs which recur only in separate sections cannot be overlooked and must in themselves indicate that the text was created by three separate "authors", and that the formulas were enlisted in the process of composition. The formulas aided in the creation of the sections of this poetry, that is clear[7].

Therefore, we side with Whallon in maintaining that the stockpile of formulas aided the creation of the poetry. But this solution answers for only *half* of the repeated pairs which we found in the poetry. The other half which occurred across the sections must be answered for in terms of textual transmission or the commonplace association of the word pairs. Whallon still may be correct in his position that all word pairs are placed in the poetry at the time of composition. But he has failed to recognize the dilemma we have here, because he neglected to apply his theory to a complete text of scripture. We now turn to examine the possibility that transmission might have an influence upon the formula, and that it might be one reason why half of the pairs recurred evenly.

B. THE UNLIKELY TRANSMISSIONAL ACTIVITY OF WORD PAIRS

Half of the word pairs in Isaiah have to do with composition, therefore, and the other half either with transmission or common association. Here we shall consider only the possibility of transmissional influence. We leave the question of the role of commonplace association for the next section of this chapter.

If we are to reckon with the influence of transmission upon the received text of scripture, we must answer the question as to who transmitted the literature. For our example, we continue with Isaiah. To review: viewed strictly in terms of poetic diction and formulaic presence alone, we have in Isaiah three distinct dictions in three historically

[7] Lest it be said that we still do not have enough material and examples to work with, we do, in fact, have many pairs which recur fifteen times, or more. For example, "hear/give ear" (Isaiah # 1) occurs 15 times in Isaiah; "Lord/holy one" (Isaiah # 13) 18 times; "Zion/Jerusalem" (Isaiah # 52) 15 times; "heaven/earth" (Isaiah # 4) 20 times; "justice/righteousness" (Isaiah # 36) 16 times "hear/see" (Isaiah # 121) 21 times.

different sections. But evenly over all the verse there exists a general diction uniting the lines irrespective of the three parts. In the first case, we see the presence of three "poets" at work, each composing his own passage. But in the second case, the presence of three poets fails to answer directly for the uniformity of formula used throughout, at least in terms of Whallon's theory of traditional diction. For as we have observed, half of the word pairs found, and even some which are rare outside of Isaiah, recur again and again across the three sections of Isaiah.

How are we to explain the standardization of many of the pairs which has occurred throughout the text? Our question might be answered in terms of the transmitted text. Either one organizer and transmitter placed his own dictional unity on the three parts, or a number of organizers and transmitters caused the unity we now have. Considering the first possibility, one or two transmitters would not have so strikingly influenced the three sections of Isaiah to the extent that half of the repeated pairs recurred evenly throughout. We do not say that a few transmitters *could not* have worked such unity on the sections, but that they probably *would not* have purposely moved in this direction to the extent to which we are speaking. It would have required at least some effort for a few men to rework the Isaianic material in such a way that the pairs recurred evenly. Therefore, it is most reasonable to speculate—at least until proven otherwise—that if transmissional influence is to answer for the evenly repeated pairs, a great many transmitters of the sections had their hands on the material, and each contributed slowly to the now present dictional unity of the book[8]. One transmitter would not have intentionally striven to rework the material into a unity. (And had one man intended to add unity to the whole of Isaiah, he could have done a far better job than our received text now indicated.) But many transmitters, each passing the sections on, could unwittingly and unconsciously have given the poetry the dictional unity it now has. It is unreasonable that just a few renditions by one or two transmitters of the parts of Isaiah would mold the diction into the uniformity as we now have it, that is, with half of the repeated word pairs recurring throughout the text. One or two transmitters could not so evenly unite the poetic diction. But it is conceivable that a group of transmitters into whose custody the book was given, certainly could.

The presence of the same word pairs throughout Isaiah might be said to reflect a "school of transmission" as some have proposed. This

[8] This suggestion is not particularly original. It is becoming more common to see groups of followers carrying the sayings of their prophets. See, for instance, E. Nielsen, Oral Tradition: A Modern Problem in Old Testament Introduction, 1954. But the suggestion is original here in terms of its origin: our research in formula criticism.

suggestion rings true to what much of the Scandinavian scholarship has offered us in recent years: the followers or "circles" of a prophet largely shape the form and diction of the poet's words[9]. However, such speculative observations on the transmission of the prophetic books in the oral and literary stages amounts to little more than hypotheses. So fluid is the question of transmissional impact upon prophecy, that it has been challenged, altered, and re-altered time and again[10].

Along these same lines, but without evidence, W. Whallon has suggested that "Isaiah stood to an Isaianidae as Homer stood to the Homeridae"[11]. Consciously or not, the followers of Isaiah constituted an Isaianidae much like the Homeridae who transmitted Homer's epic verse[12]. This he maintains as a literary comparison, and as the appropriation of a useful term in answer to his question of textual transmission. The frequent rendition of the book by this Isaianic school, he says, gave to it a certain standardization of diction throughout, and so the same word pairs recurred evenly.

Once again, however, as with the Scandinavian hypothesis of "prophetic circles", the existence of an Isaianidae cannot be proven. The presence of transmissional influence upon the poetry cannot be properly measured in the absence of textual evidence. And as convincing as such scholarly observations may sound, they rest upon speculation, and the belief that such schools of followers *could* have existed. While the Isaianidae may go a long way toward suggesting the reason for the relatively even recurrence of the word pairs throughout Isaiah, it cannot be proven. The need for a transmissional school to answer for the repeated word pairs rests upon the reality of a traditional diction. How-

---

[9] This fits well the Scandinavian ideas on the origin and transmission of the prophetic books. "Circles", or "complexes" of followers are seen as orally retelling, reforming, and crystallizing the prophet's words. A fine summary of the Scandinavian school is by O. Eissfeldt, The Prophetic Literature, in: The Old Testament and Modern Study: A Generation of Discovery and Research, 1961, 126–134. Also A. Bentzen, Skandinavische Literatur zum Alten Testament, 1939–1948, ThRv 17 (1948–1949), 272–328; H.S. Nyberg, Studien zum Hosebuche, 1935, 8; H. Birkeland, Zum hebräischen Traditionswesen, 1938; I. Engnell, The Call of Isaiah, 1949.

[10] I. Engnell, Profetia och tradition, SEÅ 12 (1947), 110–139; J. van der Ploeg, Le Role de la tradition orale dans la transmission du texte de l'Ancien Testament, RB 54 (1947), 5ff.; O. Eissfeldt, The Prophetic Literature, 126–134, but especially 131–133.

[11] Whallon, Formula, Character, and Context, 139. This is an idea which he deduces from H.S. Nyberg, Studien zum Hosebuche, 8.

[12] J.A. Davison, The Homeric Question, in: A Companion to Homer, 1962, 234–265; A. Lesky, Die Homerforschung in der Gegenwart, 1952; A. Lesky, Die homerische Frage, in his: Geschichte der griechischen Literatur, 1958, 49–58.

ever, and this we shall support in the next chapter, once the need for a traditional stockpile falls by the wayside, so will fall away the need for the influence of transmission activity as we seek to determine why word pairs are used in the poetry.

C. TRADITIONAL DICTION VERSUS COMMON ASSOCIATION AND LIMITED VOCABULARY

We often encounter the theory in the work of Whallon, Culley, and Gevirtz that the Hebrew poet who composed his verse orally, of necessity required a "stockpile of formulas" at his disposal as he created[13]. The stockpile was handed down to the poet from past versemakers, and for the new poet, there was little variation from the traditional. The formula, or at least its archetype, is ready-made; all the poet need do is draw it to mind[14]. The fact that formulas repeat themselves and often, is the primary proof which the authors point to when the case is argued that such a stockpile exists. Since there are repeated word pairs and phrases in the literature, the writers say they are most easily accounted for by ascribing them to a traditional diction. It is our task here to examine this theory, and to determine whether or not such a traditional diction, such a stockpile, is the fabrication of modern scholarship, or actually has basis in the texts of scripture. The existence or non-existence of such a traditional diction will allow us to make a judgment with regard to the influence of transmission upon the text of Isaiah.

Whallon especially promotes the argument of a traditional diction. He does not believe poets created word pairs independently or spontaneously. And he affirms his argument for a traditional stockpile of formulas by pointing to the particularly rare word pairs which recur in the literature. By rare or odd word pairs, Whallon means such pairs as "dragon/owl" ("יענה/תנים" Job # 343) in Job 30 29, which he believes could only have been created by association of habit, common practice, or customary agreement[15]. And we can certainly reinforce his observations by saying that we have come across many more peculiarly associated recurrent word pairs in the texts. "Wild ass/ox" ("שור/פרא" Job # 68, 277) in Job 6 5

[13] Whallon, Formula, Character, and Context, 151–152. 157–160. R. Culley, Oral Formulaic Language in the Biblical Psalms, 1967, 6ff. S. Gevirtz, Patterns in the Early Poetry in Israel, 1963, 11.

[14] Whallon's idea of a stockpile of phrases is older than his own investigation. He has simply drawn the idea together. See, for example, The Oxford Annotated Bible, H.G. May and B.M. Metzger, eds., 1962, where in a note on Micah 4 1-5 15 (p. 1126), the editors recognize independent, free-floating strata in the prophecy.

[15] Whallon, Formula, Character, and Context, 145.

and 21_{10}, for example, would probably be accepted by him. These he cites as proof that all word pairs were traditional, because these repeated word pairs contain words which would not normally be associated together. But to this line of thinking we reply by saying that there are equally rare and outstanding word pairs which *do not recur* in the literature, but are found only once. Some examples from Job are: "wise/wily" 5_{13}, "mark/burden" 7_{20}, "heavens/waves of the sea dragon" 9_{8}, "skiffs/eagle" 9_{26}, "snow/lye" 9_{30}, "shoot/mouth" 15_{30}, "pit/worm" 17_{14}, "food/gall of asps" 20_{14}, "moth/watchman" 27_{18}, "Mazzaroth/bear" 38_{32}, "Leviathan/tongue" 41_{1}. What is more, there are even commonly associated pairs made up of words of daily use which *occur only once* in the literature: Again, some examples from Job might be: "shake/tremble" 9_{6}, "small/very great" 8_{7}, "bray/low" 6_{5}, "disappear/vanish" 6_{17}, "grass/fodder" 6_{5}, "shut/hide" 3_{10}, "sign/groan" 3_{24}, "perish/cut off" 4_{7}, "plow/sow" 4_{8}, "righteous/pure" 4_{17}, "dust/ground" 5_{6}, "scare/terrify" 7_{14}, "maxim/defense" 13_{12}, "straw/chaff" 21_{18}, "children/offspring" 27_{14}, "bush/nettle" 30_{7}, "olive row/wine press" 24_{11}, "bird of prey/falcon" 28_{7}, "thorns/foul weeds" 31_{40}. Though we would *expect* these pairs to recur, they are found only once in all the poetry. Therefore, if we freely attribute the rare and odd *recurring* word pairs to a fixed fund of formulas for poets, we must at the same time reckon with those peculiar word pairs which do not recur and are found only once. Whallon's theory and approach to the Old Testament poetry fail to do this. He answers only for the pairs in the poetry which repeat. The presence of *all* "rare" and "common" word pairs must be answered for if we are to understand their presence in the composition of poetry.

Next we must consider the results of our own research, namely, that of the word pairs present in the text of Isaiah—the longest text we use—only about six out of every ten word pairs found, repeat themselves; and in Job, only four out of every ten word pairs found repeat themselves. This means, for example, that in Isaiah alone, there are 1278 word pairs which do not occur more than once in the text. In Job,

TABLE 2

JOB

Total Word Pairs Found	1474
Pairs Found Only Once	850
Individual Pairs which Recur	127
Total Repetitions in Text	624

850 pairs occur just once in the text or elsewhere in all the poetry. We must also answer for the use of non-recurring word pairs as well as for the use of the pairs that recur. Were these pairs which do not now repeat also a part of a poetic stockpile, but just rarely used by Hebrew poets? Can we say that half of all the word pairs we now have and which do not

repeat, repeated once? Did half of the word pairs in Job, which do not now repeat, repeat once? These arguments from silence do not satisfy us. For the theory of a fixed traditional diction answers only for the word pairs which repeat, not for the equally many which do not repeat. We have just as many examples of "rare and odd" word pairs which do not repeat, as we have those which do recur; and we have just as many examples of commonly associated word pairs which do not repeat, as we have those which do recur. If the poet of the unfixed form is allowed to be creative only insofar as the use of a stock diction, from whence do all the non-repeated pairs come? Whallon's theory does not answer this question, and concerns itself only with the pairs which repeat.

It will be recalled from Chapter I, that we said Whallon answers for the presence of the many non-repeating word pairs by saying that there were many more poets and much more verse afoot once than we now know about. By this he is suggesting that if we had more material from more Hebrew poets, many of the now non-recurring word pairs would be found to repeat. Or the view may be put in another way. We might say that given the extant material we now have, when a pair recurs only once, we have the only instance where that traditional pair fits the content of the verse. If we had the same sentiments expressed elsewhere, the pair would have occurred.

Such arguments are appealing, and gain weight from Gevirtz's similar theory that word pairs which now do not recur in Ugaritic poetry, but do in Hebrew poetry, probably once did in Ugaritic also, when more texts were circulated. The argument, which is one from silence, is persuasive in its generalities as are most positions which ascribe unavailable data to a *Vorlage*. But unfortunately, it does not fit the results of our research. Let us take Job as our text again. We have found that the ratio of repeated word pairs to non-repeated pairs in Job is about 1 : 2. That is, for every one repeating pair which we found, we found two more pairs which did not repeat. As a matter of fact, so few word pairs actually repeat compared to the whole of the word pairs in the text—in Job, 127 word pairs account for 624 recurrences!—as to cause Whallon's entire theory to fall into question. The individual word pairs which repeat, and so would be called traditional by Whallon, are rather small in comparison to the total number of pairs which are present in the text. In Job, for example, the ratio is 127: 1474. To say that those pairs which repeat are more important than those many more which do not repeat is to beg the question. In fact, when we thoughtfully consider the matter, we realize that Whallon's argument is in itself circular: oral composition requires a traditional diction; traditional diction is said to prove the presence of oral verse-making. But as we have shown in Chapter II, the formula recurs in both oral and written poetry. Hence, the need for the hypothesis of a traditional diction falls immediately into question. If oral verse-making is not the only focus for the word pairs and the purpose of their existence, then the word pairs must find a new *raison d'e'tre*.

Then too, we must once again look to our conclusions in the Second Chapter. We concluded that formulas are found in both oral and written verse. If this is true, we need a new explanation for the traditional diction which has been said to be necessary because the oral poet was composing on the spur of the moment, and did not have time to create phrases and word pairs to fit the verse. On the contrary, however, the writing poet, the literate poet who had the time to create each verse as he went, still more often than not, resorted to the formula repeated elsewhere. The theory of a traditional stockpile, therefore, seems shaky. Our study of Lamentations, and the presence of formulas in written poetry there, begins to indicate that.

All this is not to mention that the scholars are at odds to say how such a traditional diction of one literature was perpetuated and passed on in time. Culley claims that different men living in separate areas in diverse times have peculiarities and differences in their diction[16]. Whallon counters by saying that all men from all areas and periods in a given literature use the same word pairs, even over thousands of years[17]. And in his study of Ugaritic and Hebrew verse, Gevirtz shares Whallon's position[18]. Which is it to be, therefore? Are we to say that all men in all times and all places possess but one stockpile in any given literature from which to pull formulas at will? Or are we to say that different areas and periods have different stocks of diction? If we affirm the first, we shall be forced to explain how the diction was successfully passed. If we agree with the second, we must explain how the word pairs recur across the board in texts irrespective of age or locale. The concept of a traditional diction brings with itself more questions than answers to the textual evidence.

It has been a primary assumption of the foregoing studies that if a phrase or word pair is repeated, it is formulaic and hence a part of a traditional diction. But in so saying, we have failed to recognize the simple possibilities of borrowing, not to mention coincidence as likely factors in repetition[19]. We speak here not of word pairs or phrases which recur closely together, within say, two or three verses. Nor do we mean formulas which are simply idiomatic, for example, "Thus saith the Lord" ("כה אמר יהוה"). Rather, we speak of word pairs or phrases taken

[16] Culley, Oral Formulaic Language, 16–17.

[17] Whallon, Formula, Character, and Context, 171–172.

[18] Gevirtz, Patterns in the Early Poetry of Israel, 10–12.

[19] Though Culley notes the influences which borrowing might have on Hebrew verse, he makes light of it. Oral Formulaic Language, 36.

by one poet from another[20]. We mean such full assertions as Psalm 14_{2} which is later found at 53_{2}(3), which we would say comes from borrowing, not from traditional diction:

The Lord looks down from heaven
upon the children of men,
to see if there are any that act wisely,
that see after God.

יהוה משמים השקיף על בני אדם
לראות היש משכיל דרש את אלהים

And it cannot be doubted that borrowing must surely come into play in the case of many of the minor prophets who borrow full lines and series of lines from Job and Isaiah. The full assertion of Isaiah 13_{6} recurs in Joel 1.15:

Wail, for the day of the Lord is near;
as destruction from the Almighty it will come.

אהה ליום כי קרוב יום יהוה וכשך משדי יבוא

Isaiah 2_{4} (Isaiah # 54. 55) repeats in Micah 4_{3}:

He shall judge between the nations,
and shall decide for many peoples;
and they shall beat their swords into plowshares,
and their spears into pruning hooks;
nation shall not lift up sword against nation,
neither shall they learn war anymore.

ושפט בין הגוים והוכיח לעמים רבים
וכתתו חרבותם לאתים וחניתותיהם למזמרות
לא ישא גוי אל גוי חרב ולא ילמדו עוד מלחמה

Likewise, it is much the same with innumerable word pairs: "hear/listen" ("קשב/שמע" Job # 157) repeats at Job 13_{6} Hosea 5_{1} Micah 1_{2}; "lion/young lion" ("כפיר/אריה" Job # 35) repeats at Job 4_{10} Amos 3_{4} Micah 5_{8} Nahum 2_{11}. And Whallon's observation that some pairs are too rare to be borrowed, does nothing to confirm the existence of a traditional diction instead of the simple process of borrowing or even common association[21]. It is closer to the evidence to ascribe such repeated pairs to common association or borrowing than it is to regiment them into a traditional diction.

---

[20] A. Guillaume, Studies in the Book of Job: with a New Translation, 1968, 15, proposes a common stock of Hebrew phrases and idioms in terms of borrowing among the poets of Hebrew verse.

[21] Whallon, Formula, Character, and Context, 145.

Culley admits that some phrases recurring twice may be due to borrowing, coincidence, or idiom[22]. How many is impossible to say. And he maintains that there are far too many instances of repeated phrases to be explained away by mere borrowing. But if we allow phrases and word pairs which recur twice to be a consequence of borrowing, coincidence, or idiom, why not three times or more? If the phrase or word pair was particularly good, the chances would be great that another author would indeed pick it up and reuse it. Actually, many of Culley's "formulaic phrases" amount to little more than idiomatic necessities. How else, for example, can a person at prayer say, "Hear my prayer, O Lord", than "אלהים שמע תפלתי"? No, the simple suggestion of borrowing, coincidence, and idiom as active participants in the literature, weakens the theory of a traditional diction. More than likely, these factors have a far greater hand in the poetry than those who favor a traditional diction are willing to admit. Culley, for instance, in setting aside the influence of borrowing, says his locating that of the formulaic phrase in the biblical psalms proves the theory of a common heritage of established phraseology which has also been set forth by A.R. Johnson[23]. But it does nothing of the kind. His ability to locate the formulaic phrase in the biblical psalms does not alone answer for their use. And the presence of the formula there neither negates the influence of borrowing, nor does it confirm a traditional diction with any degree of certainty.

To review: So far, our own research into Hebrew formula has uncovered the following observations which strongly suggest that a traditional diction did not exist and is not expressed in the literature:

1) The word pairs recur without regard for type or genre. Types or genres may have some similar formulas only because the subject matter changes, and words are restricted to their applicable use.

2) Word pairs are not an aid solely to oral verse-making, but are also found in written poetry as well.

3) The word pairs certainly assist in composition of the verse, but do not find an active life in the transmission of the text.

4) Many recurring pairs may be ascribed just as easily to borrowing, coincidence, or idiom. The better the phrase or word pair, the more likely it would be borrowed by other poets.

These four observations regarding traditional diction are made based upon the direct results of our own research. Taken singly, they

[22] Culley, Oral Formulaic Language, 99.
[23] Ibid. 116.

may appear to be of no direct consequence with regard to a judgment on the existence and usefulness of a traditional diction. But together, and properly understood, they should at least make us suspicious of the traditional diction hypothesis.

In the first case, we have found that for the poet, the formulas are not restricted in any discernible way. They seem to come about freely, anywhere and anytime that the poet needs them. In short, nothing seems sacred about their location or use. The second point observed that we have found formulas in both oral and written verse. We differentiated between oral and written verse based upon the complexity of the formula's use. And we noted time and again that the hypothesis of the stockpile rests entirely upon that pile's usefulness to the *oral* poet, composing on the spur of the moment, before an audience. Yet we have found that literate poets resort to the fixed pair much as the oral poets do. This observation alone undercuts the *need* for the formula in a traditional diction, at least in terms of Culley and Whallon's arguments. The third point observes that we have found that it is very unlikely formulas were used in the living transmission of the poetry, even after its oral performances. This is to say, the poetry does not indicate that other agents had their hand on our received texts drastically organizing it after the primary poets created the verse. And fourth, we have found that the simple practices of borrowing, coincidence, and idiomatic repetition may have played a far greater part in the recurrences in the poetry than our scholars are willing to admit. Such participants in the formation of the poetry mitigate against the traditional diction's usefulness.

These conclusions from our research force us to find unacceptable the theory of a fixed traditional diction passed on in time from poet to poet. The theory is untenable because it fails to answer the central question of its necessity for the poet, since the poet, we have shown, need not be an oral performer. While it is the oral poet who uses formulas as a critical device in his creation process, the literate poet employs the pairs as well. Moreover, the theory makes unusually complex a phenomenon in the literature which is in fact quite simple. A "traditional diction" seems to be pure fiction and fabrication, and unnecessary based upon the evidence in the texts. But the above observations are little more than serious misgivings about the matter, and certainly not conclusive evidence. We shall be forced, therefore, to look to our own studies for the origin of the formula and its reason for existence in biblical Hebrew poetry. We must now strengthen and add to the above four observations so that there will be little doubt in our minds as to the existence of a traditional diction. For more evidence, we turn to our examination of Job and Isaiah: our quantitative investigations may be able to tell us about the quality of the diction involved.

We must remind ourselves at the outset that we have found that in Job and Isaiah, repeated word pairs are actually outnumbered 2:1 by those pairs which do not repeat[24]. And the repeated pairs amount to only about half the *total* number of word pairs present. So their number is not large at all. But if a poet, supposedly creating orally in performance, did have a stock-in-trade of fixed pairs to draw upon, we should rightly expect the author of a poem of such great length as Isaiah 1–39 to frequently repeat pairs used before: even the most gifted of speakers repeats dictional phrases and words from time to time in a long speech. But this is not the case in Isaiah, nor is it in Job. Many of the pairs repeat fairly evenly throughout the book of Isaiah as a whole. The repeated word pairs are indeed small in number compared to those which do not repeat. The pairs either repeat or they do not; they cannot be only slightly different from another word pair and still repeat. This then we take as our fifth observation on the theory of a traditional diction as the locus of the formulas, and say:

5) The actual number of word pairs which repeat is very small in comparison to the number which do not repeat.

And as our sixth and final observation, we shall turn again to our work in the books of Isaiah and Job and show that:

6) Pairs which are deemed "rare associations" by modern scholarship, were but common associations to the poet and his public.

When we closely examine the word pairs which repeat in Isaiah or Job, we are immediately struck by the common, everyday analogies which are drawn by the poets. The pairs of most frequent repetition are words of most common and natural union. For example, in Job: "iniquity/sin" ("חטא/עון" Job # 117) 10_{6}, "heaven/earth" ("שמים/ארץ" Job # 243) 11_{8-9}, "day/year" ("שנה/יום" Job # 10_{5}, "land/desert" ("מדבר/ארץ" Job # 404) 38_{26}, "mother/father" ("אב/אם" Job # 212) 17_{14}, "widow/fatherless" ("תום/אלמנה" Job # 262) 22_{9}, "hear/give ear" ("שמע/אזן" Job # 363) 33_{1}, "earth/world" ("תבל/ארץ" Job # 373) 34_{13}. Just because "water/thirst" recurs together, we say, does not at all imply a traditional diction, but common association freely made in any age or locale. For about 90% of the word pairs which we found, in fact, there seems to be no great mystery as to how the words came to be associated. That "die/bury" were associated, requires not the creation of a traditional diction, but simply an understanding of human life and death. These words of daily usage seem to recur most often to the Hebrew poet. So it is a personal diction of each poet, without being a *traditional* diction, which is not only possible, but what we are arguing

[24] See the Numerical Summary and explanation in the Appendix.

for[25]. Therefore, no fixed and rigid stock of traditional diction is needed or implied: the pairing of the vast majority of word pairs comes from their common associations[26].

But there are also a number of recurring pairs which, as we have said, have struck our scholars as odd, and as being unable to have been brought together by common association in so many poet's minds on the spur of the moment. These few pairs have been taken as concrete proof of a traditional diction by Whallon, for one[27]. For example, the association of "jackal/ostrich" in Job (# 343), and "dragon/owl" ("יענה/תוים" Isaiah # 247. 248) in Job and Isaiah, are such pairs. We suggest that the difficulty of associating these words, however, lies in our own minds, and more than likely not in the mind of the author with which it is found. Whallon classifies those word pairs he understands as common, and those word pairs which have no relationship in his *own* frame of reference as peculiar. But those pairs which seem odd to us are so only because we do not understand their relationship today.

One might ask, however, along these lines of reasoning, what, for example, would make such a pair as "dragon/owl" common? To us, there seems to be no relationship whatsoever. Likewise, what possible relationship could the words in the pair "serpent/lion" have? Our own experience does not commonly relate these words together. Yet Mowinckel has been able to show, through the examination of reliefs, how the words "serpent" and "lion" were associated together[28]. The oddity of the existing pair results not from the poet's point of view, but from our own understanding of contemporary relationships. And while we cite here Mowinckel's research with a single word pair, we are convinced that of the few pairs which seem strange to us in association, further study may also be able to determine their appropriate relationship. But since the vast majority of the pairs have understandable association for us, we choose to give the poets the benefit of the doubt, and say that those very few pairs which we do not understand today, were more than likely common associations to the poets. The number of pairs in which the association is uncertain is very small. What could

---

[25] See G.R. Driver, Hebrew Poetic Diction, SVT 1, 1953, 26–39, in which he discusses diction in terms of individual poets.

[26] Our position is supported by the efforts of such writers as J. Muilenburg who speaks of repetition in the poetry without the necessity of a traditional diction. See, A Study in Hebrew Rhetoric: Repetition and Style, SVT 1, 1953, 97–111.

[27] Whallon, Formula, Character, and Context, 145.

[28] Mowinckel has been able to show how שחל once meant "serpent" or "lizard", and was paralleled to the lion. See, שחל, in: Hebrew and Semitic Studies Presented to G.R. Driver, 1963, 95–103.

be more reasonable than the pairs: "vine/olive tree" ("זית/גפן" Job # 195) Job 15_{33}, "light/dark" ("אור/חשך" Job # 208) Job 17_{12}, "dream/vision" ("חלום/חזיון" Job # 90) Job 7_{14}, "beast/bird" ("עוף/ בהמה" Job # 140) Job 12_{7}. It is simplest, we think, thus to associate these "odd" or "rare" pairs also with common usage of the day rather than fabricate a non-existing stockpile to contain them.

When we have agreed that it is easier to ascribe all formulas to common usage, it is possible to account for *all* word pairs and phrases whether they repeat or not. If the formulas represent common associations of the poet which are easily united to compose the parallelism, then we may allow the poet to be more creative than Culley or Whallon would ever permit him to be. So our research indicates, and so shall we maintain below.

Let it not be said that there is little difference between common usage and association, and traditional diction. On the one hand, the word pairs arise out of the commonality of speech and the free association of things which are easily synonymous or antithetical. But on the other hand, the word pairs arise not so much from the poet as they do from a rigidly fixed container of acceptable word pairs passed down as the tools of the contemporary poet. The one view is free and easy in associations; the other is rigid and inflexible in associations.

The formula comes from common association to satisfy the need of the parallelism. No traditional diction is necessary or provable. The common association supplies the basic necessities of the parallelism in Hebrew poetry, that is, the word pairs[29]. And the quality of those word pairs which recur confirm this, as do the simple associations of the pairs. It remains only for us to determine why *the same words* so often repeat throughout the literature, for we recall that actually very few words repeat.

This question, we think, is easily answered. The origin and frequency of word pairs have been said to occur in Hebrew poetry to satisfy the basic architecture of the poetry, namely, its parallelism. The pairs appear to be just as easy for the poet to create as epithets were for the Homeric bard. But a major difference between the Homeric epithet and the Hebrew word pair, is the more frequent repetition of word pairs in the Hebrew poems. For the common word pairs recur much more frequently in Hebrew than the epithets do in Greek. We believe that the word pairs are more frequent than their (supposed)

---

[29] For a very complex assessment of the nature of parallelism in Hebrew poetry, in contrast to our simple one, see S. Mowinckel, Real and Apparent Tricola in Hebrew Psalmic Poetry, 1957, 6. He says that Hebrew parallelism conforms to the "law of duality" a common psychological-esthetical-stylistical "law" in the Near East.

Greek counterparts because of the limited vocabulary of Hebrew as compared to Greek. A triconsonantal language necessarily mitigates against the breadth of vocabulary as in, say, the Greek language. For example, the root word צדק may occur in pairs in verbal, nounal, participial, etc., forms, but in all cases be classified under צדק. The Hebrew poet, therefore, was able to circumvent the problem of limited vocabulary by using the same root in a great number of forms. Yet the fact remains that the theoretical maximum of basic Hebrew root words only 10,164[30].

Because the verbal roots in Hebrew are fewer, and the other classes of words reveal the verbal roots more easily, the word pairs seem to recur more often. But the traditional diction has been proposed mainly in answer to the Hebrew poet's love of repetition of word pairs and phrases. "Why", we might ask, "do the poets more often than not, unerringly pair משפט with צדקה to explain the concepts of justice and righteousness?" Those scholars who maintain a traditional diction would say in answer, that the Hebrew poet was held by the limits of the poetry which went before him, and which was passed down to him. We answer the question by saying that the poets consistently pair שפט and צדק simply because of the limited basic vocabulary of Hebrew, and the sparseness of its root words. Pairs appear to, and do, frequently recur because there are fewer synonyms to explain a notion in another way. The less root stems there are in a language, logically, the more repetition, and the more nuances each root stem must take. It may well be argued that even the Hebrew poet has more choice than our discussion makes him out to have. Yet even if the Hebrew poet should have a great deal of choice in selecting associated words, he certainly does not exercise that freedom. For example, why does the author of Job, with nine Hebrew verbs available for "shine" (אהל קרן, עשת, נגה, יפע, זרד, זהר, הלל, נגה) elect to use in Job 18_{5}, in a word pair "put out/shine" ("נגה/רעך")? We answer, simply because that was the association which was most common in usage for him. We say that the word pairs have their origin in common association in a limited vocabulary.

We shall end our discussion with the conclusion that word pairs which *repeat* are common associations fostered by limited vocabulary. Those pairs which *do not repeat* were probably created by the author with which they are found.

D. CONCLUSION AND ANTICIPATION

We have tried to move somewhat further along toward understanding the Hebrew formula. Earlier we said that word pairs are the dominating element of the poetry. And we concluded that word pairs

30 The permutation allows for two letters to recur in the same word, but, of course, not three: $(22)^2(21)$.

are most common in and stem from an oral verse-making society. But we also noted that the pairs are to be found in literate verse as well.

In this chapter, we have considered the question of whether the word pairs take part in the composition of the poetry, in the transmission of the poetry, or perhaps in both situations. We noted that in the case of the book of Isaiah, the word pairs could be grouped into two categories: those which repeat in one section of the book; and those which were found to repeat across the three sections. In the first instance, we concluded that those word pairs which occur in but one section of Isaiah must be considered to have been placed there at the creation of the verse. But in the second instance, those pairs which repeat throughout the book of Isaiah caused us to account for the influence of transmission upon the use of the word pairs.

However, in the second section of the chapter, we decided that there is no reason to believe that formulas had an equally active life and usefulness in the transmission of the poetry. We observed that the evenness which half of the word pairs reflected throughout such a dis-associated poem as Isaiah, *could* be ascribed to a school of followers of the poet, analogous to the Homeridae. This suggestion of William Whallon's would help explain the *presence* of a uniform diction in one book which also evidenced three clearly different poetic dictions as well. But Whallon and those who support the idea of a transmissional influence upon the poetry were able to marshal little textual evidence to support their view. In fact, we found that there is no reason to ascribe those word pairs which occur evenly throughout Isaiah to the so-called Isaianidae. And we offered a better reason for the recurrence of the pairs in terms of common association.

We have discovered that the concept of a stockpile of readymade phrases and word pairs for the poet does not fit the results of our own research, and lacks substance. For it fails to explain the vast majority of pairs which do not recur anywhere else, but are present in the text at the ratio of 2 : 1 to those pairs which do not recur. Rather, we suggested that it is closer to the evidence to conclude that the formulas occur in Hebrew poetry from common usage and association, and from the exigencies of a limited root vocabulary in Hebrew. And we showed how our view handles both peculiar associations (peculiar in our own minds), and the fact that many pairs do not occur more than once. The situation in the Hebrew verse was not found to be the way Gevirtz would make it when he says that the Ugaritic-Hebrew word pairs are so frequent as to preclude coincidence[31]. There simply are many more non-repeated word pairs than repeated ones.

---

[31] Gevirtz, Patterns in the Early Poetry of Israel, 3.

W. Whallon was correct, therefore, in his assumption that the word pairs (and so formulas) assisted in the composition of the poetry. Insofar as we are able to ascertain, the pair had no life in the transmission of the poetry, nor is their activity in the transmission of the poetry needed to understand why the pairs repeat across different sections of Isaiah: the pairs are the result of common association fostered by a limited root vocabulary, and are freely created by the poet whenever and wherever he wished.

Having now liberated the Hebrew poet from membership in the regimentation of the "stockpile of traditional diction", we are able to view his efforts in the creation of the verse in a far more creative light. No longer is he restricted to fixed formulas of verse which required him only to manipulate the pieces into some coherent whole. He may be regarded as creator of verse in the highest and fullest sense. It is to this subject of creativity that we now turn.

Chapter IV

Word Pairs and the Creativity of the Hebrew Poet

A. THE CREATIVITY OF THE POET AS AUTHOR

We have observed from our research that formulas do not arise from a traditional diction, but from common association promoted by a limited root vocabulary. We may now turn to deal directly with the question of creativity among the Hebrew poets. In our view, which has dispensed with a stock diction, the poet is first of all, freed from the responsibility of regurgitating a traditional diction, and being held to it. He relies only upon his own creativity and the common, everyday associations of his language.

It will be recalled that Whallon's central thesis in his chapter on formulas in the Old Testament was that no element of Old Testament poetry is more likely than not to have been created for the passage in which it now stands, since all passages are, in his view, formulaic[1]. This idea seemed especially reasonable given the observation that the Hebrew verse was full of formulas, phrases and word pairs, repeating everywhere and often. The way Whallon tells it, it would seem that every line of Hebrew poetry is formulaic. But this theory was not demonstrated, nor was it explained to our satisfaction. And the fact that every text contains twice as many non-repeated word pairs as repeated ones was overlooked by him.

Whallon's view leaves us with the impression that the Hebrew poet was not especially creative. This in itself is a traditional view in Old Testament scholarship which sees the poets adhering as close to the verse-making patterns of their predecessors as possible[2]. And as

[1] This is the theme of Whallon's entire chapter on formula in the Old Testament in: Formula, Character, and Context: Studies in Homeric, Old English, and Old Testament Poetry, 1969, 139–172.

[2] The "traditionalism" of the Hebrew artists is often discussed in modern scholarship. See, J. Muilenburg, A Study in Hebrew Rhetoric: Repetition and Style, SVT 1, 1953, 97ff., in which the rhetorical principle is applied to the Hebrew adherence to tradition. In: Form Criticism and Beyond, JBL 88 (1969), 1ff., Muilenburg discusses creativity and rhetorical principle in the poetry. The best work on tradition is B.S. Childs, Memory and Tradition in Israel, 1962.

Culley agrees with him, he says that the Hebrew poet's creativity—assuming the oral traditional diction—lies in his ability to rework acceptable phrases (and word pairs). Culley even pushes the idea of "non-creativity" so far as to say that there is no single author of a poem, nor original text of a verse[3]. For Culley, the singer of verse is nothing more than a preserver of tradition[4]. Creativity is measured by the poet's closeness to tradition. However, this union of bard and tradition does not, once again, explain the non-recurring formulas in the text. To suggest, as Gevirtz does, that those pairs which do not now repeat in the extant literature repeated once in literature now lost, is certainly an argument from silence. In addition, the argument for limiting the poet's creativity to a stock diction is more tenuous than convincing. Oral poets, says Culley, do not have the time to compose new lines and formulas before an audience[5]. But if this is the case, the questions then come to mind: If the poets themselves did not create their traditional diction in oral verse-making, who did? If the traditional diction was not created in public performance, then where? We have rejected the hypothesis of a traditional diction, for the poets may be allowed more creativity than Culley is willing to give them. What, we ask, is more contradictory than the view that the poet is a creative artist, but at the same time is saddled to the limitation of a strictly traditional diction? If the poets did not compose formulas in performance, who did compose them and when? Culley's opinions fail to satisfy completely[6].

Culley and Whallon's view on creativity considers only those pairs which repeat. Such observations fail to take into account *all* of the lines, phrases, and word pairs which were not repeated in the poetry. Their theories ascribing non-recurring word pairs to a Hebrew *Vorlage*, once again fail to withstand textual examination. On the other hand, however, our conclusion relating common association and the formula in all instances, releases the poet from membership in such a restrictive position as Whallon and Culley would place him. The pairs, we say, were made by the poets, whenever they pleased. This we have surmised based upon the great number of pairs which do not recur anywhere, but are found only once.

When we examine the Appendix summary for Job, we see that those pairs which were found only once are balanced against those pairs

---

[3] R. C. Culley, Oral Formulaic Language in the Biblical Psalms, 1967, 9.

[4] St. Gevirtz, Patterns in the Early Poetry of Israel, 1963, 14. According to his appraisal, and as we have said elsewhere, the Hebrew poet is not to be thought of as creatively "original" in our sense of the word.

[5] Culley, Oral Formulaic Language, 16. See also, Whallon, Formula, Character, and Context, 160.

[6] Culley, Oral Formulaic Language, 9. 10. 21.

which do recur throughout the literature at a ratio of 2 : 1. 850 pairs in Job recur only once in the whole of Hebrew literature, and 386 pairs recur either in Job or elsewhere. And the ratio for Isaiah is much the same. The weight of this evidence alone would lead us to question seriously the thesis of Whallon that no element of the Old Testament poetry is more likely than not to have been created for the passage in which it now stands. Pairs which do not recur number twice as many as those which do repeat. In fact, there are so many non-recurrent pairs in the literature, that not even a small number of them could have been once "traditional" as the scholars claim. Surely we must conclude that passages and lines which occur but once in extant biblical poetry must have been created for the place in which they are now found, at least until proven otherwise by new evidence. This we believe is far closer to the evidence than holding those phrases and word pairs which do not repeat as suspect and without authorship; the pairs which do not repeat anywhere seem to tell us that creativity is very much present in the texts, twice as much present as the repeated pairs. Clearly, and now we turn against Whallon, Culley, and even Gevirtz, there is more originality and creativity in the text of scripture, than there is repetition, even while repetition is a predominant aspect of the literature. We take as sound criticism of these scholars' failure to deal extensively with the texts before reaching conclusions, the words of Cassuto. While he criticizes the Graf-Wellhausen expository method, his remarks are precisely applicable to Whallon and Culley: "This method which establishes a given principle *a priori*, without taking into consideration what is expressly stated in the text, and then, placing the passages upon the Procrustian bed of that principle, hacks off the textual limbs that do not fit into the bed, can hardly be accepted as valid."[7] Whallon and Culley have, in effect, hacked off the non-recurring word pairs from the body of the formulas of the Old Testament.

We shall even go so far as to ascribe creativity to the poet himself. That the word pair is the dominating element of the "parallelistic" form of the poetry, does not disallow the fact that the poets were creative with the formation and the use of the formulas. We can only conclude that the majority of the verse was written for the place in which it now appears, and that a given verse, until it is proven otherwise, was written for the place in which it now appears. Just how creative the Hebrew poet was in terms of both form and freedom of association, must now be considered.

---

[7] U. Cassuto, A Commentary on the Book of Genesis: From Adam to Noah, I, 1961, 190.

B. CREATIVITY AND THE ASSOCIATION OF WORDS IN PAIR

The concept of a traditional diction ruling the verse-making of Hebrew poets implies that he is not especially creative. A traditional diction also implies that the Hebrew poet is not in control of the form of the verse which he is creating, nor is he able to influence the fixed pair associations which the parallelism requires. The traditional diction is said to rule and guide the poet.

But our study has indicated that the Hebrew poet is not dependent upon a stereotyped traditional diction in any way since such a stockpile does not exist. Therefore, the poet must be seen in a new light of individual creativity. Such creativity requires us, then, to look more closely at the form of the poetry and the associations which the poet makes.

We have assumed thus far in our discussion that formulas require repetition of words in fixed pairs or repetition of phrases. When two words are repeated at an even distance from each other, and stand in relationship to one another, we have a word pair. For example:

Surely there is a mine for *silver*,
  and a place for *gold* which they refine.

(Job 28_{1} 3_{15} Job # 18)

כי יש לכסף מוצא ומקום לזהב יזקו

Therefore, I will make the *heavens* tremble,
  and the *earth* will be shaken out of its place.

(Isaiah 13_{13}; so 1_{2} 14_{12} Isaiah # 4)

על כן שמים ארגיז ותרעם הארץ ממקומה

The *form* of the formula, namely that it repeats words evenly distanced, would seem to be more important than the *ease of association* of "silver/gold" ("זהב/כסף" Job # 18) or "heavens/earth" ("ארץ/שמים" Isaiah # 4) itself. But this is not always the case, in fact, quite often is not the case, and so far, no writer has taken notice of this fact[8]. While it is certainly true that the form of the fixed pair which repeats is important, we have found that this single form does not answer for a special class of repeated words which stand adjacent to each other.

As we have just observed, word pairs formed by common association are by nature very easy to create. Take, for example, the word pair "distress/anguish" ("מצוקה/צר" Job # 191). This pair recurs often in

[8] Whallon discusses the fact that many words in fixed pair recur adjacently. But he relegates the phenomenon of adjacent pairs to the prose alone, overlooking the fact that adjacent words recur often in the poetry. Adjacent words in the poetry become immediately apparent when an entire test is examined—which Whallon failed to do. See, Formula, Character, and Context, 148.

the literature, and we may well assume that the way in which these words are presented by the poet—as a word pair with the words at a fixed distance from each other—is critical:

> Then they cried to the Lord in their *distress*,
> and he delivered them from their *anguish*.
> (Psalm 107$_{6}$; so 107$_{19.28}$ 25$_{17}$)
>
> ויצעקו אל יהוה להם ממצוקותיהם יצילם

But it is not critical. Our Appendix lists of Isaiah, Job, and Lamentations indicate that[9]. For we find these same words, "distress" and "anguish" used an equal number of times next to each other as "distress and anguish" where the relationship of the words cannot be by chance either. For instance:

> Distress and anguish terrify him;
> (Job 15$_{24}$ Zephaniah 1$_{15}$ Psalm 119$_{143}$ Job # 191)
>
> יבעתהו צר ומצוקה

In the case of "silver/gold" ("זהב/כסף" Job # 18) above, we cite Psalms 105$_{37}$ 115$_{4}$ as examples of instances where the words are adjacent. For "heavens/earth" ("ארץ/שמים" Isaiah # 4) found adjacently, see Isaiah 65$_{17}$ 66$_{22}$. And one final example of the countless instances of words found in fixed pair recurring adjacently:

> The *ox* knows its owner,
> and the *ass* its master's crib;
> (Isaiah 1$_{3}$ Isaiah # 5)
>
> ידע קנהו וחמור אבוס בעליו

> Happy are you who sow beside all waters,
> who let the feet of *the ox and the ass* range free.
> (Isaiah 32$_{20}$)
>
> אשריכם זרעי על כל מים משלחי רגל השור והחמיר

This leads us to submit that since many, many words in pair recur just as often in the poetry as words yoked by conjunction, it is the *ease and importance of association* which is foremost in the poet's mind, and not necessarily the form in which the words are presented[10]. The form is an aftermath of the ease of association. Furthermore, considering the types of associations, we observe something equally very interesting:

---

[9] In our Appendix lists, citations in parentheses are usually places where the fixed pair recurs adjacently.

[10] Or another example, "wisdom/understanding" ("תבונה/חכמה" Job # 146) which is a word pair found in Job 12$_{12}$, but found adjacently in Ezekiel 28$_{4}$ and elsewhere.

we find that most popular word pairs in the poetry are found equally as often as coupled words in the poetry and the prose. "Sing/rejoice" ("שמח/שיש" Isaiah # 169, Job # 22, 250) found as a word pair at Isaiah 24_{11} 65_{13-14} 66_{10}, becomes "sing and rejoice" elsewhere (Isaiah 22_{13} 35_{10} 51_{3}). "Eat/drink" ("אכל/שתה" Isaiah # 330) is a word pair in Isaiah 29_{8} 36_{16} 62_{9} 65_{13}, and is found as "eat and drink" elsewhere (Isaiah 21_{5} 22_{13} 36_{12}). Specifically, it will be noticed that in Job and Lamentations, a great number of the word pairs occur as yoked adjacent pairs[11]. Many of these adjacent pairs, interestingly enough, recur in Genesis, Exodus, Numbers, and Deuteronomy, both in their prose and in their poetry. Could the Torah, then, provide the impetus for free association and repetition in the later poetry? That "righteousness" (צדק) is seldom found without its friend "justice" (משפט) in word pairs (Job # 95) and adjacent associations; that "hungry" (רעב) and "thirsty" (עמא) are seldom found apart (Job # 287); that "evil" (חטא) and "iniquity" (און) are found often together (Job # 117); all these and many more words seem to indicate to us that it was the *association* of the words in the author's mind which was important, and only secondarily the form which that association took in a given instance. We certainly do not mean to suggest that the Torah stamped out a fixed diction for the Hebrew poet in any way, or that the Torah could be a "traditional diction" or "stockpile", for these latter concepts were invented by scholarship to answer for oral verse-making alone. The poets were not so rigidly dependent upon past tradition. But we do wonder if the Torah did not in some way influence the *extent* of common associations and the poet's interest in repetition.

Whallon believes that the poetry influenced the prose because the words in the poetic line were critical in their organization[12]. But our observations and research indicate just the opposite. Certainly the words in the poetic line are critical in their organization. But words were associated anywhere in the literature by the Hebrew poet. The same words are repeatedly associated in the prose or in the poetry. However, freely associated words recur in the prose as adjacent pairs, and in the poetry as both fixed and adjacent pairs. It is the ease of association which seems critical to us, not so much the form in which the association is found. The poet was not bound to a fixed diction which forced him to resort to specific associations in limited forms. In the prose, words frequently repeat adjacently which are held in association. In the poetry, the associations had to satisfy the requirement of parallelism by having the words placed at an even distance from each other. But

[11] Even in the book of Ruth, to which we shall later turn, there are more words which recur as adjacent pairs than fixed pairs.

[12] Whallon, Formula, Character, and Context, 144–154.

nevertheless, the associations still occurred just as often adjacently. And herein, once again, lies our answer to the question of the repeated word pairs in the whole of Isaiah: some word pairs recur throughout that entire text, even across three poets, because they were so commonplace and routine in their association. The ease of association for the creative poet is the critical factor which was overlooked by the other scholars investigating the Hebrew formula.

C. DIFFERENT GENRE, FORMULAS, AND SUBJECT MATTER

Culley maintains, and this is a significant part of his book, that different genre have their own special formulas, different types (elements within the genre) have their own formulas[13]. This is to say, the poet is limited in the formulas which he may use in any instance, and his "stockpile" is categorized with certain pairs for certain situations. The vast majority of the repeated phrases which he located in the biblical psalms recur in individual complaints, individual thanksgivings, and hymns. For example, "65%" of Psalm 96, a hymn, repeats elsewhere. The formulas, he argues, therefore, are limited to the *Gattungen* of the biblical psalms which he studied, and formulas found in one *Gattung* differ from those found in another. He says that this is the case because the poets had their traditional diction compartmentalized in their own minds. A song, a narrative, a lament may have formulas which are used exclusively in one type of poetry or another. For instance, many formulas are found in the lament *Gattung* and nowhere else in the biblical psalms. This, again, is due to the traditional diction, the stockpile of formulas which must have been catalogued in the poet's mind: words of sorrow and woe are stored up for use in the laments; words of gladness are enlisted for hymns of praise.

This observation is at least appealing. Were it not for the fact that Culley is unable to marshal but a few examples of restricted formulaic usage in the biblical psalms, we would allow it to go unchallenged: he is able to locate just 73 phrases in the 150 psalms which repeat more than twice[14]. And he is able to locate but 10 psalms out of the 150 which have "40%" formulas or better. These 10 psalms, then, are located in the individual lament and thanksgiving, and hymn *Gattungen*[15].

---

[13] Culley, Oral Formulaic Language, 16–17.
[14] Ibid. 32.
[15] Ibid. 103.

In addition to the above problems in Culley's research, his selection of the biblical psalms alone as the focus of his type of study appears to us a poor choice. The psalms, first of all, account for only 8% of the poetry of the Old Testament, and second, represent but one genre among many in the scripture[16]. On both points, his investigation is necessarily restrictive in scope. Third, the psalms are made up of short songs coming from diverse periods in history, and hence created by many different people. But what we must consider to be most problematic in Culley's examination of the psalms is his failure to check to see if the formulas which he locates in the psalms recur in other texts and genres. This in itself would have supported or refuted his theory of "certain formula for certain types". His failure to examine the poetic literature as a whole we regard as suspicious when Culley makes the comment that a look at one author in terms of formula is best[17]. For by limiting himself to the psalm genre, he is unable to say with finality that certain formulas are used exclusively in certain genre and types. And when he later says that we cannot be certain of the psalms' exact relationship to oral formulaic composition[18], we feel as though we must look more closely into the matter.

From our own studies as well as from the observations of Whallon, we begin to see that things are not the way Culley would have them. Whallon says, without sufficient proof however, and in opposition to Culley, that word pairs are not limited to a particular genre or *Gattung*. Word pairs and phrases may appear anywhere without regard for type[19]. Hence, we must decide who is correct in his viewpoint: either the word pairs recur anywhere, without dependence upon type or genre, or they are restricted to the various types and genre, and so have limited usage.

In terms of our study, first we must consider the recurrences of the formula in Old Testament genre. Looking at the Appendix list for the book of Job, we are once more, as with Lamentations, interested in the attestation of the word pair both in the book itself and throughout the Hebrew poetry in general. Job is a part of the wisdom genre of poetry. If Culley is correct in his theory of restricted usage, we should rather easily see that the word pairs of Job repeat most frequently in the rest of the wisdom literature. But if the same pairs recur everywhere in the Hebrew poetry, Whallon's theory will be vindicated.

In checking our results, we find that the vast majority of the word pairs which are found in Job and which repeat elsewhere, repeat without

---

[16] M. Tsevat, A Study of the Language of the Biblical Psalms, 1955, 79 note 27.
[17] Culley, Oral Formulaic Language, 16.
[18] Ibid. 113.
[19] Whallon, Formula, Character, and Context, 161–162.

regard for genre whatsoever. The same word pairs recur in the older, isolated poems of the Old Testament; they recur in the prophets, and they repeat in the wisdom literature including the psalms, without bias for one genre. At least in terms of genre, then, Culley is in error, and Whallon is correct: the word pairs recur without respect to genre.

Moreover, a great many of the individual word pairs which repeat in Job, repeat elsewhere. In fact, 259 of the 386 individual word pairs, or about 3/5 of the individual pairs, repeat elsewhere. This is not immediately important here, but will be in our next chapter. Nevertheless, it does indicate the extent to which the pairs are versatile and used throughout the poetry.

In terms of the genre, the word pairs seem to recur wherever the poet has occasion to use them. And examining the smaller types within the genre, the *Gattungen*, we are led to quite the same conclusions. Here we turn once again to our Appendix list on Lamentations. The poems of Lamentations are part of the lament *Gattung*, loaded with affirmations of grief and sorrow. If Culley is correct with respect to type, we should find frequent repetition of the same word pairs used in the national or individual laments of the biblical psalms and in Lamentations, both being members of one *Gattung*[20].

We do indeed notice a number of word pairs—eleven to be exact—which recur both in Lamentations and in the lament psalms[21], but as our list shows, certainly no more than occur elesewhere in the other psalms, and elsewhere in the poetry as a whole. *Gattung* or genre, it appears, has little to do with the recurrence of the word pair[22]. But this is not to preclude the fact that different types may have different amounts of specific word pairs depending upon their usage, as, for example, in the frequent recurrences of a few of the same word pairs in Lamentations and some of the psalms. But different genres and types will have different formulas *only* because the subjects of the poems change from type to type, genre to genre, and because words are naturally restricted to their applicable use. The word pair "languish/lament" ("אבל/אמלל" Lamentations # 33, 25) is a commonplace in the lament *Gattung*, only because such pairs as "joy/gladness" are in-

[20] The national and individual laments which Gunkel classified and with which we compared Lamentations are: Individual: 3; 4; 5; 6; 7; 13; 14; 17; 22; 25; 26; 27.7–14; 28; 31.1–9, 10–25; 35; 36; 38; 39; 40.14–18; 42, 43; 44; 51; 52; 54; 55; 56; 57; 58; 59; 61; 64; 69; 71; 77.1–16; 86; 88; 102; 109; 120; 130; 139; 140; 141; 142; 143. National: 12; 60; 74; 79; 80; 83; 85; 90; 94.1–11; 123; 126; 137. H. Gunkel and J. Begrich, The Psalms: A Form-Critical Introduction, 1967; or also, H. Gunkel, Die Psalmen, RGG 4, 1913, 1927ff.

[21] Lamentations word pairs # 6, 13, 50, 60, 61, 69, 74, 80, 86, 91, 92.

[22] M. Tsevat, A Study of the Language of the Biblical Psalms, 33. He notes a uniform diction spread evenly over all the *Gattungen* of the psalms.

appropriate to the context of such passages of poetry[23]. If certain words tend to recur in definite forms and types, it is only due to the fitness of the given words in the format. No "stockpile of traditional diction" for *Gattung* or genre need be postulated, it would seem, nor can one be proven to explain the actuality of the poetry. Rather, different genres and types have different formulas peculiar to themselves only because the subject matter changes, and words are by nature restricted to their applicable use. There is no conclusive proof, therefore, neither in the few word pairs which repeat in type of genre, nor in the fact that most pairs recur throughout the literature, that a traditional diction exists[24].

D. CONCLUSION AND ANTICIPATION

We began our investigation of the creativity of the Hebrew poet by reaffirming the contention that no traditional diction or fixed stockpile of formulas existed for the poet. We noted that the hypothesis of a traditional diction answers only for those word pairs which repeat in the verse, and at the same time overlooks those pairs which do not repeat. No traditional diction is necessary to explain the presence of Hebrew formulas. Common association and limited vocabulary are able to explain both the pairs which recur in the verse and those which do not.

We next affirmed the creativity of the Hebrew poet once he had been freed from the restrictions of the "stockpile". We maintained that the majority of the verses in the texts were written for the places in which they now appear, since non-repeating word pairs outnumber those which recur in the texts and elsewhere at the ratio of 2 : 1. Need we suppose, therefore, that such a writer as Shakespeare was indebted to Job when he put into Hamlet's mouth the words[25]:

O cursed spite
That ever I was born to set it right!

No, we give credit to both authors for expressing the same, but universal idea. Both were creative. Even while we grant that Shakespeare

---

[23] "Foe/enemy" ("איב/צר" # 2, 6, 22, 23), "iniquity/sin" ("חטא/עון" # 74), "orphan/widow" ("אלמנה/יתרום" # 91), and "fierce anger" ("אף חרון" # 2) are commonplace in Lamentations because these pairs and phrases fit the subject of the author and the thoughts with which he is dealing.

[24] While our study concerned itself with the lament *Gattung*, the formula critical method could be applied easily to any genre, *Gattung*, or smaller group of related passages. For example, we also examined the so-called servant songs of Isaiah (42$_{1-4.\ 5-7}$ 49$_{1-6.\ 7-9a}$ 50$_{4-9.\ 1-3}$ 52$_{13}$-53.$_{12}$) but could see no clear relationship in the formulas used. See R.H. Pfeiffer, Introduction to the Old Testament, 1963, 454–455.

[25] A. Guillaume, Studies in the Book of Job: with a New Translation, 1968, 15.

may have known the book of Job, he was not bound to express his view in terms which violated his own creativity. Each writer, Job and Shakespeare, expressed the same, universal sentiment in their own way.

Second, we considered the creativity of the Hebrew poet in terms of the associations which he made in creating the word pairs, and in terms of the forms which these associations took. We pointed out that it is the association of the words that is more important to the authors than the form in which the words are associated. Closely associated pairs of words occur very often adjacently in the prose, and both as fixed-distanced and adjacent pairs in the poetry. If two words are associated at fixed distance from each other in the poetry as a word pair, they can almost always be found adjacent to each other, connected by conjunction, either in the prose or in the poetry. This, we concluded, is strong evidence that the associations which the authors make are more important than the form which those associations take. The strengthening of the given idea by repeating related words seems to be most important to the author.

We also suggested that while the fixed pair is critical to the poetic line, the prose may have offered associations to the poet for him to use in fixed pairs. We said that the fondness for adjacent associations in the prose, specifically the Torah, may have helped to make the desire for repetition instructional and artistic to the Hebrew poet.

Last, we held that the creative Hebrew poet is not even restricted to the use of different formulas for different situations, genre, or *Gattung*. When pairs do recur in a given genre or type of poetry, we say this is due solely to the fact that a given subject requires a vocabulary to fit that subject. Words are by their nature restricted to their applicable use. No catalogued stockpile of traditional diction to fit each and every type or genre is needed nor even probable. The poet's creativity is far more lively than that theory supposes.

In the next chapter, we shall examine the usefulness of the word pairs which do repeat, their peculiarities, and how they may better help us understand the poetry in general. Our most important observation will be that the word pair just may be the one key to our understanding of the organization of the Hebrew line, which, for want of a better word, we must call "meter".

Chapter V

Word Pairs as a Significant Index to the Poetic Line

A. BISHOP LOWTH'S CONTRIBUTION

Our aim here is to indicate the ways in which word pairs may help us to grasp Hebrew verse with greater understanding. That the pairs direct us to a deeper appreciation of the poetic line will be demonstrated. But first, it is important to observe why it has taken so long for scholarship to come to appreciate the smaller elements of the line, that is, the word pairs.

S. Gevirtz has remarked that Hebrew poetic scholarship has derived its vitality principally from two discoveries[1]. The first was R. Lowth's categories of parallelism in Hebrew verse which he suggested in the 1700's. The second was the discovery of the relationship of Ugaritic and Hebrew verse in the 1930's. However, we are interested in Lowth's work alone here.

Lowth observed that Hebrew poetry may be characterized by a divided line, one half of which says something about the other half, either synonymously or antithetically[2]. Lowth was certainly not the first to notice parallelism of the members in Hebrew poetry. As early as 960 A.D. we find Menahem ben Saruch observing that in Hebrew verse, "one half of the line teaches about the other"[3]. It was Lowth's

---

[1] S. Gevirtz, Patterns in the Early Poetry of Israel, 1963, 2–4.

[2] Two works by Robert Lowth interest us. First, Lectures on the Sacred Poetry of the Hebrews, 1829, 154–166. But we also possess a first edition of the work: De Sacra Poesi Hebraeorum Praelectiones, 1753, 177–196. But it is only in: Isaiah, A New Translation: with Preliminary Dissertation, 1778, ix, that Lowth really elaborates his views on the subject of parallelism.

[3] It is customary to note the words of such medieval writers as Rabbi Azariah de Rossi (1513–1574) for their comments on parallelism, as Lowth did: see R. Gordis, Poets, Prophets, and Sages: Essays in Biblical Interpretation, 1971, 63. But such opinions by de Rossi and Ibn Ezra are late. Menahem ben Saruch is quoted by J. Barr, Comparative Philology and the Text of the Old Testament, 1968, 62.

work, however, which led to active study of the parallelism[4]. So pervasive were his conclusions, says Gevirtz, that with minor variations over the years, his theories were refined, and the matter of Hebrew poetry was considered largely closed[5]. The parallelism, for all its intents and nuances, was assumed to be the foundation of Hebrew poetry.

To say that the matter of Hebrew poetic study was considered closed after the work of Lowth, is something of an understatement. An examination of the comparatively few works on the subject of Hebrew poetry since 1800, indicates that scholars had been lulled into thinking that Lowth had effectively spoken the last word on Hebrew poetry. Articles published on the history of poetic scholarship are as dry and lifeless as any could wish. To read one survey text or article is to have read them all[6]. The advances made beyond Lowth's investigations are few indeed. After his work on parallelism was tidied up, such topics as strophe, meter, and alliteration have claimed poetic scholarship's attention[7].

---

[4] Lowth's delineation of parallelism is seen as his *primary* contribution to Old Testament poetic study. However, this is not so. Even a cursory reading of his *Lectures* will reveal that his discussion on parallelism is nestled in chapter xix, a point which R. P. Fitzgerald totally overlooks when he emphasizes the idea of parallelism as Lowth's greatest hour. See, The Place of Robert Lowth's De Sacra Poesi Hebraeorum Praelectiones in Eighteenth Century Criticism, Ph. D. Dissertation, University of Iowa, 1964, 87–125. Lowth's greatest contribution to us is his neo-Classical esthetic appreciation of the poetry.

[5] For great praise of Lowth, see T.H. Robinson, Hebrew Poetic Form: The English Tradition, SVT 1, 1953, 128–149. For a picture of Lowth as a "bland figure" in eighteenth century criticism, see Fitzgerald, The Place of Robert Lowth's De Sacra Poesi Hebraeorum, 183.

[6] See W.O. Osterley and T.H. Robinson, An Introduction to the Books of the Old Testament, 1963 (1934), 139–149; T.H. Robinson, Hebrew Poetic Form: The English Tradition, 128–149. The surveys of poetic scholarship reveal painfully little progress in the field. Long considered the textbook on Hebrew poetry, T.H. Robinson's The Poetry of the Old Testament, 1947, is a small text of only 216 pages. Yet the author runs out of the technical aspects of the poetry to discuss on page 46, and must resort to exegesis of individual poems and books thereafter. The bibliography in that book (compiled by A.R. Johnson) combined with Eissfeldt's bibliography on poetry in: The Old Testament: An Introduction, 1965, 57, amounts to no more than a few hundred books and articles written on Hebrew poetry in the past two hundred years! And we might add, a Jewish survey of the scholarship offers the reader nothing new. See, R. Gordis, Poets, Prophets, and Saga, 61–94.

[7] Studies since Lowth may be grouped in the following way: on strophe: H. Möller, Der Strophenbau der Psalmen, ZAW 50 (1932), 240–256; C.F. Kraft, The Strophic Structure of Hebrew Poetry as Illustrated in the First Book of the Psalter, 1938; F.B. Kösters, Die Strophen, TSK 6 (1831), 40–114; A. Condamin, Poèmes de la Bible, 1933; J.A. Montgomery, Stanza Formation in Hebrew Poetry,

Lowth's approach to the poetry was, we might say, prematurely form-critical for his age. For Lowth established categories into which the verse could be fit, based upon the nature of the parallelism which was present[8]. And growing interest in categorizing and typing texts and passages after Lowth's death probably had a lot to do with the feeling that once verses were classified as to their parallelism, the scholar's job was done[9]. It was left only until recently, and the discovery of the formula in Hebrew poetry, to show us that we might move beyond Lowth's categories.

W. Whallon's comments on Lowth are different and refreshing because he is perhaps the first writer to oppose the bulk of scholarship stemming from Lowth's observations[10]. Whallon criticizes Lowth's "*Gattungen*" of parallelism because they have failed to take us behind the larger elements of the poetry (the parallelism) to examine the components of the poetry (the repeated phrases and word pairs). On the face of it, Whallon's is a harsh, but enlightened, approach. He is correct in saying that because Hebrew poetic scholarship has spent its time fitting verse into categories, it has failed to go behind the parallelism. Yet Whallon blunders in blaming Lowth alone for this state of affairs. For Whallon has failed to observe—as have all authors following Lowth—that Lowth *himself* took note of the parts of the line which make up the parallelism. Whallon is, therefore, not unlike all other writers who have discovered the importance of the elements of the poetry from an indirect approach (comparative literature). But he is mistaken in saying that Lowth himself led modern scholarship up a blind alley until the present

---

JBL 64 (1945), 379–384; P. Ruben, Strophic Forms in the Bible, JOR 11 (1899), 431–479. On anacrusis: T.H. Robinson, Anacrusis in Hebrew Poetry, BZAW 64 (1936), 37–40. On alliteration: O.S. Rankin, Alliteration in Hebrew Poetry, JTS 31 (1930), 285–291. On meter: F. Horst: Die Kennzeichen der hebräischen Poesie, ThRv 21 (1953), 97–121; P. Cummins, Rhythm, Hebrew and English, CBO 3 (1941), 27–42; S.T. Byington, A Mathematical Approach to Hebrew Meters, JBL 64 (1947), 63–77; J. Begrich, Zur hebräischen Metrik, ThRv 4 (1932), 67–89.

[8] G.B. Gray, The Forms of Hebrew Poetry, 1915, 37–83, is an examination and expansion of Lowth's parallelism. The most industrious undertaking on parallelism is L.I. Newman and W. Popper, Studies in Biblical Parallelism, 1918.

[9] It is to be noted how little form-critical scholarship has contributed to the ongoing study of the poetic line and the elements of the line. See, for example, F. Crussemann, Studien zur Formgeschichte von Hymnus und Danklied in Israel, 1969. Form criticism has occupied its time studying the larger elements of the poetry. O. Eissfeldt's survey of the "types" of poetry, for example, tells us little about of the verse or the elements of the line. The Old Testament: An Introduction, 64–127.

[10] W. Whallon, Formula, Character, and Context: Studies in Homeric, Old English, and Old Testament Poetry, 1969, 140–144.

discovery of formulas. Rather, Lowth merely clouded the issue in poetic research by emphasizing the parallelism rather than calling equal attention to the elements of the parallelism. A close examination of Lowth's definition of parallelism clearly shows that he was fully aware of the components of the verse which go together to make up the parallelism:

> The correspondence of one verse or line with another, I call parallelism, when a preposition is delivered, and a second is subjoined to it, or drawn under it, equivalent, or contrasted with it sense, or similar to it in the form of grammatical construction, these I call parallel lines; and the words or phrases answering one to another in the corresponding lines, parallel terms[11].

These "words or phrases answering one to another in the corresponding lines", we now call word pairs and phrases, and in the extended sense, the formula. That later scholarship following Lowth pursued "the parallel lines", instead of "the parallel terms", is the fault of succeeding scholarship, not Lowth[12]. Lowth must be viewed, therefore, as one of the very first to point out the components of the line which go to make up the parallelism. And we must note that, as we have said before, "the parallel terms" (the word pairs) in his definition do not have to repeat to be detected.

It is our purpose here only to say that the observation of word pairs in the line is as old as Lowth, but not until recently has it been under close examination. Lowth recognized that the word pair is valuable in understanding Hebrew poetry. That the examination of the formula to learn more about the poetry is long overdue is not Lowth's fault, as Whallon would have it, but our own. That the formula assists in our understanding of the poetry must now be shown.

B. THE PECULIARITIES OF POETIC CONSTRUCTION AS REVEALED BY WORD PAIRS

1. Long Tours

The exegesis of texts for word pairs has turned up a number of peculiarities of poetic construction. These constructions might otherwise go unnoticed, or their importance be misunderstood, if it were

---

[11] R. Lowth, Isaiah, ix.

[12] In the first two volumes of their three volume work, Newman and Popper, Studies in Biblical Parallelism, occasionally deal with the parallel terms in the line, but do not see these elements to be of great importance. In their work, the ability to classify a line as to parallelism is what is critical.

not for our approach. One example of this is what we have named "long tours". By this we mean that in Hebrew poetry, we occasionally encounter a series of one or more verses where the poet lists pairs of from three to ten words all meaning roughly the same thing, or having something to do with the same subject, or being in some way related[13].

Since the word pair by nature is made up of two words in association, the simplest tour would consist of instances where there are three words which act in association. For example, Isaiah 1.8 (Isaiah # 14):

And the daughter of Zion is left
like a *booth* in a vineyard,
like a *lodge* in a cucumber field,
like a besieged *city*.

ונותרה בת ציון כסכה בכרם
כמלונה במקשה כציר נצורה

Here the parallel words "both" ("סכה"), "lodge" ("מלונה"), and "city" ("עיר") cohere[14]. Where two words would have sufficed to explain what the poet had to say, he instead used three. And it has been suggested in the past that these instances where there seems to be a hemistich attached to two hemistichs with complete word pair, the third hemistich is an addition[15]. But we have found that in Job and Isaiah, the addition of more words pairing to the first or initial word pair is very common and may well be intrinsic to the original work.

They have forsaken the Lord,
they have despised the Holy One of Israel,
they are utterly estranged. (Isaiah 1_4)

עזבו את יהוה נאצו את קדוש ישראל נזרו אחור

They lift it up upon their shoulders, they carry it,
they set it in its place, and it stands there;
it cannot move from its place. (Isaiah 46_7)

ישאהו על כתף יסבלהו ויניחהו תחתין ויעמד ממקומו לא ימים

[13] R. Gordis, The Book of God and Man: A Study of Job, 1965, 160, cites some of the long tours in Job, but only to show the poet's vast knowledge in many fields.

[14] The triplets found are: Job: 4_{17} $5_{2.\ 6.\ 10.\ 13.\ 14.\ 17.\ 24}$ 6_5 $7_{2.\ 3.\ 11}$ 8_{11} 11_{14} 12_{11} 13_{12} 14_2 15_{33} 18_{16} 20_5 $22_{6.\ 7}$ 23_{12} 24_3 26_{12} $27_{16.\ 18}$ 29_{11} 30_{15} $31_{7.\ 22}$ 33_4 34_3 40_{23} $41_{2.\ 21.}$ Isaiah: $1_{4.\ 6.\ 8.\ 10.\ 16.\ 29}$ 2_{11} $5_{13.\ 16.\ 17.\ 20.\ 23.\ 24}$ 9_2 $10_{1.\ 2.\ 3.\ 15}$ 11_1 13_{11} 14_6 21_{14} 25_7 $29_{4.\ 19}$ 30_2 $32_{1.\ 5.\ 9.\ 16}$ 33_3 34_7 35_5 40_3 44_{26} 49_{22} 54_4 58_8 $59_{1.\ 17}$ $61_{10.\ 11}$ $66_{8.}$ Lamentations: 2_5 $5_{13.}$

[15] See S. Mowinckel, Real and Apparent Tricola in Hebrew Psalmic Poetry, 1957. He argues for the actually sparse existence of tricola in psalmic poetry.

These third lines may not add anything new to the otherwise complete parallelism and word pair, but they still seem to be important. These third lines which have sometimes been regarded as nothing more than additions to the text, may, in fact, often turn out to be massing of word pairs to an initial fixed pair. And a good method of checking to see if a hemistich is purposely added to an otherwise complete distich, might be to determine if the newly associated words recur as word pairs elsewhere. For instance, do "booth", "lodge", and "city", or any two words thereof, recur elsewhere?

TABLE 3. LONG TOURS

Job:

4_{10-11}	lion, fierce lion, young lion, strong lion, whelp, lioness
16_{12-14}	break asunder, seize, dash, set up, surround, slash open, spare not, pour out, break, run upon
18_{8-10}	net, pitfall, trap, snare, rope, trap
19_{13-15}	brethren, acquaintance, kinsfolk, close friend, guest, maidservant
28_{15-19}	gold, silver, gold of Ophir, onyx, sapphire, gold, glass, jewels, fine gold, coral, crystal, pearl, topaz, pure gold
31_{1-3}	covenant, portion, heritage
33_{23}	angel, mediator, one of the thousand
41_{26-30}	sword, spear, dart, javelin, iron, bronze, arrow, slingstone, club, javelin, potsherd, threshing sledge
28_{1-6}	silver, gold, iron, copper, ore, stone, sapphire, gold

Lamentations:

1_{13}	send, descend, spread, turn back, stun, faint
2_{2-3}	destroy, break down, bring down, cut down, withdraw, burn
3_{28-30}	sit in silence, put mouth in the dust, cheek to smiter, be filled with insults

Isaiah:

1_{11}	rams, fed beasts, bulls, lambs, he-goats
1_{17}	good, justice, oppression, fatherless, widow
2_{12-14}	proud, lofty, lifted up, high, pride, exalted, haughtiness
3_{2-3}	mighty man, soldier, judge, prophet, diviner, elder, captain of fifty, a man of rank, counselor, skillful magician, expert in charms
3_{4-6}	boys, princes, babes, people, man, fellow, neighbor, youth, elder, base fellow, honorable man, brother, father
3_{18-23}	finery of anklets, headbands, crescents, pendants, bracelets, scarfs, headdresses, armlets, sashes, perfume boxes, amulets, signet rings, nose rings, festal robes, mantles, cloaks, handbags, garments, gauze, linen garments, turbans, veils
3_{24}	perfume/rottenness, girdle/rope, well set hair/baldness, rich robe/sackcloth, beauty/shame
5_{27}	weary, stumble, slumber, sleep
9_{6}	Wonderful Counselor, Mighty God, Everlasting Father, Prince of Peace

10_{28-32}	Rimmon, Aiath, Migron, Michmash, Geba, Ramah, Gibeah of Saul, Gallim, Laishah, Anathoth, Madmenah, Gebim, Nob, Zion, Jerusalem
11_{2}	wisdom, understanding, counsel, might, knowledge, fear of the Lord
11_{6-8}	wolf, lamb, leopard, kid, calf, lion, fatling, cow, bear, lion, ox, asp, adder
14_{13-14}	heavens, stars of God, on high, on the mount of assembly, far north, heights of the clouds
16_{6}	pride, proud, arrogance, pride, insolence, boasts
8_{14}	stone of offence, rock of stumbling, trap, snare
24_{2}	people, priest, slave, master, maid, mistress, buyer, seller, lender, borrower, creditor, debtor
24_{18}	terror, pit, pit, snare
25_{6}	fat things, wine on the lees, fat things, wine on the lees
34_{11-15}	hawk, porcupine, owl, raven, jackals, ostriches, wild
34_{11-15}	hawk, porcupine, owl, raven, jackals, ostriches, wild beasts, hyenas, satyr, Lilith, owl, kite
35_{5-6}	blind, deaf, lame, dumb
41_{18}	rivers/bare heights, fountains/valleys, pool of water/wilderness, springs of water/dry land
43_{23-24}	sheep, sacrifices, burnt offerings, frankincense, sweet cane, fat, sins, iniquities
41_{19}	cedar, acacia, myrtle, olive, cypress, plane, pine
65_{25}	wolf, lamb, lion, ox, serpent

But there are many more tours in the literature which run much longer than just three associated words. These long tours may run for as many as ten associated words at one time. It is interesting to see that the long tours of most of the poets settle around different subjects: animals, plants, minerals, trees, agriculture, war, weapons. Our above list of long tours catalogues all the tours which we found in our texts. Animals, the implements of war, precious metals and jewels, and so on, are all expanded to long tours.

What we can make of the content of these lists is hard to say, but rather easy to speculate upon. But this is not our task here. Exactly *why* these long tours take place is worth investigation, however, and so will be discussed in section C of this chapter. The point to be made at present is that this phenomenon of massing many associated words together for long tours is the direct result of the nature of the word pair and the ease of association for the poet. Furthermore, it offers us a new means of analyzing the diction of an author.

2. *Standardized Patterns*

Even more intriguing for the formula critic as he works through the texts, is to notice how the word pairs are placed in the line. After working with the word pairs for a time, we are struck by a number of standardized and formal constructions which the application of the word pairs to the line follow more often than not. It is not within the scope of our discussion to consider the problems associated with meter in the verse. Nor will we be able to discuss the many different kinds of meter which have been proposed for Hebrew poetry. It is nevertheless quite apparent that the word pairs are not free spirits when they are used, but rather, conform to quite a number of stylistic principles hitherto unnoticed, so far as we know. We may at least take note of these principles in the hope that others may interpret them.

Like Culley, Whallon recognizes that there is something more basic and fundamental to the poetry in the meter[16]. Behind the *Gattungen* and types of parallelism, lie the repeated word pair and phrase. But behind even these smaller components lies meter—a set of guidelines which the use of parallelism must follow. And Gevirtz suggests that the word pairs are controlled to some extent by meter[17]. The use of different names for the deity may be some indication of this, as often the titles for the godhead conform to the length of the line[18]. But for reasons unknown to us, none of the scholars wish to dig deeply into the subject of meter and its relation to Hebrew formula.

Now it must be said at the outset of our discussion on meter, that we are not sure at all what constitutes an "Hebraic meter". A primary problem in our even beginning to understand the nature of Hebrew meter is the fact that the case endings in many instances have been dropped long ago in the Hebrew verse. The result is that our received text quite likely is missing syllables in the lines of verse[19]. And the word "meter" itself is an unfortunate use of terminology, for it implies some sort of Classical Greek measure in the poetic line, be it in terms of syncope, rhythm, or beat[20]. Moreover, the number of ways the scholars have looked at the poetry, and have proposed various meters, is unending and astonishing. Cobb is certainly justified in saying, "How strange it is to see how far these critics have gone with their systems, which transform the

---

[16] R. Culley, Oral Formulaic Language in the Biblical Psalms, 1967, 119. Whallon, Formula, Character, and Context, 158f.

[17] Gevirtz, Patterns in the Early Poetry of Israel, 12–13.

[18] Ibid. 13. He relates the various names of the deity to metrical values.

[19] We cannot trust our present text for forming the meter of the line. So say S. Morag, The Vocalization Systems of Arabic, Hebrew, and Aramaic, 1962; D.N. Freedman, Archaic Forms in Early Hebrew Poetry, ZAW 72 (1960), 101–106. On the problems with the suffixes, see Z. Ben-Hayyim, Pronominal Suffixes KĀ, HĀ, TĀ, in his: Studies in the Traditions of the Hebrew Language, 1954, Part I. Freedman and Ben-Hayyim are well read together because Freedman's article criticizes the accentuating theory of meter.

[20] The most influential work in Hebrew meter has come from men who were either Classicists themselves, or who were strongly influenced by Greek meter. E. Sievers, the most important Hebrew poetic scholar in meter, was an Indo-European

exalted poetry of the Bible to inferior prose, so that thorns grow instead of wheat, and thistles instead of barley."[21] And we too, at least, are not convinced that the organization of Hebrew verse has its nucleus in Classical Greek forms and terminology. We would prefer to begin from scratch, as it were, and evaluate the poetry based upon the nature of the line itself[22]. No positive results can be obtained by the evaluation of one poetic literature based on the rules and requirements of another poetic corpus.

Let us consider what we have found while looking for the word pairs in the texts. For one thing, there is an obvious and characteristic balance in most lines of Hebrew verse. This balance of one hemistich to another, one distich to another, appears to follow certain patterns which are enlightening in themselves.

First, it is a frequently encountered phenomenon that two nouns will occur with one verb in one half of the line, and two verbs and one noun will occupy the other half of the line. For example, Isaiah 35$_1$ reads[23]:

The wilderness and dry land *will be glad*,
the desert *will rejoice and blossom ;*

ישׂשׂום מדבר וציה ותגל ערבה ותפרח

"Wilderness and dry land/desert" ("ערבה/ציה ומדבר" Job # 279; Isaiah # 490), and "be glad/rejoice and blossom" ("גיל ופרח/שׂישׂ" Isaiah # 168. 491. 492), are both word pairs but with this "two noun —one verb/one noun—two verb" balance to the line. The examples of this structure are unending in Job and Isaiah, but are very hard to locate unless we are

philologist who knew little about Semitic languages. Sievers built much of his theory of Hebrew meter around the work of J. Ley who saw Hebrew verse in terms of strictly anapestic meter. For a review of Ley, see T.H. Robinson, Some Principles of Hebrew Metrics, ZAW 54 (1936), 37ff. The most original attempt at understanding the meter has come lately from S. Mowinckel who argues for an early Hebrew meter based upon words, a middle Hebrew meter based upon accentuation, and a late Hebrew meter based upon alternation with Aramaic influences. See his: Marginalien zur hebräischen Metrik, ZAW 68 (1956), 97–123. But there have been many other attempts at handling the meter. Maecklenburg, Einführung in die Probleme der hebräischen Metrik, WZKM 46 (1939), 1–36; E. Lund, Eine metrische Form im Alten Testament, AcOr(L) 17 (1939), 250–263; H. Kosmala, Form and Structure in Ancient Hebrew Poetry: A New Approach, VT 14 (1964), 423–445, and VT 16 (1966), 152–180; E. König, Metrum als Mittel der Textkritik in der althebräischen Poesie, JBL 47 (1927), 331–343.

[21] W.H. Cobb, A Criticism of Systems of Hebrew Meter, 1905, vii.

[22] For the problems of trying to come to grips with meter in practical exegesis, see J. Bright, Jeremiah, 1965, cxxvii–cxxxviii.

[23] The examples which we now list are the product of our research in Isaiah and Job.

directly examining the nature of the words in pair. And the structure occurs in reverse order, of course, as "one verb—two nouns/two verbs one noun", as in Isaiah 59 13 (Isaiah # 733. 734):

Speaking oppression and revolt,
conceiving and uttering from the heart lying words.
דבר עשק וסרה הרו והגו מלב דברי שקר

Thus the phenomenon is frequently encountered in the poetry, and certainly says something about the question of necessary balance between hemistichs, for such a delicate balance of "two—one/one—two" (or variations thereof) cannot be attributed to mere coincidence: it will be noticed that in most instances where such an arrangement occurs, the verbs and nouns in the Hebrew will be symmetrical, that is:

verb – verb – noun/noun – noun – verb

The form (or some variation of it) is not fortuitous. And it will be seen that in this type of balance, both elements involved exhibit the "adjacent characteristic" of the poetry which we spoke of earlier: two nouns or verbs united by conjunction are usually found elsewhere as words in fixed pairs. "Wilderness and dry land", for example, is also found as "wilderness/dry land" ("ציה/מדבר" Isaiah # 490; Job # 297).

Second, we have also noticed how frequently one half of a word pair in one hemistich, where there are other items, will be balanced by two parts in the other hemistich. Isaiah 52 1 (Isaiah # 14. 52) reads:

Awake, awake, put on your strength, O Zion;
put on your beautiful garments,
O Jerusalem, the holy city;
עורי לבשי עזר ציון
לבשי בגדי תפארתך ירושלם עיר הקדש

Where the noun "Jerusalem" would have sufficed to balance the noun "Zion", as it usually does, both "Jerusalem" and "holy city" are marshaled out to balance "Zion". And why does the poet need two terms here to balance out one? We say that it is because "Jerusalem" and "the holy city" offset the extra weight of the longer first line which includes "Awake, awake". A double set of words are used to balance a single word in pair when that single word is set in a line (or hemistich) which is longer than the former. More examples will make this principle of construction clearer:

transgressing and denying the Lord,
and *turning away* from following our God,
(Isaiah 59 13 Isaiah # 20)
פשע וכחש ביהוה ונסוג מאחר אלהינו

In the haunt of jackals is *her resting place*,
the grass shall become *reeds and rushes*.

(Isaiah 35$_{7}$)

בנוה תנים רבצה חציר לקנה וגמא

Behold, you fast only *to quarrel and to fight*
and *to hit* with wicked fist

(Isaiah 58$_{4}$)

הן לריב ומצה תצומו ולהכות באגרף רשע

It cannot be valued in *the gold of Ophir*,
in precious *onyx or sapphire*. (Job 28$_{16}$)

לא תסלה בכתם אופיר בשהם יקר וספיר

In each case, the line or hemistich with two words of the fixed pair balances the extended length of the line or hemistich with one word of the fixed pair. And the examples of this ordering of the pair are endless. (See also, Isaiah 55$_{4}$ 57$_{3}$ 58$_{4.5}$ 59$_{13}$ 60$_{9}$ Job 28$_{6}$, to cite only a few examples.)

We can only conclude that patterns existed which ruled the use of the word pair and instructed the poet in filling out the line. That the pairs have to conform to rules in their application to the line, now appears to be clear enough, but the relationship of these patterns of application is another question. Let us continue with our findings.

Third, we see that in many instances in our texts, the word pairs seem to be the most important aspects of the hemistichs and so, the lines. For example, Isaiah 60$_{4}$:

Your sons shall come from far,
and *your daughters* shall be carried in the arms.

בניך מרחוק יבאו ובנתיך על צד תאמנה

"Son/daughter", and "come/carry" are word pairs and primary to the meaning of the line. Without the pairs, the line would make little sense. And so it is in many other instances:

Then *you shall call*, and the Lord will answer;
you shall cry, and he will say, Here I am. (Isaiah 58$_{9}$)

אז תקרא ויהוה יענה תשוע ויאמר הנני

The foot tramples it, *the feet* of the poor,
the steps of the needy. (Isaiah 26$_{6}$ Isaiah # 195)

תרמסנה רגל רגלי עני פעמי דלים

I have spoken, and I will bring it to pass;
I have proposed, and I will do it. (Isaiah 46$_{11}$)

אף דברתי אף אביאנה יצרתי אף אעשנה

In these and many other instances, it is the word pair which is central and critical to the line; without the pairs the line has no content at all.

And in a great many instances, the line is made up of nothing but word pairs:

For *you shall be ashamed* of the oaks
IN WHICH YOU DELIGHTED,
And *you shall blush* for the gardens
WHICH YOU HAVE CHOSEN.

(Isaiah 1₂₉ Isaiah # 46, 47)

כי יבשו מאילים אשר חמדתם
ותחפרו מהגנות אשר בחרתם

But *the Lord of hosts* is exalted IN JUSTICE,
and *the Holy God* shows himself holy IN
RIGHTEOUSNESS.

(Isaiah 5₁₆ Isaiah # 20, 36, 109)

ויגבה יהוה צבאות במשפט והאל הקדוש נקדש בצדקה

Then *the lambs* shall graze as IN THEIR PASTURE,
fatlings and kids shall feed AMONG THE RUINS.

(Isaiah 5₁₇ Isaiah # 110, 111)

ורעו כבשים כדברם והרבות מחים גרים יאכלו

Fourth, we cannot fail to take notice of how many lines are *perfectly* counterbalanced in the Hebrew (and often even in the English), "verb-noun/noun-verb" or vice versa, in a precise way:

He makes stiff his tail like a cedar;
the sinews of his thighs *are knit* together.

(Job 40₁₇)

יחפץ זנבו כמו גידי פחדו ישרגו

Those who *lavish* gold from the purse,
and *weigh out* silver in the scales,

(Isaiah 46₆ Isaiah # 59)

הזלים זהב מכיס וכסף בקנה ישקלו

To bring back Jacob to him,
and that Israel *might be gathered* to him,

(Isaiah 49₅ Isaiah # 179)

לשיבב יעקב אליו וישראל לא יאסף

Clothed is my flesh with worms and dirt;
my skin *hardens*, then breaks out afresh.

(Job 7₅ Job # 82, 83)

לבש בשרי רמה וגיש עפר עורי רגע וימאס

In each of these examples, the verb-noun order in each hemistich is strictly regular. This observation is applicable to a great number of lines.

We have concentrated upon the word pair in the line in our study. But in so doing, we must take great care not to overlook the other elements of the line which augment the word pairs. This, then, is our fifth observation, namely, that many times it is not the word pairs which fill out the line and aid in the balance, but it is the extra phrases and words which are added to the hemistichs:

He slashes open his kidneys, *and does not spare;*
he pours out my gall *on the ground.* (Job 16_{13})

יפלח כליותי ולא יחמול ישפך לארץ מררתי

"Does not spare", and "on the ground", while not essential to our understanding of the line, nor are they in fixed pair, seem to fill out and assist the strength of the line already created by the word pairs. Other examples of the same stylistic principle are:

For the arrows of the Almighty are in me;
my spirit drinks their poison;
the terrors of God are arrayed against me (Job 6_4)

כי חצי שדי עמדי אשר חמתם שתה רוחי בעותי אלוה יערכוני

Do you know the balancings of the clouds,
the wondrous works of *him who is perfect in knowledge,*
(Job 37_{16})

התדע על מפלשי עב מפלאות תמים דעים

The haughty looks of men shall be brought low,
and the pride of men shall be humbled;
And the Lord alone will be exalted in that day
(Isaiah 2_{11} Isaiah # 68, 69)

עיני גבהות אדם שפל ושם רום אנשים
ונשגב יהוה לבדו ביום ההוא

The point here simply is that often the part of the line or hemistich *not* composed of word pairs, is critical to the balance of the whole. Yet the entire line operates under rules which somehow must be regular, or at least an option in the poet's mind as he constructs his verse.

The most convincing proof that there are guidelines by which the word pairs are used in a line, comes from the observation that usually word pairs in a particular line *cannot* be reversed without upsetting the balance of the line[24]. Take Job 18_{21}:

Surely such are the dwellings of *the ungodly,*
such is the place of *him who knows not God.*

אך אלה משכנות עול וזה מקום לא ידע אל

To reverse the word pair "ungodly/him who knows not God" in the Hebrew would increase the first hemistich to six words or ten syllables, and reduce the second hemistich to three words or five syllables:

אך אלה משכנות לא ידע אל וזה מקום עול

[24] See the work which has been done by A. J. Ehlen, The Poetic Structure of a Hodayah from Qumran; an Analysis of Grammatical, Semantic, and Auditory Correspondence in 1QH 3.19–36. Th. D. Dissertation, Harvard University, 1970, 10–12.

The balance of the line's hemistichs, which originally was very close at 7/8 syllables, would, therefore, be destroyed. Illustrations of this fact are endless:

Who says of *Jerusalem*, 'She shall be inhabited',
and of *the cities of Judah*, 'They shall be built',
(Isaiah 44₂₆ Isaiah # 82)

האמר לירושלם תושב ולערי יהודה תבנינה

And I will make *boys* their princes,
and *babes* shall rule over them. (Isaiah 3₄ Isaiah # 78)

ונתתי נערים שריהם ותעלולים ימשלים בם

Therefore *snares* are round about you,
and *sudden terror* overwhelms you; (Job 22₁₀ Job # 263)

על כן סביבותיך פחים ויבהלך פחד פתאם

When the word pair in Isaiah 3₄ is turned around in the line, the 10/9 syllable balance of the line is changed to 12/7; when the members of the pair are reversed in Job 22₁₀, the balance of syllables as 9/8 is changed to 11/6.

This sixth observation we take to be conclusive evidence that the construction of the line and the use of the word pair follow definite patterns and principles, and that this is the case more often than not. The balance of the line is destroyed more times than it is preserved by a reversal of the words which are held in fixed pair. We must surmise that the poet planned out his lines of verse around the differences in length of the words in pair.

Seventh, there seems to be a built-in means of balancing words in pair where one word might be longer than another in terms of syllables. The poetry is literally loaded with cases where one half of a word pair is plural and the other half is singular. Yet in most all instances, the use of singular or plural has no impact upon the *understanding* of the line. By so varying the singular-plural aspect of the words in pair, the lines are balanced in more uniform lengths. For example, Job 38₃₉ (Job # 35):

Can you hunt the prey for *the lion*,
or satisfy the appetite of *the young lions*,

התציד ללביא טרף וחית כפירים תמלא

By making the word pair "lion/young lion" singular and plural respectively, the distich is better balanced with respect to the number of syllables in the line. The change in number does nothing for the content and meaning of the line: the pair and distich could just as meaningfully be rendered entirely in the plural or in the singular. Hence, we say that the "singular/plural" (or vice versa) relationship in so many lines must be due to a more sophisticated need for what we, for want of a better word, must call meter. The examples are unending, but a close check on the Hebrew text is often necessary to spot them:

So *man* is humbled,
    and *men* are brought low— (Isaiah 2_{9} Isaiah # 62, 63)

וישח אדם ותשפלו אנשים

And I will lead the blind in *a way* that they know not,
    in *paths* that they have not known I will guide
(Isaiah 42_{16} Isaiah # 558, 559)

והולכתי עורים בדרך לא ידעו בנתיבות לא ידעו אדריכם

For he has clothed me with *the garments* of salvation,
    he has covered me with *the robe* of righteousness,
(Isaiah 61_{10} Isaiah # 752)

כי הלבישני בגדי ישע מעיל צדקה יעטני

(See also such examples in Isaiah as: 2_{11} 44_{26} 49_{7} 53_{3} 56_{3} 57_{1} $59_{5.8.21}$ 60_{8} 66_{12}; in Job: $5_{10.19}$ 6_{15} 38_{39} 4_{10} 6_{23} 10_{11} 12_{10} 13_{23} 8_{20} 25_{5} 7_{21}?)

Eighth, we have found from our research of word pairs that there are numerical pairs which operate in the same way as the regular ones:

A thousand shall flee at the threat of *one*,
    at the threat of *five* you shall flee,
(Isaiah 30_{17} Isaiah # 293 Job # 366)

אלף אחד מפני גערת אחד
מפני גערת חמשה תנסו

In this example, the numerical word pair would be "X/X + 4" in pattern. But the numbers and the patterns are, of course, variable:

Two or three berries
    in the top of the highest bough,
Four or five
    on the branches of a fruit tree, (Isaiah 17_{6})

שנים שלשה גרגרים בראש אמיר
ארבעה חמשה בטעפיה פריה

Here the numerical pair is "X/X + 2". (See also Isaiah 19_{18} 37_{30} 47_{49}.) Number values, it seems, were commonly used as pairs, and interchanged freely[25].

And finally, we must mention that often the same word is used in pair, many times in different tenses. The pair "perfect/imperfect" is rather common in the poetry.

---

[25] See W. M. W. Roth, The Numerical Sequence x/x + 1 in the Old Testament, VT 12 (1962), 300–311; and: Numerical Sayings in the Old Testament, 1965. Gevirtz deals with and counters the article of Roth in: Patterns in the Early Poetry of Israel, 15–24, but especially 17–18 note 8.

Will you *speak* falsely for God,
and *speak* deceitfully for him? (Job 13_{7} Job #158)
הלאל תדברו עולה ולו תדברו רמיה
No shepherds will make their flocks *lie down* there.
But wild beasts will *lie down* there, (Isaiah 13_{20-21})
ולא יהל שם ערבי ורעים לא ירבצו שם
ורבצו שם ציים ומלאו

In Job 13_{7}, the pair is "imperfect/imperfect," and in Isaiah 13_{20-21}, the pair is "imperfect/perfect" in form. And so it is not only with verbal word pairs, but also with nounal pairs, that the word pairs are made up of the same word. (See Job 7_{8} 24_{15} עין; 13_{7} דבר; 8_{3} עות; 11_{7} מצא; 15_{31} שוא; 17_{15} תקוה; Isaiah 13_{20-21} רבץ.)

In regard to these pairs composed of the same words, it is interesting to notice that when the Septuagint translators encountered a parallelism made up of the same words in pair, they usually sought to change one member of the pair to a synonymous word, thereby effectively hiding the redundancy of the original word pair[26]. And we see this same practice done in the modern translation efforts of today, for in many instances, it is difficult to see that the words in pair are the same when examining the translations. Nevertheless, this principle of the poetry—that pairs may be made up of the same word—we take as our ninth and final observation.

Let us review the statements which we have made, above and previously, regarding the use of the word pair in the line of poetry:

1) Fixed words in pair almost always recur as adjacent words connected by conjunction, and found in prose and poetry.

2) Lines are regularly found as "noun–noun–verb/verb–verb–noun".

3) Lines are regularly found "one half of a word pair—extra words/two synonymous words answering as the second half of the pair".

4) Words in fixed pair always are the most important part of the parallelism and line. Without them, distichs and hemistichs lose all meaning.

5) Word pairs sometimes fill out otherwise complete lines created by other word pairs.

6) Lines are regularly found as "verb–noun/noun–verb" or vice versa, in perfect symmetry.

7) Extra phrases often fill out otherwise complete lines created by the word pairs of the line.

8) Word pairs, more often than not, cannot reverse themselves within a given line without upsetting the balance in the number of words and syllables in the hemistichs.

---

[26] U. Cassuto, A Commentary on the Book of Genesis: From Noah to Abraham, 1961, 128. In: Biblical Literature and Canaanite Literature (Conclusion), (in

9) Pairs frequently fill out the balance of the line by being rendered "singular/plural" or vice versa.

10) There are numerical word pairs which operate in sequential patterns freely and exactly like regular word pairs.

11) Often, the words in a fixed pair are the same, differing only in verbal tense. Frequently, when this occurs, translators unwittingly hide this fact by not rendering the word the same way twice.

Therefore, the list points, at least, to the fact that there is a certain control over the use of the word pairs in the line, of which the poets were conscious. And we defend our results because we have proceeded from our textual research to the observations which we have made, not from preconceived theories to the text as Whallon and Culley have done.

As to what these observations mean with regard to general rules governing the poetic line in Hebrew poetry, we are not at all sure. For neither the word pairs nor the rest of the poetic line is so ordered that syllables are always equally balanced. In fact, it is rarely the case that hemistichs are perfectly balanced with respect to the syllables of the line. Even in the example of Job 38 39 used previously, where we said that the "singular/plural" pair aided balance, a counting of Hebrew syllables reveals an 8/9 imbalance:

Can you hunt the prey for the lion,
or satisfy the appetite of the young lions,
התצור ללביא טרף וחית כפירים תמלא

But this is about as balanced as most Hebrew verse is ever found. However, of one thing we are sure, and this stems from our research: the use of word pairs in the line was not, as a rule, haphazardly formulated. There appear to be far too many technical ways of balancing the line at the Hebrew poet's disposal, as we have shown.

C. VIOLATING THE ECONOMIES OF COMPOSITION AND TRANSLATION

The examples of the regularity of word pairs in the line are easy to see and understand once pointed out. But for the novice, hunting the text of scripture for similar characteristics can be unnerving and compli-

Hebrew) Tarbiz 14 (1942), 9–10, he states that parallelism with word pairs with the same word in different tenses is common. See also his: The Goddess Anath, 1971 (1953), 46–47. M. Held, The YQTL-QTL (QTL-YQTL) Sequence of Identical Verbs in Biblical Hebrew and in Ugaritic, in: Studies and Essays in Honor of A. A. Neuman, 1962, 281–290, deals with the perfect-imperfect use of the same word in pair.

cated. And as we shall see, the difficulty of seeing the way in which word pairs operate in translation is not always the fault of the reader.

W. Whallon emphasizes what he calls "violation of economy" in the Hebrew poetry[27]. By this he is referring to the numerous instances, discussed previously, where poets are fond of massing more than two associated words in a word pair chain[28]. He says these instances are violations in economy because the normally economic word pair consists of but two (or perhaps three) words at most associated together. Isaiah 1_{11} is a violation of economy, as we have said: "rams, fed beasts, bulls, lambs, he-goats", are all used. Where two of the words would have sufficed to say what the poet had to say, he became carried away and used five. And Isaiah 3_{2-3} is an extreme violation on the poet's part: "mighty man, soldier, judge, prophet, diviner, elder, captain of fifty, man of rank, counselor, skillful magician, expert in charms." Eleven items were used by the poet to get his point across.

These violations of economy would not be so important if they were few in number. But they are not. In Isaiah alone, we count over twenty-five instances where the author allows himself to expand his word pairs to include a long list of repeated words. Whallon ascribes this phenomenon to the desire on the poet's part to keep alive many words which would otherwise have passed into oblivion from disuse. But this seems unlikely. For the view requires the poet to be concerned with the conservation of his words, and requires him to be mindful of his future followers. Such a theory of foresight must come from the sophistication of hindsight — Whallon's, not the Hebrew poet's. Rather, a more reasonable explanation for the lapses of economy would be the simple enjoyment and artistry derived from creating such long tours, and the impressiveness of the finished product. The point which could be made with two words in pair is made in more stunning effect with six or eight words in pair. And, we would add, such a viewpoint conforms to the central purpose of the word pair and the parallelism in the Hebrew poetry, and that is to produce an ornate and artistic product.

Whallon (and Culley and Gevirtz) is reluctant to allow the Hebrew poet any sign of creativity outside the traditional diction[29]. In keeping with this line of thinking, Whallon places the violations of economy within the realm of traditional diction. By saying that the poet was

---

[27] Whallon, Formula, Character, and Context, 154–157.

[28] Whallon also deals with violations with respect to popular word pairs. For example, since "משפט/צדקה" is a common pair in the poetry, "דיך/צדקה" (Isaiah 10_{2}) is a violation on the part of the poet because משפט and דיך have about the same meaning, and are substituted one for the other. But with violations such as these, we are not interested.

[29] Whallon, Formula, Character, and Context, 157ff.; Culley, Oral Formulaic Language, 9; Gevirtz, Patterns in the Early Poetry of Israel, 14.

concerned with the availability of poetic words and pairs for future generations, the poetaster comes off as "The Defender of the Verse", which seems to us very unlikely indeed. We think that the violations of economy mainly are due to the creativity of the poet alone, and perhaps were aided to some degree by common association and limited vocabulary. We believe that the latter is the case, because a number of these long tours recur throughout the whole of Isaiah, repeating tours found nowhere else. The tour in Isaiah 11_{6-8}, for example, recurs at 65_{25}, that is, in the historically different sections. It appears, therefore, that there are certain subjects upon which the versemakers enjoy elaborating: precious metals, jewels, objects of war, and the animal world all appear again and again. But in any event, the violations are due to the creativity of the poets, and have their origin and framework in the poet's thought.

Whallon also points out in passing, a violation of translation in which modern translators also engage[30]. This type of violation may occur in three ways. First, many times translators of the Hebrew render one word in many different ways in lines which seem to be very much alike in content. For instance, in Isaiah, the verbs שלם, רחם, and נחם, are frequently used by the poet, but translated in innumerable ways. As another example, רוח is translated as "breath" in Isaiah 40_{7} (Isaiah # 220), as "spirit" in Isaiah 40_{13} 61_{1} 63_{14}, and as "wind" in Isaiah 59_{19}, in all but the same contexts. And the same thing occurs with word pairs. "עמל/און" is translated in (RSV) Job 4_{8} (Job # 30) as "iniquity/trouble". But in Job 13_{35}, that same pair is translated as "mischief/evil". Moreover, the freedom of translation has nothing to do with the tenses or states of verbs: גוע (Kal future) is translated as "expire" in Job 3_{11} (Job # 13), as "breathe one's last" in Job 14_{10}, as "die" in Job 10_{18}, and as "perish" in Job 34_{15}. The verb ילד is translated in a number of different ways, all roughly analogous: in Job 3_{3} (Job # 9) it is "born", in Job 15_{35} it is "bring forth", and in Isaiah 13_{8} it is "travail". משפט is translated now "ordinances" in Isaiah 58_{2} (Isaiah # 36), "aright" in Isaiah 28_{26}, "justice" in Isaiah 1_{17}, and "judgment" in Isaiah 34_{5}. נחל is rendered "brook" in Job 40_{22} (Job # 71), "torrent bed" in Job 6_{15}, "stream" in Job 20_{17}, and "valley" in Job 21_{33}. נוע is expressed as "fold" in Job 5_{24} (Job # 64), "dwelling" in Job 5_{3}, "habitation" in Job 18_{15}, and "haunt" in Isaiah 34_{13}. To express both the literal monotony *and* the quality of the verse in translation is, of course, difficult for the modern translator[31]. But such liberties with the poetry as these we have listed above seem extreme to say the least.

---

[30] Whallon, Formula, Character, and Context, 155.

[31] The task of translation is not an easy one. For one example of how one scholar deals with translation of the poetry, see J. Bright, Jeremiah, cxxv–cxxxviii, but especially cxxvi. He has to deal with large sections of prose and poetry in

Second, translators are wont to translate two or more Hebrew words which are synonymous into one English word. אשם, עון, פשע, חטא, (Job # 117, 98) are each translated interchangeably at the whim of the translator: now "sin", now "iniquity", now "transgression". רום, גבה, שפל, נשא, גאה, are each and severally translated as "proud", "high", "haughty", "lifted up", in a great many places (Isaiah # 69, 70, 71, 72, 73).

Third, there is a violation in the economy of translation whenever the translator successfully hides a word pair or phrase which is significant to the diction of the author of the text[32]. Were we not able to read the Hebrew text, we would not recognize easily that "earth/they who dwell in it" was a word pair in Isaiah 51_{6}:

The earth will wear out like a garment,
and *they who dwell in it* will die in like manner,
והארץ כבגד תבלה וישביה כמו כן ימותון

And in reading (RSV) Job 3_{11} (Job # 14), we would not at all be aware that the word pair "womb/belly" ("רחם/בטן") is even so much as present in the line:

Why did I not die *at birth*,
come forth from *the womb* and expire?
למה לא מרחם אמות מבטן יצאתי ואגוע

Nor would we know that in Isaiah 62_{3}, the word pair "hand/hand" ("כף/יד") contains two different words for "hand" in:

You shall be a crown of beauty in *the hand* of the Lord,
and a royal diadem in *the hand* of your God.
והיית עטרת תפארת בידי יהוה וצנוף מלוכה בכף אלהיך

The translator unwittingly hides the very elements of the line which we consider to be important. The limited vocabulary of the poet and the poetry, which we discussed before, is overlooked by the translator as he attempts to fill that vocabulary out. This we take to be a tragedy of translation efforts insofar as formula criticism is concerned.

Woe to you, destroyer, who yourself have not been destroyed;
you treacherous one, with whom none has dealt treacherously!

Jeremiah. The problems of translation come most clearly into view when one examines more than one translator's attempt at handling the same material.

[32] On economy and translation, see T. J. Meek, Hebrew Poetic Structure as a Translation Guide, JBL 59 (1940), 1–9.

When you have ceased to destroy, you will be destroyed;
and when you have made an end of dealing
treacherously, you will be dealt with
treacherously. (Isaiah 33:1)

הוי שודד ואתה לא שדוד ובוגד ולא בגדו בו
כהתמך שודד תושד כנלתך לבגד יבגדו בך

In some cases, however, as in the verse from Isaiah above, the translation shows us clearly the limited vocabulary used by the poet. The restricted vocabulary of the poet seems highly repetitious to us, but at least it shows us precisely how the poet constructed his parallelism. Nevertheless, it seems that most translators, when encountering pairs made up of the same word, more often than not, resort to synonyms rather than render the line literally. And this practice, we noted, was even common in the Septuagint translation.

Now it is the understandable concern of the modern translator to conceal much of the repetition and what might seem in English to be the monotonous use of a limited vocabulary available to the poet[33]. But the result of this practice is that the average reader of the English Bible is led astray by such translations into thinking that the original text of scripture contains many more *different* words than there really are. And, as we have shown in the above examples, even the scholar can be lured from recognizing the poet's limited root vocabulary in the text. But it is this limited vocabulary which, we believe, contributes to the need for the word pair's repetition and its commonplace associations. The violations of economy in composition and translation, therefore, effectively prevent us from seeing the key words in the Hebrew poetic line.

D. THE HOMERIC EPITHET AS DISTINCTIVE FROM THE HEBREW WORD PAIR

It has been suggested time and again in Old Testament scholarship that we may understand the regulation of Hebrew verse by a close analysis of Greek poetry. A comparison of things Greek and Semitic has been quite common. And a same such analogy has been made in terms of the Hebrew word pair and elements of Greek verse. Our question is, therefore, will a Greek-Hebrew comparison of formulas teach us about the Hebrew word pair?

---

[33] The tension between literalism and freedom of translation is best expressed as a problem for the modern translator in H. S. Gehman, Adventures in Septuagint Lexicography, Textus 5 (1966), 125–132.

Whallon, with his comparative expertise, says that the epithet is to Homer, what the word pair is to Isaiah[34]. Hebrew synonymy was a prosodic device analogous to the Homeric epithet, and the Anglo-Saxon kenning. "Swift-footed Achilles" is to Homer, what "inhabit/dwell" is to Old Testament bards, such as Isaiah and Job[35]. This seems, on the face of it, a just comparison, one which recognizes the idiosyncrasies of each literature, keeps them apart, and respects each for what they are. But under scrutiny, we have found that the comparison does not hold up, because Whallon has once again failed to examine a large cross-section of the Old Testament literature itself.

Parry has shown that epithets are commonplace in Homer, and that they are a mark of oral verse-making. Though epithets are not common in Hebrew verse, they are, nevertheless, present. And it mystifies us why Culley, with all his concern for forcing Indo-European oral characteristics upon the biblical psalms, and his knowledge of Parry's work in epithets, did not force the epithet to be a mark of oral versemaking in Hebrew. But he did not.

The comparison between the epithet and the word pair, first of all, fails to recognize a distinctive difference between them. The Homeric epithet is in itself an artistic creation; the Hebrew word pair is not. The epithets, for their creation, require contemplation of characterizations and their deeds; word pairs are common associations of synonymous or antithetical words requiring nothing of the kind. "Hector of the shining helm" (Il. 6.263), "Atreides Menelaos of the great war cry" (Il. 16.656), "swift-footed Achilles" (Il. 1.364; 16.5), and "Apollo who strikes from afar" (Il. 1.75), are poetic creations of the highest order, not made on the spur of the moment, but directly related to the characterization[36]. In them are found essential elements of the Homeric

[34] W. Whallon, Formulaic Poetry in the Old Testament, CL 15 (1963), 2; also Formula, Character, and Context, 157f.

[35] Whallon's contrasting of some aspect of the Old Testament and Homeric prose and poetry is not new. E. Auerbach, Mimesis, The Representation of Reality in Western Literature, 1957, contrasts Odysseus and Abraham in his first chapter, concluding that Hebrew poetry "is real and elevated in style". But also, among seventeenth and eighteenth century authors, it was common practice to compare Homer and the Bible. Pope's preface to the Iliad compares the Bible to Homer, says Fitzgerald, The Place of Robert Lowth's De Sacra Poesi Hebraeorum, 81. And de Wette cites older scholars who made the same comparison in H.H. Rowley's article. The Book of Job and Its Meaning, BJRL 41 (1958–1959), 167–207.

[36] This is Whallon's thesis in: The Homeric epithets are significantly true to the individual character, in: Formula, Character, and Context, 1–32. But his idea that the epithets fit the characters is not new. Lattimore describes the characters of the Iliad in terms of their epithets in: The Iliad of Homer, 1951, 45–52.

essential elements of the Homeric epics, and clues to the character's importance. "Cloud gathering Zeus" (Il. 1.511) tells us something essential about the nature of Zeus. The Hebrew word pair, on the other hand, is certainly created and used by artists, but it is utilitarian in purpose, and certainly not monumental in scope of implication. The epithet endures throughout the literature, while the word pair may be used just once and then dismantled. The epithet will be remembered; the word pair need not and probably will not be remembered.

Second, the Homeric bard freely enjoys the use of the epithet in his verse, but certainly is not held to it as the essential ingredient of the well-metered line. Homeric verse may easily occur without the need for the epithet in the line. But the Hebrew poet, by the very nature of the poetry, is dependent upon the word pair for the well paralleled line. The absence of the Homeric epithet in a line does not prevent the accomplishment of the hexameter. But the absence of a suitable word pair in the Hebrew line or lines, prevents the parallelism from occurring. This Whallon overlooks.

That the Homeric meter is analogous to the Hebrew parallelism seems generally true, for these are what guide the formation of the line, and are the obvious requirements of the poetry. But the Greek epithet is not analogous to the Hebrew word pair, nor is the comparison a help to us in understanding either of the poetries any better. The word pair is necessary for the parallelism; the epithet is not necessary for the meter. Rather, it is more correctly said that the Homeric formula, comprised of repeated phrases (of which epithets are a part), is analogous to the Hebrew formula, comprised of repeated phrases and words (of which the word pair is a part). The similarity of the two literatures rests in their repetition of elements of the poetic lines, nothing more.

There are few epithets in Hebrew verse, for reasons which are not obvious at first. In the Homeric epic, the action centers around characters human, semi-human, and divine. As they move, so moves the narrative. And the characterizations—depending upon the hero—have varying degrees of depth. Those heroes in the foreground of the literature have splendid epithets epitomizing their life and style. "Hera of the white arms" (Il. 8.381), and "manslaughtering Hector" (Il. 18.149) provide us with graphic clues as to the character's appearance and activity. In the Old Testament, however, it is not so much the activities of the characters that are important, but rather, movements on a more universal scale. For action revolves around the godhead, nations, and man in general. For this reason, it is not specific men who get the biblical epithets so much as God, nations, and generic man. We hear not so much of "much-afflicted Job", or "Isaiah, bearer of God's omens", but of "man, he that was born of woman" ("אדם ילוד אשה" Job 14$_{1}$ 15$_{14}$), "Lord, the God of Jacob" ("יהוה אלהי יעקב" Isaiah 2$_{3}$), "Jerusalem, city of David, mount Zion" ("ציון עיר דוד ירי״" Isaiah 18_{7} 22_{9}; etc.), and "God, the holy one of Israel" ("אלהיםקדוש ישראל" Isaiah 5_{24}; etc.). We hear nowhere of "commandment-carrying Moses", or "father of us all, Abraham". But we do find the important elements in the biblical tales, such as Jerusalem, receiving such epithets as: "the mountain house of the Lord" ("הר בית יהוה" Isaiah 2_{2}), "the city where David encamped" ("קרית חנה דוד" Isaiah 29_{1}), and "mount of the daughter of Zion" ("הר בת ציון" Isaiah 10_{32}). Or we hear Israel called, among many other names, "daughter of Zion" ("בת ציון" Isaiah 1_{8}). In these and other instances, a great many biblical epithets recur in the form of word pairs: "Jerusalem/mountain house of the Lord", and "Ariel/city where David encamped", are epithetical.

So we conclude that the Homeric epithet is not the striking analogue to the Hebrew word pair. The word pair and the epithet are quite different. The word pair assists in the mechanics of the line of parallelism and is essential to that parallelism; the epithet is artistically composed, and speaks directly to us about the content of the narrative and is not essential to the Greek line. It is the quality of repetition in the two literatures which, if anything, is analogous. Yet we must say that there is no need or real value in determining such analogues, since, as we have maintained all along, the literatures cannot be directly compared. The Hebrew word pair must be examined on its own terms if we are to understand the rules behind Old Testament poetry.

E. CONCLUSION AND ANTICIPATION

Here we have attempted to indicate ways in which word pairs are useful in poetic research. We have said in this chapter that contrary to Whallon's opinion, it was not R. Lowth who led us down the path away from the components of the poetry, and into a false sense of security in organizing the whole lines of verse. On the contrary, he was one of the first to point out the elements making up the whole. Unfortunately, those who followed after him were more taken with his categories of parallelism than with the true basics of the poetry, the component elements, which he himself pointed out: Lowth saw the word pair as the essential element of the parallelism.

Next we said that the study of the word pairs reveals a great deal concerning the nature of the poetry. The numerous long tours reveal a fondness for running the word pair out as far as possible, but in controlled order. And the way in which the word pairs are employed in the line leads us to believe that there are definite standardized patterns governing their use. These principles of construction, we said, have to do with "meter" for want of a better term.

But if there is some order in the use of the word pair and the application of it to the line, that order is certainly often well hidden by violations of economy of composition and translation. The former seems to be a breech of the usual two-word word pair for the enjoyment of constructing more elaborate lines, that is, the long tours; the latter prevents us from coming to grips with the abundant repetition which will ultimately lead us to a better understanding of "Hebrew meter". The ambiguous translation practices only lead us further away from the true nature of the verse.

Finally, we observed that any understanding of "Hebrew meter" must come upon its own foundation, for the analogy of the Greek epithet and the Hebrew word pair does not hold. The fact that the Old Testament poetry actually contains its own kinds of epithets was overlooked by our scholars[37]. Relating the synonyms in Hebrew to the epithets in Greek, only leads us off into an application of one literature to another, without profit to either. If any analogue exists, it simply is that the two literatures have elements in their lines which repeat. The subjects of Hebrew word pair and meter are not advanced by the comparative method.

We are next going to consider the usefulness of the word pair in the practicalities of textual criticism. While we have questioned and denied the word pair's origin and locus in the traditional diction—based upon our research, we have all along maintained the word pair's presence in the literature. The word pairs in oral and written literature are the product of the creativity of the poet with which they are found. We will now concern ourselves with the word pair's ability to help us answer a number of questions: Can word pairs point to additions in texts? Can they help us distinguish the prose line from the poetic line? Can the word pairs sometimes assist in repairing obscure words and passages? We now turn to a consideration of these questions.

---

[37] Whallon should have been aware of work done on biblical epithets. On epithets for the godhead, see M. Tsevat, A Study of the Language of the Biblical Psalms, 1955, 39. סלע Psalm 22; עז Psalm 27; מגן Psalm 57; עזר Psalm 110. Also, B. Albrektson, Studies in the Text and Theology of the Book of Lamentations, 1963. He notes the epithets for Zion in Lamentations, 221–228; and for God in Lamentations, 228–229.

Chapter VI

The Usefulness of Word Pairs in Evaluating Poetry

A. INTRODUCTION: THE USEFULNESS OF FORMULA CRITICISM

We have said that parallelism is the dominating characteristic of Hebrew poetry, and that the component parts of the parallelism are the word pair. But even the word pairs, when they are isolated out of lines, do not tell us the whole story, for as we have just seen, they follow definite standardized patterns in the way in which they are used in the line. These rules, until we understand them more fully, are called metrical. But we suspect that the rules have little to do with what we know as Classical Greek verse-making given to syllables, beats, and measures.

A development of "Hebrew meter", however, is not what we are seeking in this study. For we have striven only to test the theories on formula criticism in Hebrew poetry by way of our own research, and where needed, adjust aspects where our studies have shown others to be in error. We have found that word pairs occur in oral and written literature; we have determined that the word pairs stem from the creativity of the poet; and we have concluded that no traditional diction is necessary or provable in the literature. Yet despite our assertion that no traditional diction exists, but rather, that formulas constitute commonplace associations, we believe formula criticism to be methodologically sound and useful. And in spite of our differences of opinion with other scholars in the past, we wish here to indicate the many ways in which we have found the formula remains a useful tool in textual criticism. And we must add that our purpose here is only to interest others in our methological approach to the scriptures by suggesting paths to take in the future; our minimal efforts *must not* be seen as attempts to solve the large questions which we consider. Our work is merely a beginning and a rough outline of studies which we believe might be valuably pursued by others. And even when full projects are undertaken using formula criticism, the results obtained must be added to the existing fund of evidence on any one question, and cannot be used to form conclusions alone.

B. WHAT IS PROSE? WHAT IS POETRY?

In the same chapter of *Formula, Character, and Context* which we have discussed before, W. Whallon sets down a rather simple, yet persuasive, means for distinguishing Hebrew prose from Hebrew poetry[1]. He says that in passages which lack parallelism, and are customarily referred to as prose, certain key elements recur in series, adjacently. Examples of this would be:

You shall conceive and bear a son (Judges 13_3)

והרית וילדת בן

And again *she conceived and bore* a son. (Genesis 29_{34})

ותהר עוד ותלד בן

In these lines of prose, the key words, "conceive" and "bear" are found adjacent to each other, separated only by conjunction. But in passages which have parallelism and which are usually called poetry, the key elements of the lines do not usually recur in series, but are more regularly the word pairs joining together the successive hemistichs. For example:

Let the day perish wherein *I was born*,
and the day which said, 'A man-child *is conceived*'.
(Job 3_3 Job #9)

יאבד יום אולד בן והלילה אמר הרה גבר

You conceive chaff,
you bring forth stubble; (Isaiah 33_{11} Isaiah #450)

תהרו חשש תלדו קש

The key words in these lines are not adjacent to each other, but are more evenly balanced in the lines. Therefore, prose to Whallon is a passage or verse in which the key terms of the line are adjacent to each other; poetry is a passage in which the key terms stand, as a rule, at an even distance from each other. By "distance", Whallon does not imply a degree or measure, but only that the key terms in the poetic line are separated into different phrases, hemistichs, lines, etc.

This proposal, as we have seen earlier, is not altogether true, since related words recur both adjacent to each other *and* as fixed pairs about equally often in the poetry. But where both word pairs and adjacent key words occur together in lines, the text is probably always poetry. What is significant about Whallon's observations, however, and what he himself does not realize, is the possibility that the recognition of *distance* between key elements in the line may be a useful way of distinguishing the Hebrew prose from the Hebrew poetry.

---

[1] W. Whallon, Formula, Character, and Context: Studies in Homeric, Old English, and Old Testament Poetry, 1969, 148–150.

There are certainly other ways of distinguishing the prose line from the poetic verse[2]. Whallon himself, following Auerbach, engages in a rather lengthy comparative analysis of Hebrew prose and poetry in terms of content and style[3]. On content he says: the content of the prose implies a background and develops with suspense; events occur vertically with chronological development; great lengths of time pass with appropriate changes in the characters involved. But the content of the poetry unfolds in the foreground and has no suspense; events occur horizontally without chronological development; little time passes without much change in the characters involved. On style he says: Old Testament prose style suggests a background by using only essential descriptive elements; style is vertical because it deals only with the moment at hand; it is a low style typified by naturalistic speech and historical interests, and deals with specifics. The Old Testament poetic style suggests a foreground by having the leisure to include any descriptive elements; the style is horizontal because it is timeless; it is high style typified by non-naturalistic speech and philosophical interests, and deals in generalities.

Such may be designated as an esthetic analysis of the essence of Old Testament prose and poetry. But while the comparison of the prose and poetry does set one against the other, it fails to evaluate the structure of the verse and prose. However, Whallon's proposal of key word distance may help us to understand the structure of the prose and the poetry.

This distinction as to distance between key words becomes more than something of passing interest when we consider the amounts of respective prose and poetry translated into English over the past one hundred years. And an inspection of both Hebrew and English editions of the Old Testament over this same period reveals that as editions become more recent, more and more previously prose lines appear in poetic form in the editions. At each new publication of the Hebrew scriptures in any language, more lines are seen as poetic than ever before.

We shall consider Isaiah as our example. In the past century, more and more of Isaiah's words have been printed as poetry. But the criteria which the translators have used in deciding whether or not a particular passage is prose or poetry is difficult to determine, to say the least. There is much in the RSV edition, for example, which is regarded by the editors as prose, but which is regarded by Kittel's edition as verse[4]. Isaiah 22 8b-11. 15-25, for instance, is printed as prose

[2] R. Gordis compares prose and poetic stylistic differences in: Qoheleth and Qumran—A Study in Style, Biblica 41 (1960), 402ff.

[3] Whallon, Formula, Character, and Context, 173–210.

[4] Biblia Hebraica, ed. by R. Kittel: Isaiah – R. Kittel; Ruth and Lamentations – T.H. Robinson; Job – G. Beer.

in the RSV, but as verse in Kittel. Conversely, there are many lines in the Kittel edition which are written in prose, but are rendered poetically in the RSV text. For example, see Isaiah 24$_{4}$. And there are yet other passages which are prose in both the Hebrew as well as the English, but which seem to have key word balance which suggests to us a poetic line following Whallon's theory. What, then, are the criteria which translators use to edit their texts as prose or poetry? Minimally, their means of selection is ambiguous, if not downright contradictory. Why, for example, is Isaiah 22$_{15-25}$ rendered as prose by the RSV when it is placed as a poetic line in Kittel? To explain the matter by saying that each translator has his own views on what is and is not poetry, is to place poetic study entirely in the subjective realm. Formula criticism and key word distance, we suggest, may help us here.

Let us then apply Whallon's theory to the text of scripture. It would be preferable to use the blocked page of Hebrew text of the earlier editions when we begin an exhaustive examination of the scriptures to determine what is prose and what is poetry[5]. With such a text, we would be uninfluenced by the work of previous scholars. But for our purposes of merely suggesting the usefulness of formula criticism and the text of scripture, we shall compare select passages of the RSV and Kittel editions. In this way we shall be able to see quickly where points of difference exist. We must note, however, that in any event, we do not have the luxury of Greek meter, Old French assonance, or Old English alliteration to guide us in our search of the true poetic line.

Moreover, we must also be suspicious of Masoretic cantillation marks as a help in the selection of the poetry. Kahle, for one, has pointed out the recentness of the marks and the many ways in which they are contradictory[6]. We propose now to test Whallon's theory about the distance of key words as an index to determining what is poetic and what is not. To recall: prose has its key words adjacent to each other; poetry has the key words at an even distance from each other and in some kind of tension between phrases, hemistichs, lines, etc.

We shall look, first of all, at a few passages which appear as prose in the RSV text of Isaiah, but are printed as poetry in Kittel's text. We mentioned one such instance above, Isaiah 22$_{8b-11.\ 15-25}$, but there are

[5] At hand we have Biblia Hebraica, ed. by E. van der Hooght, 1867, and The Massoretic Bible, ed. by C.D. Ginsburg, 1894.

[6] S. Gevirtz believes the cantillation marks to be useless for such study. Patterns in the Early Poetry of Israel, 1963, 12. P. Kahle's views on the marks are much the same: Masoreten des Ostens, 1966 (1913); so K. Levy, Zur masoretischen Grammatik, 1936; G.R. Driver, Abbreviations in the Massoretic Text, Textus 1 (1960), 123.

many others: 4_{1-2} 7_{18-25} 8_{6-10} 10_{20-22} 24_{4} 30_{20}[7]. Looking at these prose RSV passages in terms of "key word distance", we are often struck by the word pairs in the lines, and take $22_{8b-11.\ 15-25}$ as our example. As we examine the lines, we find that word pairs do indeed exist, and adjacent pairs are few: "look/see" 22_{8b-9}, "weapon/breech" 22_{8b-9}, "count/break down" 22_{10}, "look/have regard" 22_{11} (Isaiah # 103), "hew/carve" 22_{16}, "tomb/habitation" 22_{16}, "hurl violently/seize firm hold" 22_{17}, "whirl/throw" 22_{18}, "thrust/cast down" 22_{19}, "office/station" 22_{19}, "clothe/bind" 22_{21}, "robe/girdle" 22_{21}, "habitation/house" 22_{21} (Isaiah # 340), "Jerusalem/Judah" 22_{21} (Isaiah # 82), "open/shut" 22_{22} (Isaiah # 341), "peg/throne" 22_{23}, "give way/cut down/fall/cut off" 22_{25}. It would seem that from the presence of the word pairs in these lines, not to mention phrases which we did not list, that the translators of the RSV edition had no justifiable reason for placing such passages in prose form. Word pairs are present and so, indicate poetic verse.

And we are able to apply these same principles to passages which are printed as poetry in the RSV edition, but as prose in Kittel. The English translator's guidelines for placing the lines into poetry seem inconsistent in view of what we have just found regarding lines which they print in prose. Isaiah 51_{13-16} and 65_{24-25}, are both printed as poetry in the RSV edition, but as prose in Kittel. Yet the following word pairs turn up in those verses: "release/die" 51_{14}, "die/fail" 51_{14}, "Lord God/Lord of hosts" 51_{15} (Isaiah # 20), "mouth/hand" 51_{16}, "planting/laying the foundations" 51_{16} (Isaiah # 667), "heavens/earth" 51_{16} (Isaiah # 4). The word pairs here show that whatever reason Kittel had for printing these verses as prose escapes us, for they certainly are poetry.

And we must examine a few passages which are prose in both Kittel's text of Isaiah, and in the RSV edition. Perhaps they both could be wrong in some cases, and we trust that our word pair criterion will tell us this wherever the translators are in error. The following passages are printed as prose in both editions: Isaiah 4_{3-6} $7_{1-6.\ 10-17}$ 8_{1-4} 14_{1-3} $19_{16-20.6}$. Taking 4_{3-6} as our test ground: "left/remains" 4_{3}, "Zion/Jerusalem" 4_{3} (Isaiah # 52), "wash away/cleanse" 4_{4}, "filth/bloodstains" 4_{4}, "daughters of Zion/Jerusalem" 4_{4} (Isaiah # 52), "judgment/burning" 4_{4}, "cloud/smoke and shining of a flaming fire" 4_{5}, "day/night" 4_{5} (Isaiah # 333), "canopy and a pavilion" 4_{5}, "shade/refuge and shelter" 4_{6}, "heat/storm and rain" 4_{6}. So these lines, at least, which are written as prose in both editions, also have word pairs, and necessarily should be translated as poetry.

---

[7] These are the substantial passages, but there are many other individual lines which are also questionable in this respect.

But let us not be fooled into thinking that our method always turns up word pairs and hence, poetry. Job $1_{1-2.13}$, which is universally printed as prose, contains scarcely any word pairs. In fact, and in keeping with Whallon's theory, there are more adjacent key words in the section than there are word pairs: "blameless and upright" 1_{1} (Job # 3), "go and hold" 1_{4}, "send and invite" 1_{4}, "eat and drink" 1_{4}, "sin and curse" 1_{5}, "go to and fro and walk up and down" 1_{7} (Job # 2), "blameless and upright" 1_{8} (Job # 3), etc. These and many other adjacent pairs, rather than fixed pairs, lead us to conclude that Job 1_{1}ff., is not poetry.

Our findings strongly indicate, therefore, that the distance between key words in a line is critical and very helpful in determining whether or not a line is prose or poetry. Whallon's observation seems to hold up under examination of the limited passages to which we have applied it. And the criteria of the translators, Kittel included, appear ambiguous and contradictory to us. We believe that our rule of thumb for separating the prose and the poetry is not only responsible, but more accurate: in spoken verse where word pairs occur, even with adjacent pairs alongside, the passage is poetry; where word pairs are very rare, and adjacent key words are more often the case, we have, more likely than not, a prose text. Whallon's theory is quite adequate in allowing us to determine whether a line of text is prose or poetry, even more so than he himself realized.

C. WAS RUTH ORIGINALLY A POETIC BOOK?

J. Myers has written an impressive little monograph amassing evidence which he maintains indicates that the book of Ruth was once a poem, and more exactly, an oral poem passed by word of mouth[8]. That it was orally recited (or at least written) as a poem, Myers shows by pointing to any number of items, which, taken together indicate a poetic kernel in the book of Ruth[9]. He elaborates on such subjects as the picturesqueness and conciseness of the book; the orthography, morphology, syntax, and vocabulary of the text; its literary features and structure. These points collectively reveal to Myers that Ruth was once poetry. And to cap his argument, Myers lists a number of lines of

[8] J.M. Myers, The Linguistic and Literary Form of the Book of Ruth, 1955, 42–43.

[9] The belief that a prose passage has behind it a poetic original is much more effectively argued for parts of Genesis by U. Cassuto, A Commentary on the Book of Genesis: From Noah to Abraham, 1961, 128. He discusses the extent of Hebrew poetry and the poetic substratum in the narrative of Genesis. See also his same commentary, From Adam to Noah, 11.

Ruth in which he says he has found various types of parallelism[10]. These he takes as "potent argument in favour of a poetic original underlying the book of Ruth"[11].

The parallelism which Myers says that he had found in the book of Ruth, is, in fact, his only solid argument in favor of a poetic life of the book. The rest of his observations we must regard as a speculative, esthetical appreciation of the literature, which is secondary and highly subjective. But the fact that he claims to have located parallelism in Ruth is another matter: where there is parallelism, there will always be word pairs forming the parallelism. So we must check his parallelisms for word pairs.

The book of Ruth may become for us a working example of the usefulness of the formula-critical method, and at the same time another test for the "theory of key word distance" just examined. As our Appendix list to Ruth shows, we have gone through the book looking for the key words in the lines which are, on the one hand, expressed at an even distance from each other, or are, on the other hand, adjacent. In other words, we have found all the repeated phrases and word pairs which are present. And we included in our study every line of text whether it involved speech or not.

The process was very rough going in comparison to the known poetic books we have examined. The lines simply did not run smoothly as we were used to in Job and Isaiah. Ruth 4 3-6, for example, was very choppy compared to known poetry. And our results were comparably meager indeed. In the four chapters of the book, we encountered less than twenty word pairs which recur in Ruth or elsewhere. Moreover, as our Appendix list shows, the pairs are certainly no more than commonplace associations which could be created by an author forming either poetry or prose. There were also found a number of repeated phrases, but they too were not substantial, and were equally commonplace.

TABLE 4. RUTH

מצא/נתן	give/find	1 9	
אנוש/בן	son/man (husband)	1 11	Repeats
עגן/שבר	wait/restrain	1 13	
דבק/נשק	kiss/hold fast	1 14	In narrative
לין/הלך	go/stay	1 16	No key word distance
שוב/עזב	leave/return	1 16	
קרא/קרא	call/call	1 20	Same word in pair
ריקם/מלא	full/empty	1 21	
שוב/הלך	go/return	1 21	
ענה/קרא	answer/humble	1 21	

[10] Myers, The Linguistic and Literary Form, 41–42.

[11] Ibid. 42.

שדי/יהוה	Lord/Shaddai	1_{21}	Repeats
דבק/עבר	cross over/cleave	2_{8}	
משכרה/פעל	deed/reward	2_{12}	
עשה/לקט	glean/work	2_{19}	Repeats
בקר/לילה	night/morning	3_{13}	Repeats
קרא שם/אשה חיל	renoun/call the name	4_{11}	
בית לחם/אפרתה	Ephrathah/Bethlehem	4_{11}	Repeats
כול/שוב נפש	restore life/nourish	4_{15}	

Next, we looked at the examples of parallelism which Myers says are in the text of Ruth, and therefore, betray the existence of poetry. He lists some twenty-one examples of various types of parallelism, and claims that there are many more in Ruth[12]. Since he has found more parallelisms than we have found word pairs, perhaps we have overlooked some pairs in our trip through the text.

When we examine Myers' examples of parallelism, we encounter problems. Of the twenty-one examples of parallelism which he lists, and which are found above, only eighteen actually have word pairs back of them, and may justly be considered to be hemistichs in parallel. In reality, only fifteen of these eighteen pairs which he found are legitimate: there is no distance between one; one is found in the narrative of the book and not in the speech; and one has the same word repeated, from which we cannot tell much. Of these fifteen remaining pairs, only five (so marked) were found to repeat either in Ruth or elsewhere in the literature. That five word pairs which repeat are found in a text of four chapters, is certainly not significant enough to merit the conclusion that the text in question was once poetry. We find, therefore, that while Myers' parallelism is backed by some word pairs, they are not at all substantial[13]. The average chapter of poetry in Isaiah or Job has from thirty to eighty word pairs!

Hence the number of parallelisms in the book of Ruth appears to be quite few. Myers seems to be imposing his views on the book. In this regard, we must make mention of Myers' serious mistake of forcing his poetic line upon passages which are not in themselves speech. He even sets the narrative frame of the story into poetic line also. $1_{6.\ 14.\ 22}$ 4_{18-22}, are all rendered by him as poetry[14]:

She returned from the land of Moab;
And they arrived at Bethlehem
at the beginning of the barley harvest. (Ruth 1_{22})

השבה משדי מואב והמה באו בית לחם בתחלת קציר שערים

[12] Ibid. 41–42.

[13] Myers' examples of synthetic parallelism should have no word pairs, but they do. Hence they are not really synthetic.

[14] See Myers' section; The Hebrew Text of Ruth Reconstructed to Show Poetic Passages, in: The Linguistic and Literary Form, 47–53.

For Myers overlooks one essential fact of Hebrew poetry, that all Hebrew poetry is speech—the speech of God, the speech of man, but always speech[15]. Moreover, Myers even unwittingly affirms this fact by finding seventeen of his twenty-one examples of parallelism in Ruth in the dialogue of the book. And in the speech exist only the legitimate word pairs to be found in the whole story[16]. The fact that Myers fails to affirm this reality (that all poetry is speech), causes us to question his entire critical approach to the poetry.

But Myers' most obvious weakness in seeking poetry in Ruth is the fact that he fails in every way *to find as poetry* the lines of the book, and so must resort to creating verse with the contents of each line: he must alter his lines to obtain poetic verse. To explain: $1_{1.\,6b.\,8.\,9.\,11.\,13}$, etc., are all placed into poetic lines by Myers by adding and subtracting letters, words, and phrases from the verses. But few of these lines actually have word pairs in them to assure true parallelism, the mark of the poetry. So while Ruth's lines may be *emended* to resemble poetry, as Myers does, the lines themselves do not indicate that they were once poetry, nor are they in any sense found as skeletons of poetry. We could, for example, set Exodus or Deuteronomy into poetic line if we really wanted to. Selecting at random, Exodus 14_{21}, from an equally as exciting story as Ruth, may be easily placed in poetic line as Myers does with the lines of Ruth:

Then Moses stretched out his hand over the sea,
  and the Lord drove the sea back
by a strong east wind all night,
  and made the sea dry land.

ויט משה את ידו על הים ויולך יהוה את הים ברוח קרים
עזה כל הלילה וישם את הים

But no matter how we adjust the lines, they still are without word pairs and so, are without parallelism, and are certainly not poetry. On the other hand, we have suggested that certain lines from Isaiah, long considered prose, be placed as poetic lines. But we propose this not by altering the lines in any way, but because they are found as dormant poetry, containing word pairs, but hitherto unrecognized as poetry. The few word pairs which we have found in Ruth do little to suggest that

---

15 Some of the speech of the Old Testament is prose, and some is poetry. But all the poetry is speech. This is a fact which few have taken notice of beside Paul Dhorme, A Commentary on the Book of Job, 1967 (1926), lxiv. But see his full discussion of the poetic dialogues of the book of Job, xxxvi–liii.

16 This tempts us to suggest that Ruth might once have been a play: a prose narrative with poetic lines. But the individual dialogues in the book are really too short to allow any "dramatic" intercourse between the players.

the author of Ruth measured his lines comparably to other Hebrew poetry. In fact, because we have found all of the word pairs in the text, and have judged those which Myers' parallelism contains, we have found *all* of the instances of possible parallelism in the book. And because they are so few in number, we conclude that the book was not once poetic.

Last, we must ask how our results in the book of Ruth instruct us in that book's relation to other texts which are considered to be prose. We may note, first of all, that the few word pairs which we found are comparable to any prose text, for there are at least a few word pairs per chapter in any prose passage. And certainly, in comparison to any known poetic texts, the word pairs of Ruth occur rarely, if at all. However, what is even more interesting in Ruth than the few pairs present, are the many instances of the adjacent key words which are present: the number of adjacent words found in Ruth which are found elsewhere as word pairs is significant. The adjacent terms such as "kiss and weep" ("בכה ונשק" Ruth 1 9; # 3) point to a prose diction rather than a poetic one, for as we have said, adjacent words are a characteristic of the prose, not the poetry. And such phrases which repeat as, "as the Lord lives" ("חי יהוה" Ruth 3 13 # 8) which are found only in the prose, further confirm our conclusion. We take these phrases to be but another indication of the fact that Ruth is, and always has been, prose.

We conclude, then, from the word pairs and the adjacent words which we have found in the book of Ruth, that the text does not suggest a poetic kernel, but is prose throughout.

D. FORMULA CRITICISM AND THE PROBLEM OF DATING TEXTS

We submit that formula criticism has something to say respecting the problem of dating Old Testament poetry. However, W. Whallon has cogently stated that we cannot date books or even shorter passages based upon places where repeated phrases or word pairs *which are traditional* are critical to our interpretation[17]. For example, since Jeremiah 17 8 is repeated in Psalm 1 3, and Isaiah 13 6 is repeated in Joel 1 15, we cannot be sure in which of the texts the phrases and word pairs are original[18]. We cannot date the passage in which these verses

[17] Whallon, Formula, Character, Context, 168–172. See also, U. Cassuto, The Goddess Anath, 1971 (1953), 52.

[18] R. Culley seems to be aware of the danger of dating texts based on repeated formulas. Oral Formulaic Language in the Biblical Psalms, 1967, 108. S.R. Driver and G.B. Gray date Job on that text's relation to other texts: A Critical and Exegetical Commentary on the Book of Job, I 1921, lxii.

are found if our judgment is to rest solely upon the repeated formulas in the line.

We seek here to amend Whallon's suggestion by saying that we cannot use verses containing critically repeated phrases and word pairs which occur from *commonplace association* to date passages[19]. The associations can and do repeat at any time and any place in the literature. Therefore, for instance, it is impossible to date the acrostics of Lamentations by employing passages containing word pairs repeated there and elsewhere. Whallon voices this caution because a word pair repeated one place does not prove origin or dependency. We voice this caution regarding pairs because these pairs, as common associations, could recur at any time.

But Whallon's observations here on dating texts using repeating word pairs does not answer for the use of passages with *non-recurring* word pairs as possible sources of information. For we have said before, pairs which do not repeat, are most likely original with the author with which they are found, at least until proven otherwise. It is not reasonable to assume, as some have, that if a pair recurs nowhere else, it was nevertheless once a part of a traditional diction, and therefore, once repeated. This argument from silence divests the Hebrew poet from any creativity whatsoever. Not so much as a line of the text bearing his name may be considered to be his.

Now where word pairs recur in separate books, these passages which contain the pairs certainly cannot be enlisted to date one of the texts. In this Whallon is correct. The minor prophets, for example, contain a great many of the word pairs and phrases found in Job. But on the other hand, when we are dealing with word pairs which recur but once and in one text, we believe we are better off ascribing that verse and word pair to the author in which it is found, rather than not. If the verse is useful in the dating of the passage in which it is found, then so much the better. It is best to take a non-repeated phrase, word pair, or verse seriously in the place where it is found, rather than relegate it to a time when it was repeated but which we cannot prove. To assume that a pair which does not repeat was a commonplace once in the poetry, is pure hypothesis. Take these phrases and word pairs which are found nowhere else than the locations cited:

Like a lion he breaks all my bones; (Isaiah 38_{13})

כארי כן ישבר כל עצמותי

[19] But Whallon is not the first to make this astute remark. A. Guillaume has said that when material is repeated in the poetry, as it often is, we cannot tell who created the line first. Studies in the Book of Job: with a New Translation, 1968, 15. N.H. Tur-Sinai also warns that we cannot date books based upon word pairs in passages: one hemistich or distich which repeats does not show in which place it was first created. The Book of Job: A New Commentary, 1957, 208.

As locusts leap, men leap upon it. (Isaiah 33 4)

כמשק גבים שוקק בו

You shall be *a crown* of beauty in the hand of the Lord,
and a royal *diadem* in the hand of your God. (Isaiah 62 3)

והיית עטרת תפארת ביד יהוה וצנוף מלוכה בכף אלהיך

He stretches out the north over *the void*,
and hangs the earth upon *nothing*. (Job 26 7)

נטה צפון על תהו תלה ארץ על בלי מה

He will suck the poison of *asps*;
the tongue of *a viper* will kill him. (Job 20 16)

ראש פתנים יינק תהרגהו לשון אפעה

These phrases and word pairs, to pick a few at random, are beautiful examples of Hebrew poetry. Yet they occur only once, in the places cited. Are we therefore to ascribe them to a "traditional diction" which once was said to make them available to all poets, even while we have no examples of such? We think not. There is little reason for not assigning them to the author's creativity where they are found, and to his part of the poetry alone. This can be our only conclusion if we always keep in mind that the number of word pairs in Job which do *not* repeat outnumber those which do at the ratio of 2 : 1.

Therefore, we suggest temperance in writing off single word pairs as part of a non-existent traditional diction. We allow all non-repeated pairs to be considered part of the author's creativity in which they are found, and so parts of valid verses and passages with which to date the text, at least until proven otherwise.

E. FORMULA CRITICISM AND THE PROBLEM OF AUTHENTICATING TEXTS

1. Isaiah

We have already discussed how the word pairs in Isaiah indicate the influence of commonplace association upon the text as a whole, and how they, at the same time, attest to the original efforts of three creative "authors". In the first instance, the Appendix list on Isaiah reveals that a number of the word pairs recur with some frequency in more than one of the sections, and without much bias for any one of the parts. This, we said, was not due to those who transmitted the text, but simply to the fact that most word pairs are commonplace associations which could be created by any poet without much thought on the matter. In the case of transmissionary influence, we concluded that an

Isaianidae might explain such uniformity throughout, but that there was no real textual evidence to support the "school theory". Rather, we pointed to the results of our research in the text of Isaiah which indicated that most pairs which recurred across all the sections were simple associations, easily created by any poet, irrespective of time or place.

But this was not all that the word pairs indicated in Isaiah. Quite a few recurring word pairs which were restricted to one of the three sections, 1–39, 40–55, 56–66, unquestionably confirm the originally separate authorship of the parts. These isolated word pairs in each section confirm the longstanding historical surveys of Isaiah's contents which also suggested three sections and three distict "authors" of the book[20]. So even while many of the word pairs have to do with common association, and are evenly distributed throughout, we can still see a division of three parts in the remaining word pairs.

Let us look at the three sections for a moment. 1–39 contains the word pairs which are most common throughout the whole of Isaiah. This may be due to a borrowing by the later two authors, we cannot say. Yet more pairs from 1–39 occur in 40–55 or 56–66, than either of these latter two do in each other. And we found that each section had its own favorite words in terms of word pairs: 1–39 was fond of "dwell" ("שכן") at the rate of 13–0–2 for the three sections; and "land" ("ארץ") was also a favorite word of 1–39 at the rate of 119–42–19. 40–55 contains a great number of new and different word pairs compared to 1–39, but which do not repeat at all. The many short quotations in 40–55 (43_{9} $10_{42.\ 17}$; etc.) make the sectional diction stand out from the other two parts; the numerous run-on lines present in 56–66 ($56_{4.\ 5.\ 6}$ 57_{18}) as well as its own favorite words such as "delight" ("חפץ" 3–7–11) all go together to make the section's diction different.

So we see in Isaiah that the word pairs reveal two aspects of the nature of the text: we see many word pairs repeated throughout 1–66 from common association; and in each section, 1–39, 40–55, 56–66, we find very dissimilar repeated and non-repeated word pairs which are not found in more than one section. It is this latter observation which leads us to believe that historical investigation is correct in concluding that Isaiah is not a unity of composition, but a combination of three

---

[20] The following articles dealing with the unity or division of the book of Isaiah are helpful: S. Mowinckel, Neuere Forschungen zu Deuterojesaja, AO 16 (1938), 1–40; K. Elliger, Der Prophet Tritojesaja, ZAW 49 (1931) 112–140; L.G. Rignell's commentary on II Isaiah points out the differences between the sections nicely: A Study of Isaiah Chapters 40–55, 1956. For current views that Isaiah is a unity, see O.T. Allis, The Unity of Isaiah: A Study in Prophecy, 1950, who says about all there is to say on this unpopular position.

different poems[21]. Our pairs are certainly not conclusive evidence in matters of datnig or separating passages. Nevertheless, they present us with but one more way to assist textual research.

2. *Job*

It is an important, if not burning question in Job and wisdom scholarship, as to whether or not the book of Job is made up of some parts which are not original to the principle author[22]. One of these passages is the Elihu speech (chapters 32–37)[23]. Irrespective of other means of investigation and what they have concluded, what do the formulas in the passage tell us about chapter 32–37's relationship to the whole of Job?

Our answer must come from an examination of all the word pairs and phrases which we have collected in Job. Job is an especially good text in which to seek word pairs for it is a part of wisdom literature. The sapiential literature is, as we have said, highly paratactic, loaded with self-sustaining lines of wisdom: the word pairs rarely occur between the lines[24]. And in looking to Job, we may say, first of all, that the word pairs in chapters 32–37—in comparison with the word pairs found in the rest of the book—seemed rough and choppy and particularly hard to come by. The pairs in the section arise infrequently compared to the rest of the book. What is more, of the forty-two word pairs which repeat in chapters 32–37, only ten (Job # 24, 33, 41, 94, 95, 11, 115, 133, 243, 296) of these recur elsewhere in the book of Job. This is to say that the word pairs which are found to repeat in chapters

---

21 As we said before, we could only briefly consider such smaller sections as the servant songs of II Isaiah. However, we were not able to observe a single diction in the songs.

22 The very best survey on additions to the text and what scholarship thinks is found in H.H. Rowley, The Book of Job and Its Meaning, BJRL 41 (1958–1959), 167–207. But equally informative are: W. Baumgartner, The Wisdom Literature, in: The Old Testament and Modern Study: A Generation of Discovery and Research, 1961, 216–221; R. Gordis, The Book of God and Man: A Study of Job, 1965, 104–116; A. Guillaume's notes on Job 32–37 in: Studies in the Book of Job 168.

23 R.H. Pfeiffer believes that the Elihu speech was added: Introduction to the Old Testament, 1963, 665. Driver and Gray are against Elihu based upon style and language: A Critical and Exegetical Commentary on the Book of Job, vol. I, xli–xlviii. J. Pedersen believes the Elihu speech was not a part of the original Job, but fits the book so well that it probably was written by the author of Job. Israel: Its Life and Culture I–II 1926, 531.

24 The book of Job was regarded as wisdom literature in *mashal* form as early as M. Maimonides, The Guide of the Perplexed, 1969, III, xxii, 487. And also see: Genesis Rabbah LVII. 4.

32–37, repeat more elsewhere than they do within the text of Job[25]. We might even go so far as to say that, considering the formula, these chapters stand out remarkably in relation to the rest of the chapters of Job. So, without much ado, we surmise that chapters 32–37 of Job were not penned by the same poet who created the rest of the book of Job.

But the addition of chapters 32–37 to Job is fairly obvious, even without the assistance of the word pair study. However, there are other sections of Job which tell us even more interesting things about their relationship to the book as a whole when their word pairs are examined.

The book of Job is made up of a number of dialogues given by a limited number of characters: Job, Eliphaz, Bildad, Zophar, Elihu, and Yahweh[26]. When the word pairs which have been found are examined with regard to the character who uses them, amazingly enough, a great number of the pairs occur with only one of the characters. This is to say that evidently the author of Job has constructed a more highly structured poem than we heretofore have given him credit; or, and here we certainly hazard a guess, perhaps these dialogues came to the composer of the text as full dissertations, and he worked them together into the finished form we now have: he ordered the arguments into the progression which we now have. In any event, a great number of the recurring pairs repeat over again with the same character. For example, the following word pairs recur primarily in the dialogues of Job alone: # 10, 11, 12, 13, 14, 17, 19, 67, 68, 75, 78, 80, 82, 83, 85, 87, 88, 93, 107, 110, 111, 115, 117, 119, 122, 123, 125, 142, 152, 153, 154, 158, 159, 161, 163, 168, 169, 173, 180, 198, 201, 202, 205, 208, 210, 212, 229, 231, 251. For the dialogues of Eliphaz, see Job # 30, 31, 32, 55. Therefore, as our Appendix list shows, quite a large number of the pairs have a fondness for repeating depending upon who is speaking; pairs in the first speeches of a character tend to recur again in his later speeches. This complexity of dialogue, though we have not begun to fully examine it, leads us to suspect that the author of Job was more interested in the unity of characterizations than we ever imagined.

---

25 This is seen more clearly in our method of approach than even in the work of Driver and Gray, wherein they pointed out the parallel passages of Job. A Critical and Exegetical Commentary on the Book of Job, vol. I, lxviii. —

26 The arrangement of the dialogue is best seen in B. Kennicott's edition of: Vetus Testamentum Hebraicum, 1776–1780, vol. II, and also in R.H. Pfeiffer, Introduction to the Old Testament, 660–667: Introduction 1–2. Job 3. 6. 7. 9. 10. 12. 13. 14. 16. 17. 19. 21. 23. 24_{17} 26_{1-4} 27_{1-12} 29. 30. 31; Eliphaz 4. 5. 15. 22; Bildad 8. 18. 25 26_{5-24}; Zophar 11. 20. 24_{18-25} 27_{13-23}; Hymn 28; Elihu 32. 33. 34. 35. 36. 37; Yahweh 38. 39. 40. 41. 42_{1-6}; Epilogue 42_{7-17}.

And so we come to realize that the formula may just be a new means of assessing the unity and structure of poetic texts. The pairs tell us things about the dialogues of Job, and also about the "extra" passages therein. For instance, our research has revealed that of the fifteen word pairs which recur in the hymn in chapter 28 (Job # 311–325), only six of the pairs (# 313, 314, 316, 320, 321, 325) recur in Job[27]. And most of these pairs that do recur in Job are of the most commonplace associations. These results make the hymn suspect. Other sections in Job which might be more fully explored using our methodology would be the broken parts of the Zophar speeches; the speech of Yahweh (chapters 38–41) has been questioned for its originality by such scholars as Finkelstein[28], but accepted by others such as Dhorme, based upon literary style[29]. The possibilities of exploration using formula criticism are almost endless in such texts as Job where a number of passages have long been suspect.

We conclude that our study of formulaic diction indicates that the book of Job may be made up of a number of parts, Elihu speech and the hymn of chapter 28, to name but two sure sections which were most likely not written by the author of the original composition. Furthermore, our studies show that there is more coherence in the speeches of each character, than in the successive dialogues. We see more unity in the views of each actor and the manner in which he expresses himself.

3. Lamentations

N. Gottwald submits that the four acrostics of Lamentations were written by a single poet[30], but not as a calculated entity[31]. He argues his position not from any literary evidence which he has located on the matter, but from the basic unity of subject and content throughout the four acrostics[32]. (We cannot be sure about much of anything in the fifth poem, he says.)

---

[27] R. H. Pfeiffer, Introduction to the Old Testament, 665, believes the hymn to have been added. In opposition, P. Dhorme, A Commentary on the Book of Job, lxxvi, avers that the hymn is the product of the author of Job, but inserted here because it fits the dialogues so well.

[28] L. Finkelstein, The Pharisees: The Sociological Background of Their Faith, 1964, 234.

[29] P. Dhorme, A Commentary of the Book of Job, lxxviff.

[30] Gottwald opts for one author of the four poems: Studies in the Book of Lamentations, 1962, 21. 27–28. But his is not the only opinion on the matter. See R. H. Pfeiffer, Introduction to the Old Testament, 722–723.

[31] Gottwald, Studies in the Book of Lamentations, 27–28.

[32] Against Gottwald, see B. Albrektson, Studies in the Text and Theology of Lamentations, 1963, 214–217.

Since the application of formula criticism is based primarily upon the fact that every person, be he poet or not, speaks with his own particular diction, it should be fairly obvious a determination to find out if the four poems of Lamentations contain one diction or more. If the word pairs and phrases which we have collected repeat in each of the four poems, then it will be likely that Gottwald is correct in his view that there was one author for the four poems having the same subject matter. If, however, the pairs and phrases do not repeat commonly within the poems, then a single diction and author for the book of Lamentations is at least questionable and bears further consideration.

Our Appendix list for Lamentations tells us that there are eighty-one word pairs in the book which repeat either in the text or elsewhere. However, only twelve (# 6, 24, 38, 41, 49, 52, 61, 62, 63, 74, 78, 79) of the eighty-one pairs repeat in the poems of Lamentations; only seven (# 6, 41, 49, 61, 74, 78, 79) of these twelve actually repeat in more than one of the four poems. Seven out of eighty-one repeated pairs is not a good ratio, even given the fact that Lamentations is limited in the amount of material present, and was written poetry from the beginning.

Our word pairs are certainly not sufficient enough evidence for us to make final judgments on any matter. Nevertheless, they do provide at least one further indication of a given text's nature. In the case of Lamentations, we can say, therefore, that we are suspicious of Gottwald's belief in a single author, at least insofar as a uniform diction is concerned. One author (as in the case of each of the sections of Isaiah) would more than likely betray his presence in four poems more strongly than the repetition of just seven word pairs out of eighty-one. We thus find questionable Gottwald's assumption that Lamentations 1–4 emanated from a single poet.

F. FORMULA CRITICISM AND THE PROBLEM OF RELATING TEXTS

We have shown above the value of word pairs in examining individual texts for their own peculiar construction and dictional usages. We now turn our attention to the ways in which the formula may assist us in comparing one text to another[33].

[33] This is one of the faults of Culley's investigation of the biblical psalms: he does not check to see if the phrases which recur there are also found in other texts of the Old Testament.

1. *Lamentations and Jeremiah*

For example, the book of Lamentations has been attributed at one time or another, and in mainly the early commentaries, to the prophet Jeremiah[34]. It is not necessary or desirable to enter into this argument here, for both sides believe they have weighty reasons for and against Jeremiah as the author of Lamentations. All we need note here is that the association of Lamentations and Jeremiah was early, and is indicated by the opening words of the Septuagint version of Lamentations: "Jeremiah sat weeping . . . and said . . ." ("ἐκάθισεν ιερεμιας κλαίων . . . και εἶπεν"). But oddly enough, if such early attestations of authorship are valid, the book did not find its way next to the prophet's own prophecy in the Hebrew Bible.

If Jeremiah did, in fact, have a hand in the composition of Lamentations, or even, we might add, have a hand in the transmission of the text, there should be some relationship between the word pairs used in both texts, between Jeremiah and Lamentations. As one author has but one diction, so should one author rather consistently exhibit that diction in all of his creations[35]. With our text of Lamentations, we should see more than the usual number of repeated word pairs in Lamentations and Jeremiah[36]. If, on the other hand, the repeated word pairs of Lamentations recur no more often in Jeremiah than elsewhere in the literature, that prophet's relation to Lamentations must be held to be suspect[37].

We must now consult our Appendix list for Lamentations. In Isaiah, we sought the frequency of the word pairs within that text alone; in Lamentations, we sought diversity of examples attesting to the word

---

[34] Gottwald, Studies in the Book of Lamentations, 21, is not of the opinion that Jeremiah wrote Lamentations. For a conservative view that it is better to attach Lamentations to Jeremiah, see R.K. Harrison, Introduction to the Old Testament, 1969, 1069–1070. His summary of the scholarship is excellent, but he has little reason to attribute Lamentations to the prophet. B. Albrektson, Studies in the Text and Theology of the Book of Lamentations, 214, notes the older writers who have tied the two books together.

[35] We cite as an example, the work which has been done in the area of playwriters. See H. Craig's excellent survey of the work done with the diction of Shakespeare in: The Complete Works of Shakespeare, 1961, 47–67.

[36] It may be argued that we contradict our conclusions regarding the dialogues of Job. However, there is far more unity between the dialogues of Job than there is between the acrostic poems of Lamentations.

[37] M. Löhr sees parallels between Lamentations and Jeremiah, Ezekiel, II Isaiah, and especially the psalms: Der Sprachgebrauch des Buches der Klagelieder, ZAW 14 (1894), 31–50; Threni III und die jeremianische Autorschaft des Buches der Klagelieder, ZAW 24 (1904), 1–16; Alphabetische und alphabetisierende Lieder im Alten Testament, ZAW 25 (1905), 173–198.

pair's wide use in the literature. But we were especially interested in the use of the same word pairs in Lamentations and Jeremiah. However, we must also notice that there is a fundamental difference, which we have maintained, between the prophecy of Jeremiah and the acrostics of Lamentations: whereas the poetry of the former was probably oral, we have said that the latter was probably written. The first was more easily and freely composed; the second was more complex and required a literate hand. We take as our proof of this the fact that Jeremiah contains an unusually large number of word pairs much like Isaiah and Job, while Lamentations contains significantly fewer. We have maintained all along that repetition is the characteristic of oral verse-making. Since the repetition of parallelism in Hebrew poetry requires word pairs, the word pair's frequency in the poetry instructs us in the degree of oral production. Job, Isaiah, and Jeremiah, more likely than not, have been oral compositions.

Looking now to our Lamentations Appendix, we see that in all five of the poems, acrostic and non-acrostic, the word pairs which repeat recur no more often in Jeremiah than they do anywhere else: twenty-six (# 2, 5, 10, 12, 13, 15, 20, 22, 26, 30, 33, 39, 50, 51, 52, 53, 56, 70, 78, 81, 84, 88, 89, 90, 92, 94) of the eighty-one individual pairs which repeat are found in Jeremiah. But about the same amount of the pairs are found in Isaiah and Ezekiel (Isaiah – Lamentations # 6, 11, 19, 21, 27, 33, 37, 39, 40, 41, 47, 50, 53, 54, 57, 68, 74, 81, 82, 84, 90, 91, 97; Ezekiel – Lamentations # 14, 18, 20, 21, 23, 29, 75, 78, 79, 80, 83). In fact, the repeated word pairs of Lamentations recur over a far more diversified area than we might expect. The pairs which are present, then, do not at all indicate the influence of Jeremiah upon the text any more than they indicate the influence of Ezekiel or Isaiah. We conclude that our investigation does little to support the idea that Jeremiah was the author of the text of Lamentations. It is not conclusive proof by any means, but it does point to another way of testing the poetry.

2. *Lamentations and the Lament Psalms*

So we have maintained that every poet has his own way of saying things. But given a topic, he may well use the same word pairs as simple associations which fit the subject matter. We have said elsewhere that word pairs recur throughout the literature irrespective of genre or *Gattung*. If word pairs do repeat more often in the poetry of the same genre or *Gattung*, it is only because the subject matter of like poems is the same. This fact coupled to the limited vocabulary of the Hebrew, makes the pairs seem to appear more often in one genre or *Gattung* than another, although there is nothing compelling the poet to do this. It is simply the case that when we speak of things sorrowful, for example, we use the vocabulary of sorrow, or the negation of joy.

But we have yet actually to test our theory, and this we now do. We take for our illustration, the so-called lament *Gattung* in the biblical psalms which falls into the two categories of national and individual laments[38]. If the pairs are actually restricted to the forms of the poetry, Lamentations and these particular psalms should contain a number of the same word pairs, at least more than other aspects of the literature do. But we must again remind ourselves that Lamentations was written, and so has far fewer word pairs than do the biblical psalms: the psalms conform to the one line, paratactic nature of Job, while the acrostics of Lamentations are remarkable for the complicated distance between the words in pair. So the fact that one set of poems was written and the other set orally composed will have some bearing on our conclusions.

Turning to the results of our research in Lamentations, we find, first of all, that only eleven (# 6, 13, 50, 60, 61, 69, 74, 80, 86, 91, 92) of the eighty-one individual word pairs of Lamentations repeat in the lament psalms[39]. This result alone leads us to question seriously the theory that the word pairs repeat in given genre or *Gattung*: the word pairs of Lamentations which repeat are found in the prophets (# 1, 2, 5, 6, 7, 10, 11, 12, 13, etc.), the wisdom literature (# 5, 11, 15, 37, 50, 52, etc.), the early poetry (# 28, 44, 72, 91, etc.), and the psalms (# 6, 8, 13, 21, 31, 37, etc.). And those pairs which do recur in Lamentations and the lament psalms tend also to confirm our observation that the word pairs, if restricted at all, are restricted to their applicable use. For example, Lamentations and the lament psalms speak of dangers, the word pair "foe/enemy" ("איב/צר" Lamentations # 6) is very fitting in this context (Lamentations 1_{5} Psalm $13_{4(5)}$). And so is the word pair "compassion/steadfast love" ("חסד/רחם" Lamentations 3_{31-32}; Lamentations # 60; Psalm 26_{6} $51_{1(3)}$) fitting in this context where hope is expressed as well as the loss of hope. Pairs are restricted to their applicable use, but that seems to be the only way in which they are restricted. The poets could select any word pair they wished in a situation. But the point to be made is that the more commonplace the pair, the more often it would come to mind for any poet.

G. FORMULA CRITICISM AND THE PROBLEM OF REPAIRING TEXTS

The word pairs are useful not only in terms of what they statistically indicate, but also with respect to exegesis.

[38] See above, Chapter IV, note 20. Besides Gunkel's work in classifying the lament psalms, see H. Jahnow, Das hebräische Leichenlied im Rahmen der Völkerdichtung, 1923.

[39] Our results agree largely with the findings of M. Löhr's study of Lamentations and the other poetic books of the Old Testament.

J. Barr has warned us that emendation of parallel lines where one of the key words is corrupt, is dangerous. It is dangerous because it is impossible to accomplish correctly[40]. He cautions us about repairing lines which seem parallel, but are ones in which we do not know the kind of parallelism present. The lost word may be synonymous or antithetical and so would change the whole meaning of the parallelism by improper emendation. We examine the following lines from Job and Isaiah:

What do you know that *we do not know*?
What ------ that is not clear to us? (Job 15_9)
מה ידעת ולא נרע (תבין) ולא עמנו הוא

They snatch on the right, but are still *hungry*,
and they devour on the left, but they are not -----;
(Isaiah 9_{20} $(_{19})$)
ויגזר על ימין ירעב ויאכל על שמאול ולא (שבעו)

Let us assume that the parts of the lines above which are missing are in some way corrupt or unintelligible. Barr advises us that guessing the correct words parallel to "do you know" and "hungry" is almost impossible. "See", "bear", "understand", "reveal", etc., would all be legitimate possibilities simply by looking at the first line; "starving", "thirsty", "weak", "content", "satisfied", etc., would each be possibilities in the second line depending upon whether or not the word pair is synonymous or antithetical. To guess at the correct verb or noun is hazardous to Barr.

The caution is well taken, but not entirely correct. For as Gevirtz has consistently shown, formula criticism frequently may help in emendations to the point where there is little doubt or question as to which is the missing word or words in a line[41]. We see a hemistich, or word in a hemistich, as "corrupt" usually because a form of a word or combination of letters makes no sense to us. But oftentimes, what we have in our line and what should be in its place are not far off philologically. Yet even without such philological aid in correcting texts, the word pairs may go even further in helping us make changes where they are needed. Armed with the knowledge of how word pairs repeat in the texts, and a lexicon in hand, we are many times able to make sound judgments as to the missing word in a word pair[42].

---

[40] J. Barr, Comparative Philology and the Text of the Old Testament, 1968, 277–282.

[41] Gevirtz, Patterns in the Early Poetry of Israel, 15–96.

[42] Even antithetical word pairs can be identified and filled out if only one member is known. Some examples from Isaiah are: "forget/remember" (17_{10} # 298), "smite/lift up" (10_{24} 53_4; # 209), "be secure/lead astray" (30_{15} 47_{10}; # 630), "forsake/delight" (58_2 62_4; # 685), "seek out/forsake" (58_2 62_{12}).

Our lines from Job and Isaiah, above, are our case in point. Turning to the Hebrew of Job 15_{9}, and pretending that we do not know the outcome of the word pair "know/– – –", we find from our study of Job and Isaiah, that ידע recurs most frequently with the verb בין. The other possibilities which we suggested, "see", "hear", "reveal", while they occur with "know", do not do so nearly as often as with "understand" as its partner (Job # 180). And in the second example, from Isaiah, we find that of the words which recur the most with "hungry", and in antithesis, is "satisfy" ("שבע/רעב" Isaiah # 192). The negative of the second hemistich is a fairly good indication that the word pair will be antithetical. Of course, in such studies, this is where a full listing of all the word pairs of the Old Testament, noting recurrences, would be of great help to us. But until that work is finished, we must rely upon the arduous task of checking every instance in which the known word of the pair recurs.

With these observations in mind, we have made a number of suggestions for repair work in the texts which we have considered. These appear below. We shall discuss only two of the numerous changes

TABLE 5. REPAIR WORK

Isaiah :

חפר/בוש	ashamed/blush	1_{29} 24_{23} 29_{22}* 54_{4}
פלשתים/קדם	east/Philistines	2_{6} $9_{12}$$_{(11)}$ 11_{14}
רהב/נגש	oppress/insolent	3_{5} 14_{4}*
גדי/כבש	lamb/kid	5_{17}* 11_{6}
להבה/אש	fire/flame	(4_{5}) 5_{24} 10_{17} (29_{6}) (30_{30}) 43_{2} 47_{14}* (66_{15})
ראה/שמע	hear/see	6_{9} 21_{3} etc. 42_{20}*
בין/אמן	believe/understand	7_{9}* 43_{10}
שבט/מטה	rod/staff	$9_{4}$$_{(3)}$ $10_{5.15.24.26}$* 14_{5}
יצת/אכל	consume/kindle	$9_{18}$$_{(17)}$ $9_{19}$$_{(18)}$*
שמאול/ימין	right/left	$9_{20}$$_{(19)}$ (30_{21})* (54_{3})
עני/דל	needy/poor	10_{2} 11_{4}* 26_{6}
איים/ציים	wild beasts/hyenas	13_{21}* (34_{14})
גפן/שדדה	field/vine	16_{8}* 32_{12}
ראה/שעה	regard/look	$17_{7.8}$ (32_{3}) (41_{23})*
בלע/בקק	empty/confound	19_{3} (24_{1})*
חזות/ברית	convenant/agreement	28_{15}* 28_{18}
אין/אפס	nought/nothing	40_{17} (41_{12}) 41_{24}*$_{.29}$* 46_{9}
בין/זכר	remember/consider	43_{18} (46_{8})*
ירא/פחד	fear/be afraid	(44_{8})* 60_{5}
יסד/נטע	plant/lay foundation	51_{13}* 51_{16}
לבונה/זבח	sacrifice/frankincense	43_{23} 65_{3}*
חמס/שדד	destroy/oppress	16_{4}* 60_{18}
אביון/ענו	poor/needy	41_{17}* 29_{19}

Lamentations:		
מועד/שך (סך)	booth/appointed feast	2$_{6}$* De. 31$_{10}$
כתם/זהב	gold/pure gold	4$_{1}$*; no repair needed as Kittel suggests: Jb. 28$_{16-17}$ 31$_{24}$ (Pr. 25$_{12}$)
דרך קשת Supply כשת	bend the bow	2$_{4}$*; Ps. 64$_{3(4)}$
בת עמי Add בת to עמי	daughter of my people	4$_{3}$* Je. 6$_{14}$
Job:		
אביון/מחרב	fatherless/needy	5$_{15}$* Ps. 37$_{14}$ Pr. 30$_{14}$
חזק יד/פה	mouth/hand of the mighty	5$_{15}$* 5$_{20}$ Ps. 17$_{13-14}$ 22$_{20(21)}$ 44$_{2-3(3-4)}$, etc.
תשועה/עזר	help/resource	6$_{13}$* Ps. 44$_{27}$ 60$_{11(13)}$ (108$_{12(13)}$)
חנם/שערה	tempest/without cause	9$_{17}$* Ps. 69$_{4(5)}$
ארחלה/רגל ארחוה to ארחלה	feet/path	13$_{27}$* (30$_{12}$) 33$_{11}$ (Ps. 119$_{101}$); this odd pair recurs in I and II Isaiah
טמא/בהמה טמא to נטמינו	cattle/stupid	18$_{3}$* (Le. 5$_{2}$ 7$_{21}$)
יד/חמה יד is correct	destruction/hand	21$_{20}$* Is. 51$_{17}$ (Je. 21$_{5}$ 25$_{15}$) Ek. 3$_{14}$ (20$_{33}$) (25$_{14}$)
לקט/קצר לקט to לקש	gather/glean	24$_{6}$* (Ru. 2$_{3.7}$)
נפש חללים/מתים מתים is from מות not the KJV "men"	dying/soul of the wounded	24$_{12}$* Nu. 19$_{16-18}$ Ps. 88$_{5(6)}$ Is. 22$_{2}$
שם/מקום	place/name	24$_{20}$* (Is. 18$_{7}$) Je. 7$_{12}$
ענן/כסה	moon/cloud	26$_{9}$* Ps. 97$_{2}$, Kittel's emendation is wrong
כף/אימה	fear/hand	13$_{21}$ 33$_{7}$*
אור/ברך	moisture/lightning	37$_{11}$* Hb. 3$_{11}$
לשכו/טחות	clouds/mist	38$_{36}$* Ps. 51$_{6}$
חללים/דם	blood/fat	39$_{30}$* Is. 34$_{6}$ 1$_{11}$
למס חסד מאס to למס	he who *withholds* kindness	6$_{14}$* 5$_{17}$ 7$_{16}$
שלם/עור יעיר not יעתר	rouse himself for you/reward you	8$_{6}$* 41$_{10-11(2-3)}$
ארץ עיפתה כמו אפל צלמות	land of gloom as darkness	3$_{5}$ 10$_{20}$* 10$_{21}$ 12$_{22}$ 16$_{16}$ 24$_{17}$ 28$_{3}$ 34$_{22}$
בטח שכב/חפר	look around/take your rest	11$_{18}$* Pr. 3$_{24}$
חכמה/דעת ידע to עם	understanding/wisdom	12$_{3}$* Ec. 8$_{1}$ (Da. 1$_{4}$)

which we have suggested, as our general method of repairing passages follows the two examples. Our first illustration is Isaiah 11$_{4}$ (Isaiah # 195):

But with righteousness he shall judge *the poor*,
and decide with equity for *the meek* of the earth.
ושפט בצדק דלים והוכיח במישור לענוי ארץ

As the line stands, with the word pair "poor/meek" ("ענו/דל"), there is not much trouble in understanding the author's point. Yet we find that the word pair "ענו/דל" occurs only once in all the Old Testament poetry. And the word "ענו" is a philological oddity. A much more common pair, however, is "עוי/דל" (Isaiah # 195, Job # 377) which repeats some seven times in the poetry, and two times in Isaiah alone (10_{2} 26_{6}). These facts are found by examining all the uses of the word "דל". The change in the meaning of the line is not great when "ענו" is changed to "עני". But nevertheless, the change makes even more clear the comparison which the author is trying to make: "דל" and "עני" seem to be but two ways of speaking of poorness, and the concept of meekness has nothing to do with the line.

Another example of a change which is made in a text by us, comes not so much from difficulties which we have with the meaning of the line, as from the fact that often words are found which are obviously corrupt in that they occur only once in all the literature. Isaiah 41_{24} reads:

Behold, you are *nothing*,
and your work is -----.
הן אתם מאין ופעלכם (מאפע)

The word "אפע" in the word pair "אפע/אין" (Isaiah # 518), occurs just once, here. All too frequently, the problem words in the line, as in this case, are *hapax legomena* or *dis legomena*. However, "אפס/אין" recurs a number of times in Isaiah (40_{17} (41_{12}) 46_{9}). The two words, "אפע" and "אפס" are very close in form, and it is easy to see how a corruption might take place. We take the liberty, therefore, of changing the pair to "אפס/אזן". The line then reads:

Behold, you are *nothing*,
and your work is *nought*.

Many of the repairs of lines which we suggest are dependent upon the recurrence of but a few instances of repeated word pairs. But we defend our work by saying, once again, that we have not had the privilege as Gevirtz had, namely, of picking particularly ripe verses for our repair work: we have limited ourselves to the texts we began with, and our results, though meager and incomplete, reflect our study of word pairs alone.

H. CONCLUSION

We have tried to show in this chapter that formula criticism is useful in evaluating the poetry of the Old Testament, both in statistical survey and in general textual exegesis. Especially helpful are the word pairs. While they are not the only means available for distinguishing the prose line from the poetic verse, they certainly aid us in determining which lines are poetry and which are not. Sometimes they are even able to help us decide which entire books are poetic. And they are able to do so in a manner which is at least much more consistent than the criteria which previous translators have used. We conclude in this respect that the book of Ruth never existed as poetry.

We pointed out that the lines containing repeated word pairs were not useful in attempting to date the poetry. Those pairs which repeat in more than one book are common associations made freely by poets, and we cannot tell who made a word pair first in the respective verses. But on the other hand, we also maintained that we should also take seriously those passages containing pairs which do not recur elsewhere. We allowed them to be the creation of the poet with which they are found, and so may be used to help date a text, if the line in question can be of any help in that respect.

We showed how the word pairs may be instrumental in adding to the collective evidence for or against additions to one text. And we indicated how the pairs may be helpful in relating one text to another. Finally, we listed those repairs which we were able to make in the texts consulted, mainly based upon the word pairs which we have previously found.

We believe that the essential value and usefulness of formula criticism lies in its ability to test the uniform diction of a given book or author. And it can do this even better than it can compare the dictions of two or more books. But we have shown that it is fully able to assist in that also. Formula criticism, while useful, is certainly not the panacea for Hebrew poetic study we might wish. Nevertheless, it is able to help answer the question of a uniform diction in a given text in a way no other method can do.

Chapter VII

Conclusions and Suggestions for Further Study

A. CONCLUSIONS

In this study, we have sought to evaluate the theories of formula criticism put forth by other scholars and to indicate the ways in which formula criticism is a useful tool in the continuing research of Old Testament poetry.

In the first instance, we have described the history and theory behind the various studies in the area of formula. We reviewed the Homeric studies of Parry and Lord on repeated phrases; the work of Ginsberg and Gevirtz on the word pairs found in Ugaritic-Hebrew literatures; and the comparative efforts of Whallon in terms of the repeated phrase and word pair in Greek and Hebrew poetry respectively. We affirmed, first of all, that Old Testament poetry is replete with formulas—repeated word pairs and phrases. But we said that of the two kinds of Hebrew formula, the word pair was by far the dominating formula within the literature. And then we proceeded to discuss the nature of the word pair in general.

Next, we said, in opposition to virtually all of the scholarship in the field (with the exception of the reserve of Whallon), that the formula is used in *both* an oral and literate verse-making society. Looking to the acrostic poems of Lamentations, which were undoubtedly composed in writing, we saw that word pairs were also to be found in that verse. So we concluded that the formula is not the exclusive domain of orally created poetry: it recurs in both oral and written literature. The pairs have their locus in the oral poetry, but they are also literary devices which are intrinsic to written poetry.

We discussed at length the theory that the formula is invented and employed to assist the oral poet in the creation and performance of his verse. However, as we have just said, formulaic material was found in oral *and* written poetry. If repeated elements are located in both oral and written literature, then it follows that its existence need not rest upon the prerequisite for oral verse-making. The view that formulas are used for oral verse-making *alone*, could not be substantiated. To answer the question of the purpose of the formula in oral and written texts, we turned to the biblical poetry itself and our work in Isaiah.

We found that the word pairs recur in two different ways in Isaiah. First, we noted that a great many of the repeated pairs recur evenly throughout the whole of Isaiah. But second, we found that an equally large number of the word pairs which repeated occurred in three separate sections of the book, 1–39, 40–55, 56–66, conforming to what scholars have long suspected of a threefold division of Isaiah. In the first case, concerning the pairs which repeated throughout the whole of Isaiah, we followed Whallon's suggestion that they might have to do with the transmission of the text more than with its original composition: the existence of pairs which recurred evenly throughout, he said, was due to transmissional influence. He even went so far as to posit an Isaianidae to explain this evenness. But this hypothesis of a transmissional activity on the poetry could not be supported. The hypothesis was supported by another theory which gave to the "school of transmission" following Isaiah a "course of study" in the form of a traditional stockpile of formulas. But once the concept of a traditional diction was invalidated, the idea of the Isaianidae fell by the wayside.

In the second case, concerning those pairs which were restricted to separate divisions, we suggested that this was due to the presence of three separate "authors" who composed the historically distinct sections. These pairs obtained existence at the creation of the verse.

A traditional diction, a "stockpile" of word pairs, has been suggested by our scholars as the locus and container of the pairs in the poetry. The stockpile was used by the poets of one generation, and then passed on to the poets of the next. Poetasters were said to be creative only insofar as they worked and reworked the traditional diction handed down to them. But when this theory was set against the results of our research in the book of Job, it was found seriously wanting.

It will be recalled that in the book of Job, we discovered a great many word pairs which did not recur either in that book or elsewhere for that matter. And this was not only the case in Job, but rather, in every book we looked at, and we suspect in the Old Testament in general. The non-recurring word pairs were more prolific than those which recurred—at a ration of 2 : 1. While the theory of a traditional diction allowed for all those word pairs which repeated in the poetry, it said no more about the pairs which did not repeat than to state that they probably also repeated once. And we would have accepted this argument from silence, if there were but a few pairs which did not repeat. But our data told us that the non-recurring pairs were *twice* as many as those which recurred. Thus the theory of a traditional diction was supported by only limited evidence, and did not take into account the pairs which did not repeat. And the amendment to the theory which said that those pairs which do not repeat, repeated once, was viewed as begging the question. In addition, when we began to apply it, the traditional diction theory was found to be unusually restrictive in terms of the creativity of the Hebrew poet: for those who upheld the traditional diction hypothesis, the poet became no more than the overseer of the stockpile.

But we noted at the same time that the vast majority of the pairs which repeat are made up of relationships which are nothing more than common usage from everyday life, and simply associations which most any poet would make. The notion that rare and obscure repeated pairs proved a traditional diction to be present in Hebrew poetry was found wanting: all but very few of the words in pair associate themselves for no discernible reason to us today. And those few pairs which seem indeed to be peculiar, we are willing to say were probably very much related in the mind of the author and his contemporaries at one time. To strengthen our argument, we pointed out the fact that those pairs which repeated frequently, did so because of the limited root vocabulary in Hebrew which gives the reader the idea that the pairs recurred far more often than they actually did. Those pairs which do not repeat anywhere, we ascribe to the creativity of the poet with whom they were found. And we concluded that the theory of a traditional diction just did not fit the results of our own research, nor Hebrew poetry in general. We found, rather, common associations and creativity more at work in the poetry. And this we concluded was a far better explanation for the even repetitions in Isaiah than the Isaianidae or transmissional influence William Whallon proposed. The purpose of the formula, then, was to fill out the line in such a way that the basis of the poetry, the parallelism, was fulfilled. No traditional diction was needed to explain this. Therefore, the origin of the Hebrew formula rested in the poet's creativity, common association, limited vocabulary, and prose associations. The reason for the use of the formula in the poetry was to fill out the parallelism, written or oral.

Finally, we considered the Hebrew poet as a creative artist freed from the bondage of a fixed traditional diction which allowed for no originality: every phrase and word pair was seen as traditional. We at least allow for the fact that the poet may have an original or universal idea which he expresses in his own way. And we went so far as to say that until evidence is located to the contrary, we view most verses which do not repeat as having been written for the place in which they are now found.

We said that while the word pair is essential to the poetic parallelism, the Hebrew bard is free to form associations as he sees fit. The association of two closely related words is more important to him than the form which that association takes. This was evidenced by the fact that associated words occur both adjacently and as fixed pairs in the poetry. But the ease of associations may have been fostered and extended by the range of adjacent associations in the Torah.

And we concluded that the creative poet was not held to use different formulas for different genres or *Gattungen* as those who opt for a traditional diction suppose. Words, on occasion, do recur in poems of a given genre or *Gattung* only because words are restricted to their applicable use. A stockpile neatly catalogued for various types of poetry was neither necessary nor provable.

Our second objective of the thesis was to show the inherent usefulness of the formula as an aid to Hebrew poetry study and general biblical exegesis. But before we explained the ways in which the formula may be an important tool of research for the scholar, we discussed the nature and recurrence of the word pairs in the poetry. We pointed out that as early as R. Lowth, the importance of word pairs and of the small elements of the line was seen. It was the form-critical trend after Lowth which led us to see only whole verses and poems. And we also discussed the violations in the economy of composition and translation which effectively prevent us from seeing the truly full extent of the formulas in the poetry. Such violations keep any order or standardization of the use of the pairs well hidden. Moreover, we understood that if the formula is to succeed in helping us understand Hebrew poetry, we must consider it on its own terms in the Old Testament alone: the Homeric epithet, for example, while it is not at all analogous to the Hebrew word pair, like most literary analogues, does nothing to help us better understand Hebrew poetry.

But turning directly to the ways in which the word pairs and the phrases may help us to understand the structure and organization of the Hebrew verse, we listed the standardized patterns in which we found the Hebrew word pairs repeat in the line. This led us to conclude that there are definite conscious or unconscious patterns available to the poet as he creates his lines. The use of the word pairs is not haphazard, and our total understanding of how the pairs are used may point us directly to the nature of "Hebrew meter". Yet we said time and again, that when we enter the area of "meter" in Hebrew verse, we are better off examining the poetry on its own terms, rather than comparing it to the meters of other literatures.

In addition to being a useful means of better understanding the Hebrew poetry, the word pairs can also help us in the exegesis of the Old Testament verse. The pairs can assist us in determining what is prose and what is poetry in a given passage of scripture. The theory that poetry is characterized by a line with the key members evenly distanced from each other, held up under scrutiny. And the theory that prose, in contrast to poetry, is characterized by a line with key words next to each other, was likewise useful. These observations provided us with a consistent criterion for assigning lines to prose or poetry. Next we applied the principle of key word distance to an entire text. And we were able to make a judgment as to whether or not the book of Ruth was once poetry. From the absence of word pairs in the text, we concluded that it was not originally a poetic piece. However, we warned that in this and in all other instances where we apply this principle, in passages or in whole texts, our conclusions must be added to other evidence and do not stand alone.

The idea that the word pair is valueless in dating passages was also checked. Whereas it was held that verses which contain repeated pairs could not be used to date passages, lines which contain pairs which do not recur may be used to date the passage, if they so prove to be useful in that respect. For the non-repeated word pairs, we said, attest to the creativity of the poet with whom they are found.

We also tried to demonstrate how the word pair may assist in adding to the collective evidence in determining additions to texts. Our work in this respect was certainly minimal, and was not meant to be conclusive. We aimed only at showing how such future studies might be carried out to fruitful ends. We sought merely to point the way to others by saying that, for example, the diction of Lamentations does not indicate one author of the five poems, or of even the first four acrostic poems. And we emphasized that our conclusions regarding the diction of a book or passage should not alone be the sole criterion for determining whether or not it is original to the text or added. The results which formula criticism bring must be included with the evidence obtained via other approaches to the texts.

And we suggested that not only may the internal diction of one book be examined, but also the dictions of a number of texts and authors. Once again, our test book was Lamentations which was compared to Jeremiah and the lament psalms. By establishing the diction of one text, we are able to note its presence in another, if it is there.

Last, we listed the repairs which we think are merited in the texts we studied based upon the word pairs alone. We discussed how the repair of a parallel line is not only possible, but with enough evidence of the use of the word pair, very rewarding.

Our general conclusion to the whole of our investigation will be, therefore, that the theories concerning formulas needed a number of alterations before they fit the textual evidence and could be justly called a methodology. But the presence and importance of the formula in Hebrew poetry stood our study well. Formula criticism is useful, and to a far greater extent than Gevirtz's work anticipates. It opens the door to a number of ways, hitherto unnoticed, of approaching classic Old Testament problems. While formula criticism is not the final solution to all the questions about Hebrew poetry, it nevertheless will go a long way toward helping us repair and relate texts. And it alone just might be the key to a better understanding of the meter.

B. FURTHER STUDY

Our work with formulas has brought to light some suggestions for further study which we think might well be pursued.

We wonder, first of all, what the nature of the word pairs might be in the Qumran literature? Are pairs present in that poetry? Do the pairs reflect an Old Testament flavor for one author or text? Or are the pairs which are found there nothing more than common associations as is the case in the Old Testament poetry[1]? It has been held, for example, that the Hodayot Hymns resemble the biblical psalms through a conscious effort on the part of the poets to copy and borrow phrases and lines[2]. This theory stems, of course, from the general belief that what was considered genuine to the ancients, was most traditional (a belief which we questioned in our arguments). The closer a new (Qumran) hymn was to existing tradition and standards (the Old Testament psalms), the more highly esteemed and accepted it was[3]. This, as we say, is a common belief among scholars today. But the problem of transmissional diction over long periods of time is much more complicated than this. Did, for example, the writers of the Qumran poetry paraphrase the scripture or simply quote it loosely in composing such poems as the Hodayot Hymns[4]? But be this as it may, it would still be of interest to catalogue all the word pairs in the Qumran literature and see what they tell us[5].

[1] Some work has been done on limited aspects of apocryphal and extra-biblical poetry. See S. Mowinckel, Die Metrik bei Jesus ben Sirach, StTh 9 (1955), 137–165.

[2] For the statement that the Hodayot Hymns are late copies of the earlier biblical psalms, see R. Gordis, Poets, Prophets, and Sages, 1971, 85; and his Book of God and Man: A Study of Job, 1965, 163. G. Morawe, Vergleich des Aufbaus der Danklieder und hymnischen Bekenntnislieder (1 QH) von Qumran mit dem Aufbau der Psalmen im Alten Testament und im Spätjudentum, RQ 4 (1963–1964), 323–356, does compare 1 QH to the psalms and post-biblical Judaism, but not in terms of word pairs.

[3] P. Skehan, Le Travail d'Edition des Fragments Manuscrits de Qumran, RB 58 (1956), 49–67. Also the back articles in S. Holm-Nielsen, Hodayot – Psalms from Qumran, 1960.

[4] See P. Wernberg-Møller, The Contribution of the Hodayot to Biblical Textual Criticism, Textus 4 (1964), 133–175.

[5] Ibid. 173–175. Wernberg-Møller has found 102 scriptural allusions in the Hodayot Hymns. An interesting study of the poetic structure of a hodayah hymn is by A. Ehlen, The Poetic Structure of a Hodayah from Qumran; an Analysis of Grammatical, Semantic, and Auditory Correspondence in 1 QH 3. 19–36, Th. D. Dissertation, Harvard University, 1970. See especially his sections on parallelism or what he calls "correspondence", 98–99, 102–103, 113–115, 119–120, 134, 127–128, 136–137, 157–163, 173–176.

A specific project might then be to see what such newly found texts as the Psalms Scroll (11 QPs[a]) tell us when compared to the last fifty psalms of the Old Testament[6]. Our studies have revealed that poets were not nearly so restricted as to tradition as many have hitherto believed: we found that the non-repeating pairs far outnumber those which repeat. We conjecture, therefore, that if the word pairs of the Old Testament poetry recur in the Qumran literature—and we suspect that they do, this is only because the word pairs have remained common associaations yoked to a language with a limited root vocabulary.

R. Culley has suggested that theme is closely related to formula, a subject which we did not discuss[7]. The former deals with the content of the poem; the latter deals with syntax, meter, and lines. Formulas allowed the poet to complete easily the parallelism of the lines; themes aided the poet in making scenes and descriptions. Theme is "a group of ideas recurring in variable form"[8]. The theme deals with content, then, and refers to the elements of subject matter or a group of ideas[9].

In the short poems, such as the biblical psalms, theme may be difficult to determine because of the limited material at hand. But in the longer poems, as in the case of narrative and epic poetry, the theme may be more prevalent and powerful[10]. The epic of the Iliad, for example, supports the theme of the "μῆνιν Πηληιάδεω 'Αχιλῆος" (Il. 1 1) throughout. But in the shorter poems, the thematic element may be harder to find. In the longer biblical texts of, say, Job or I Isaiah, to which we have turned our attention, perhaps it will be found that recurrent words and phrases result in a thematic *leitmotiv* recurring now and again in the poem to keep us on the road as we travel through the poem[11].

The study has also made us painfully aware of the need for a more efficient means of finding repeated pairs. The mechanical task, as we approached it, was tremendously time consuming: relying on the Bible of Kittel and the Thesaurus of Loewenstamm, every word pair in the Hebrew texts of our books was found and placed on individual note cards[12]. Next, every use of each word in our pairs was placed on the

[6] M.H. Goshen-Gottstein, The Psalms Scroll (11 QPs[a]): a Problem of Canon and Text, Textus 5 (1966), 22–33.

[7] R.C. Culley, Oral Formulaic Language in the Biblical Psalms, 1967, 17–20.

[8] Ibid. 18. [9] Ibid. 100.

[10] A.B. Lord, Composition by Theme in Homer and Southslavic Epos, TAPAPA 82 (1951), 71–80.

[11] One such example of a theme might be the motif of Zion in Lamentations. See B. Albrektson, Studies in the Text and Theology of the Book of Lamentations, 1963, 219–228.

[12] S. Mandelkern's Veteris Testamenti Concordantiae Hebraicae atque Chaldaicae, 1955, 2 vols. But we preferred S. Loewenstamm and J. Blau, Thesaurus of the Language of the Bible, 1957, mainly because of its clearer listing of the Hebrew occurrences of each word, and for its fine introductory articles.

card, and the number of times and the place the two words recurred close together were recorded. Finally, because such concordances as Mandelkern and Loewenstamm fail to quote more than a few words of a line, each recurrence of the two words nearby each other was examined for its use as a legitimate word pair. The process required some fourteen weeks for the book of Isaiah alone.

We believe that the determination of the word pairs could be done very easily with the aid of a computer. But because we are not knowledgeable in this field, we do not know the details of how this could be done. But we do know that human error is present when checking the seemingly endless lists of usages in the concordances as we have done. Those pairs which we finally found are certainly word pairs. But we can never be sure that we have them all because of our present means of gathering them.

We have indicated time and again that parallelism is *the* dominant characteristic of Hebrew poetry, and that the word pair is the tool with which the poet constructs the parallelism. But we also said that there is even something more basic and essential to the poetry than the word pair, and that, for want of a better term, we must call "meter". The use of the word pairs in the verse seems to indicate that standardized patterns actually existed for the poet. And there are probably many more subtle and even more obvious rules which we have overlooked in our research. But the guidelines which we have found tell us that the organization of the words in the line is not haphazard. We suggest that work needs to be done in the area of "meter". We can only earnestly recommend that the work be done without dragging in the baggage of Classical Greek verse, and that we learn to deal with the poetry on its own terms.

Appendix

Lists

A. INTRODUCTION

The results of our findings require several introductory remarks. We must make clear our criteria for selection of the word pairs and phrases. And as preface, we must repeat our definition of the formula given earlier: a formula is a repeated word pair or phrase in one or more lines of poetry, the terms distich and hemitisch having only to do with the length.

As we have said elsewhere, a number of grammatical changes in phrases and word pairs were found to be possible from our research. This was the case, since an increase or decrease in the number of syllables in a line would not necessarily destroy the poetic structure, nor would it render the formula useless. The addition or omission of the definite article, of fixed pronominal suffixes, and the -ā on the imperative and first person of the imperfect are all of no consequence to the formula[1]. Their presence or absence in a word will not affect the fact that a word is or is not a formula. And we shall allow for the free substitution of different classes of words: nouns, verbs, participles may jointly or severally occur as a formula.

The word pairs are what really interest us most, although we have listed the phrases we have found which repeat. We shall, of course, allow in our study both internal and external word pairs occuring within one line or between more than one line. Internally, the pairs may occur within one hemistich, or between the two (or more) hemistichs of the line. For example, the word pair "anger/wrath" (חמה/אף Isaiah # 576) is found in one hemistich in Psalm 37$_8$:

Refrain from *anger*, and forsake not *wrath*!
Fret not yourself; it tends only to evil.

הרף מאף ועזב חמה על תתחר אך להרע

And the same word pair is also found in the two hemistichs of one line, as in Psalm 90$_7$:

For we are consumed by your *anger*;
by your *wrath* we are overwhelmed.

כי כלינו באפך ובחמתך נבהלנו

[1] R. Culley, Oral Formulaic Language in the Biblical Psalms, 1967, 32–33.

And the pair may occur between two or more lines, as in Nahum 1 6:

Who can stand before his indignation?
    Who can endure the heat of his *anger*?
His *wrath* is poured out like fire,
    and the rocks are broken asunder by him.

לפני זעמו מי יעמוד ומי יקום בחרון אפו
חמתו נתכה כאש והצרים נתצו ממנו

That the pairs may recur in reversed order (e.g., "wrath/anger") we take to be of no consequence. All variations in the locations in the lines will be allowed, so long as the words under examination speak to each other in some way. Even pairs which recur but are separated by whole distichs will be allowed, as in Lamentations 2 10 (Isaiah # 52):

The elders of the daughters of Zion
    sit on the ground in silence;
they have cast dust on their heads
    and put on sackcloth;
the maidens of Jerusalem
    have bowed their heads to the ground.

ישבו לארץ ידמו זקני בת ציון
העלו עפר על ראשם חגרו שקים
הורידו לארץ ראשן בתולת ירושלם

Pairs which are found in the first hemistich and the third, first and fourth, etc., will all be accepted. And we must ever be aware that the verse numbering in our texts often has little to do with the progression of the poetic line and so the word pairs. Word pairs have been found to occur separated by as much as three whole lines.

The first list contains a numerical summary of our findings. We list the total number of word pairs which are found in each book; those pairs which recur only once, in the place that they are found; the total number of word pairs which repeat in the texts (one pair may recur four times, and that would count as four); the total number of individual pairs which made up the repetitions both in the book and elsewhere (one word pair which repeated two, three, or four times, etc., would be counted as one).

Next we list the necessary data which we compiled for the various points discussed in the thesis: for Isaiah, we looked at the number of times the pairs repeated in the three sections; Job's relation to the Elihu speeches, and so on. And last, we list the number of phrases which were found to repeat in the text. Their number is insignificant indeed, compared to the word pairs we located.

We looked for different things in different books. Job, Isaiah, Lamentations, and Ruth each has its own summary dealing specifically with special interests in that book. To summarize: we sought the repetitions of the word pairs in Lamentations throughout all of the Hebrew poetry in general, but especially in Jeremiah and the psalms; with Job, we checked the repetitions in the poetry in general, but also in the parts of that book; in the case of Isaiah, we looked at its sections alone; and in dealing with Ruth, we examined both the Hebrew prose and poetry.

And with regard to all our statistics, we must again remind ourselves that percentages are only relevant to the amount of text at hand. But in the case of Job and Isaiah, we possess enough text and word pairs to get a satisfactory idea of the relationship of the word pairs which recur in the literature, and those which do not. When we began our research, we accepted every word pair as potentially repeatable. This approach gave us a large number of pairs with which to work. And so our results must reflect, to a great degree, the relationship of repeated to non-repeated pairs in the poetry as a whole.

On these lists of word pairs from the texts, a few more things need to be said. We list the root verbal stems of the words in pair wherever possible, for we believe that it is the verbal root which the poet called to mind as he created the pairs for his poetry. The places where we found the word pairs to recur have been divided up into two kinds: first, those places where the words actually recur as fixed pairs without any doubt in our minds; and second, those places where known recurring word pairs are found either as adjacent pairs, as words in one phrase, or in questionable relationships. In this second case, *the verse numbers are placed in parentheses*. These parentheses, then, should indicate to the reader that the words are in some way closely related at that citation, but cannot be construed to be a word pair.

When we seek recurrences of word pairs in other books of the poetry, and when these word pairs are very popular, we need not list all outside occurrences, but only a sampling, *followed by etc*. Our object, after all, in this respect, is only to show that the word pairs repeat and do so often. Some pairs repeat thirty times or more. To report them all would require more space than is practical.

It should be recalled that we are dealing with a theory that holds that the recurring word pair (formula) is very common in the literature, so common, that the idea of a traditional diction has been built upon the recurrences. To give this theory the benefit of the doubt, which is only fair, we have extended the same benefit of the doubt to the word pairs. Indeed, many, instances of word pairs which we say repeat may be questioned. But this approach allows us to come to a concrete judgment as to the frequency of the word pair's recurrence. The more word pairs which are included, the better chance the theory will have to hold up. But we have found that the word pairs *recur rarely* compared to the total number of pairs which we have found. And in keeping with our interest in showing all the word pairs possible, we have placed no requirements of complexity upon them: the most common word pairs are included as we have observed that they tell us just as much about the diction of the texts as the most elaborate pairs do. We include two words if they in some way relate to each other, and are equal distance from each other. Whether the pair is found in what looks like prose or poetry from the organization of the page, makes no difference, as we have shown in the thesis. The words in a line become pairs based upon their relationship to each other and the balance which they exhibit in the line.

There is likelihood of our overlooking repeating word pairs throughout the literature. The concordance's lexical division of words by their grammatical forms often hides the pairs from our eye. But the recurrences of the pairs within one text are fairly easy to catalogue in the concordances. And from a comparison of our results in a single text to our results when we search the entire poetry for pairs, we are able to say that it seems no more than 2–4% of the recurrences of the word pairs in the literature have been overlooked.

B. THE LISTS

1. *Numerical Summary*

ITEM	RUTH	LAMEN-TATIONS	JOB	ISAIAH
Total Word Pairs found:	44	240	1474	3168
Total Word Pairs found only once:	33	150	850	1278
Total repetitions in text:	12	90	624	1890
Individual pairs which recur in text:	1	14	127	543
Individual pairs which recur elsewhere:	17	67	259	
Ratio of pairs which do and do not repeat:	18 : 33 1 : 2	81 :150 1 : 2	386 : 850 1 : 2.2	543 : 1278 1 : 2.3

Isaiah: pairs in	
I–II–III:	45/543
I–II:	111/543
II–III:	61/543
I–III:	62/543

Job – Elihu:	10 in Job 42 elsewhere
– Hymn:	5 in Job 15 elsewhere
– Yahweh:	20 in Job 53 elsewhere
– Minor Prophets:	85

Lamentations – Jeremiah:	26
– Lament Psalms:	11

Total Phrases:	8	20	57	80

2. *Isaiah*

WORD PAIRS

No.	Hebrew	English	I Isaiah	II Isaiah	III Isaiah
1	אזן/שמע	hear/give ear	$1_{2.10}$ 28_{23} 32_{9} (30_{21}) (32_{3}) (33_{15}) (36_{11}) 37_{17} (6_{10})	$42_{20.23}$ 48_{8} 50_{4} 55_{3}	59_{1} $64_{4(3)}$
2	קשב/אזן	give ear/harken	28_{23} (32_{3})	42_{23} 51_{4}	
3	שמע/הלך	come/hear		42_{24} 55_{3}	
4	ארץ/שמים	heavens/earth	1_{2} 13_{13} 14_{12} 13_{5} (37_{16})	$40_{12.22}$ 42_{5} $44_{23.24}$ $45_{8.12.18}$ 48_{13} 49_{13} $51_{6.13.16}$ (55_{9}) 55_{10}	(65_{17}) 66_{1} (66_{22})
5	חמור/שור	ox/ass	1_{3} (32_{20})		
6	עם/ישראל	Israel/people	1_{3} (10_{22}) 11_{16} 14_{2} 19_{25}		
7	בין/ידע	know/understand	1_{3} 11_{2} 6_{9} (32_{4}) (29_{24})	$40_{21.14}$ 43_{10} 44_{19} (44_{18})	(56_{11})
8	עם/גוים	nation/people	1_{4} $2_{2\text{-}3.4}$ 10_{6} 11_{10} 13_{4} $14_{6.32}$ $18_{2.7}$ $25_{3.7}$ 30_{28} 33_{3}	42_{6} 49_{22}	61_{9} $65_{1\text{-}2}$
9	גוים/ממלכה	kingdom/nation	13_{4}		(60_{12})
10	עון/חטא	sin/iniquity	1_{4} 5_{18} 6_{7} 27_{9}	40_{2} 43_{24}	$59_{2.12}$
11	בן/זרע	offspring/son	1_{4}		57_{3}
12	שחת/רעע	evil/corrupt	1_{4} (11_{9})		(65_{25})
13	קדש/יהוה	Lord/holy one	1_{4} 5_{24} 10_{20} 29_{19} 31_{1}	$41_{14.16.20}$ $43_{3.14}$ 45_{11} 47_{4} 48_{17} 49_{7} 54_{5} 55_{5}	$60_{9.14}$
14	ציון/עיר	city/Zion	1_{8}	52_{1}	60_{14} $64_{10(9)}$
15	קדוש/גאל	redeemer/holy one		(41_{14}) (43_{14}) 47_{4} (48_{17})	
16	סרה/נכה	smite/rebel	1_{5} 14_{6}		

No.	Hebrew	English	I Isaiah	II Isaiah	III Isaiah
17	ראש/רגל	foot/head	(1_{6}) 7_{20}		
18	עמרה/סדם	Sodom/Gomorrah	$1_{9.10}$ (13_{19})		
19	תורה/דיר	word/teaching	1_{10} 2_{3} 8_{20}		
20	אלהים/יהוה	Lord/God	1_{10} 2_{3} (7_{11}) (17_{6}) $21_{10(17)}$ 24_{15} (25_{1}) 25_{9} (26_{13}) (30_{18}) 35_{2} (36_{7}) $36_{18.20}$ $37_{(4).16.(20).(21)}$ (38_{5})	$40_{3.27.(28)}$ (41_{13}) 41_{17} (43_{3}) 44_{6} $45_{3.5.14.18.21}$ $48_{1.2(17)}$ $49_{4.5}$ 50_{10} $51_{15.20(22)}$ $52_{7-8.10.12}$ $54_{5.6}$ (55_{5}) 55_{7}	59_{13} (60_{9}) 60_{19} $61_{2.6.10}$ 62_{3} 66_{9}
21	ישראל/צבא	host/Israel	1_{24} 5_{24} 21_{10} 37_{16}	44_{6} 47_{4} 48_{2} 54_{5}	
22	עם/קצין	ruler/people	1_{10} (3_{7})		
23	עה/זבח	sacrifice/burnt offering	1_{11}	43_{23}	(56_{7})
24	חלב/עלה	burnt offering/fat	1_{11}	43_{23-24}	
25	דם/חלב	fat/blood	1_{11} $34_{6.7}$		
26	מריא/כבש	beast/lamb	1_{11} 11_{6}		
27	עתוד/איל	ram/he-goat	1_{11} 34_{6}		
28	עתוד/פר/איל	ram/bull/he-goat	1_{11} (34_{6-7})		
29	שבת/חדש	new moon/sabbath	(1_{13})		66_{23}
30	יטב/רעע	do evil/do good	1_{16-17} (5_{20}) (7_{15})		
31	חשך/רעע	evil/darkness	5_{20}	45_{7}	
32	ריב/שפט	defend/plead	1_{17}	50_{8}	
33	אלמנה/יתום	fatherless/widow	$1_{17.23}$ (9_{17}) 10_{2}		
34	שמע/אבה	willing/obedient	(1_{19}) (28_{12}) (30_{9})	42_{24}	
35	מרי/שמע	obedient/rebel	1_{19-20} 30_{9}		
36	צדק/משפט	justice/righteousness	$1_{21.27}$ $5_{7.16}$ $(9_{7(6)})$ 16_{5} 26_{9} $32_{1.16}$ 28_{17} (33_{5})	50_{8} 51_{4-5} (54_{17}) 58_{2}	56_{1} 58_{2} $59_{9.14}$
37	עשה/שמר	keep/do			$56_{1.2}$
38	נקם/נחם	vent wrath/avenge	1_{24}		61_{2}
39	איב/צר	enemy/foe	1_{24} $9_{11(10)}$		59_{18}

40	יעץ/שפט	judge/counsel	1_{26} 3_{2-3}		
41	קריה/עיר	city/city	1_{26} 22_{2} 25_{2}		
42	נאמנה/צדק	righteous/faithful	$1_{21.26}$		
43	חטא/פשע	rebel/sin	1_{28}	$43_{25.27}$ 44_{22} 53_{12}	58_{1} 59_{12}
44	עזב/חטא	sin/forsake	$1_{4.28}$		
45	כלה/שבר	destroy/consume	1_{28} 27_{10-11}		
46	חפר/בוש	ashamed/blush	1_{29} 24_{23} 29_{22}	$54_{4a.4b}$	
47	גנה/איל	oak/garden	$1_{29.30}$		
48	בית/הר	mountain/house	(2_{2}) 2_{3} (10_{32})		56_{7} 66_{20}
49	גבעה/הר	mountain/hill	$2_{2.14}$ 10_{32} $30_{17.(25)}$ (31_{4})	(40_{4}) 40_{12} 41_{15} (42_{15}) 54_{10} (55_{12})	65_{7}
50	הר/גיא	valley/mountain	(22_{5})	40_{4}	
51	ארח/דרך	way/path	2_{3} (3_{12}) 30_{11}	40_{14}	
52	ירושלים/ציון	Zion/Jerusalem	2_{3} $4_{3.4}$ (10_{12}) 10_{32} (24_{23}) (30_{19}) 31_{9} 33_{20} $37_{22.32}$ 31_{4-5}	40_{9} 41_{27} $52_{1.2}$	62_{1} $64_{10(9)}$
53	בת/בתולה	virgin/daughter	(23_{12}) (37_{22})		
54	יכח/שפט	judge/decide	2_{4} $11_{3.4}$		
55	מלחמה/חרב	sword/war	2_{4} 3_{25} 21_{15} 22_{2}		
56	קשת/חרב	sword/bow	21_{15} 22_{2-3}	41_{2}	
57	בית/עם	people/house	2_{6} 14_{2} 32_{13}	(56_{7}) 58_{1}	
58	פלשתים/קדם	east/Philistines	2_{6} $(9_{12[11]})$ 11_{14}		
59	זהב/כסף	silver/gold	(2_{7}) 2_{20} 13_{17} 30_{22} 31_{7} 39_{2}	40_{19} 46_{6}	$60_{9.17}$
60	אוצר/זהב/כסף	silver/gold/treasures	2_{7} (39_{2})		
61	אצבע/יד	hand/finger	2_{8} 17_{8}		
62	איש/אדם	man/man	2_{9} 5_{15} (31_{8})	(44_{13}) 52_{14}	
63	שפל/שחח	humble/bring low	$2_{9.11.17}$ 5_{15} 25_{12} 26_{5} 29_{4}		
64	נגע/שחח	bring low/cast down	25_{12} 26_{5}		
65	עפר/צור	rock/dust	$2_{10.19}$		

No.	Hebrew	English	I Isaiah	II Isaiah	III Isaiah
66	מן/מפני	from before/from	$2_{10.19.21}$		
67	גאון חדר פחד/יהוה	terror of the Lord/ glory of his majesty	$2_{10.19.21}$		
68	אנוש/אדם	man/man	$2_{11.17}$ 13_{12}	51_{12}	56_{2}
69	רום/גבה	haughty/proud	$2_{11.17}$ 10_{33}	52_{13}	
70	שפל/רום	proud/high	$2_{12 (17)}$ (10_{33})		
71	נשא/רום	proud/lift	2_{12} 37_{23} $2_{13.14}$ (6_{1}) 13_{2} 33_{10}	49_{22} 52_{13}	57_{15}
72	שפל/גאה	proud/high	2_{13} (13_{11}) (25_{11})		
73	שפל/נשא	proud/lift	$2_{9.12}$	40_{4}	
74	מים/לחם	bread/water	3_{1} 21_{14} 30_{20} 33_{16}		
75	איש מלהמה/גבור	mighty man/man of war	3_{2}	42_{13}	
76	נביא/זקן	elder/prophet	3_{2} $9_{15 (14)}$		
77	יעץ/צר	captain/counselor	3_{3} $9_{6 (5)}$ 19_{11}		
78	משל/צר	prince/rule	3_{4}	49_{7}	
79	איש/עם	people/man	3_{5} 6_{5} $9_{19 (18)}$ (13_{14})		(63_{3})
80	רהב/נגש	oppress/insolent	3_{5} 14_{4}		
81	רעה/איש	man/neighbor	3_{5} (13_{8}) 19_{2}	(41_{6})	
82	יהודה/ירושלים	Jerusalem/Judah	(1_{1}) (2_{1}) (3_{1}) 3_{8} 5_{3} (22_{21}) (36_{7})	44_{26}	
83	בבד/יהוה	Lord/glory	3_{8} (4_{2}) 6_{3} 24_{23} (35_{2})	(40_{5}) 42_{8} ($_{12}$)	(58_{8}) 59_{19} (60_{1}) 60_{2}
84	אשה/עללה	child/woman	3_{12} 13_{16}		
85	משל/נגש	oppress/rule	3_{12} $14_{4\text{-}5}$		
86	בלע/תעה	mislead/confuse	3_{12} $19_{16 (15)}$ 28_{7}		
87	עני/עם	people/poor	$3_{14.15}$ (10_{2}) 14_{32}	49_{13}	
88	יהוה/אדון	Lord/Lord	3_{17} 22_{14} 25_{8}	49_{14}	(56_{8}) 61_{1}
89	אבל/אנה	lament/mourn	(3_{26}) (19_{8})		
90	אמלל/אבל	lament/languish	19_{8} $24_{4.7}$ (33_{9})		

91	שמלה/לחם	bread/clothes	(4_{1} (3_{7})		
92	שם/קרא	call/name	(4_{1}) (7_{14}) (8_{3}) ($9_{6(5)}$) (12_{4})	(40_{26}) (41_{25}) ($43_{1.7}$) (44_{5}) ($45_{3.4}$) (48_{1}) 48_{2} 49_{1} 54_{5}	(62_{2}) (63_{19}) ($64_{7[6]}$) ($65_{1.15}$)
93	באש/ענב	grape/wild grape	$5_{2.4}$		
94	איש/ישב	inhabitant/man	5_{3} 6_{5}		
95	שית/שמיר	briar/thorn	(5_{6}) ($7_{23.24.25}$) ($9_{18[17]}$) (10_{17}) (27_{4}) (32_{13})		
96	נטע/כרם	vineyard/planting	5_{7} (37_{30})		(65_{21})
97	יהודה/ישראל	Israel/Judah	5_{7} (7_{1}) 11_{12}	48_{1}	
98	איש/בית	house/man	5_{7} (14_{18})	(44_{13})	
99	שדה/בית	house/field	5_{8} 32_{12-13}		
100	אין ישב/שמם	desolate/without inhabitant	5_{9} 6_{11}	(49_{19}) (54_{3})	
101	יין/שכר	beer/wine	$5_{11.22}$ 24_{9} 28_{7} 29_{9}		56_{12}
102	כנור/תף	tambourine/lyre	5_{12} 24_{8} (30_{32})		
103	ראה/נבט	regard/see	5_{12} 18_{3-4} 22_{11} 38_{11}	(42_{18})	(63_{15})
104	מעשה/פעל	deed/work	5_{12}		59_{6}
105	המון/עם	people/multitude	5_{13} 13_{4} (17_{12}) (33_{3})		
106	צמא/רעב	hunger/thirst	5_{13} 29_{8} 32_{6}	(49_{10})	65_{13}
107	שאון/המון	multitude/throng	5_{14} 13_{4} 17_{12}		
108	עלז/שאון	throng/exult	(5_{14}) 22_{2}		
109	אל/היוה	Lord/God	5_{16} 12_{2} 31_{3}	(42_{5}) 45_{21}	
110	גדי/כבש	lamb/kid	5_{17} 11_{6}		
111	אכל/רעה	graze/feed	5_{17} 11_{7} 30_{23-24}	(44_{19-20})	65_{25}
112	חוש/מהר	hasten/speed	5_{19} (8_{1})		
113	בוא/קרב	draw near/come	5_{19} 13_{6}		
114	אור/חשך	darkness/light	5_{20} 9_{2} 13_{10} (5_{30})	(42_{16}) 45_{7}	(58_{10}) 59_{9}
115	בין/חכם	wise/shrewd	3_{3} 5_{21} 29_{14} 10_{13} (11_{2})		
116	פנים/עין	eye/sight	5_{21} 38_{3}		

No.	Hebrew	English	I Isaiah	II Isaiah	III Isaiah
117	צדק/רשע	guilty/innocent	5_{23} (26_{10})	(54_{17})	
118	צדק/שחר	bribe/right	5_{23} 33_{15}	(45_{13})	
119	להבה/אש	fire/flame	(4_{5}) 5_{24} 10_{17} (29_{6}) (30_{30})	43_{2} 47_{14}	$66_{15b\,(15a)}$
120	להבה/אור/אש	fire/fire/flame	10_{17}	47_{14}	
121	אש/גחלד	coal/fire		47_{14} 44_{19}	
122	חשש/קש	stubble/chaff	5_{24} 33_{11}		
123	פרח/שרש	to root/to blossom	5_{24} 27_{6}		
124	עצה/נטה	stretch out/purpose	$14_{26.27}$		
125	נטה/שוב	turn away/stretch out	5_{25} $9_{12.17.21}$ 10_{4} 14_{27}		
126	יד/אף	anger/hand	5_{25} $9_{12.17.21}$ $10_{4.5}$		
127	רום/נוף	wave/lift	10_{15} 13_{2}		
128	קצה ארץ/רחק	afar/end of the earth	5_{26} 13_{5} (26_{15})	43_{6}	
129	נתק/פתח	loose/break	5_{27}		58_{6}
130	קשת/חץ	arrow/bow	5_{28} (7_{24})		
131	כפר/סור	take away/forgive	6_{7} 27_{9}		
132	ראה/שמע	hear/see	6_{9} 21_{3} 33_{15} 37_{17} 38_{5} 11_{3} 32_{3} 29_{18} 39_{5} 6_{10} 18_{3} 33_{19} 30_{30} 30_{21-22}	$42_{18.20}$ (52_{15})	$64_{4\,(3)}$ $66_{8.19}$
133	אזן/עין	eye/ear	6_{10} 11_{3} 32_{3} 33_{15} 35_{5} 37_{17} 30_{20-21}	43_{8}	
134	לב/עין	eye/heart	6_{10} 38_{3}	44_{18}	
135	בין/שמע	hear/understand	$6_{9.10}$ 33_{19}	40_{21} (52_{15})	
136	בין/ראה	see/understand	$6_{9.10}$ 14_{16}	44_{18} 52_{15}	
137	אדמה/בית	house/land	6_{11} 32_{13}		
138	אדמה/עיר	city/land	6_{11} 1_{7}		
139	אדם/ישב	inhabitant/man	6_{11} 38_{11}		
140	שמם/שאה	lay waste/desolate	6_{11} 24_{12}		
141	דמשק/ארם	Syria/Damascus	7_{8} 17_{3}		

142	שמרון/אפרם	Ephraim/Syria	7_{9} ($9_{9(8)}$)		
143	בין/אמן	believe/understand	7_{9}	43_{10}	
144	דבש/חמאה	curds/honey	($7_{15.22}$)		
145	אשור/מצרים	Egypt/Assyria	7_{18} 10_{24} (11_{11}) 11_{16} ($19_{23.24}$) 19_{25} 20_{4} 27_{13}	52_{4}	
146	סלע/נחל	ravine/rock	7_{19}		57_{5}
147	הר/ארץ	land/hill	7_{24-25} 14_{25} 16_{1} 18_{6} (27_{13})	44_{23} 49_{13}	57_{13}
148	שמרון/דמשק	Damascus/Samaria	7_{8-9} (8_{4}) (10_{9})		
149	רמליהו/רצין	Rezin/Remaliah	($7_{1.4}$) (8_{6})		
150	אשור/נהר	river/Assyria	(7_{20}) 8_{7}		
151	רב/עצום	mighty/many	8_{7}	53_{12}	
152	הלך/עלה	rise/go over	8_{7} (2_{3}) (35_{9})—	40_{31}	
153	עבר/שטף	overflow/pass on	8_{8} (28_{15})	43_{2}	
154	דבר/עצה	counsel/word	8_{10} (36_{5})	44_{26}	
155	ערץ/ירא	fear/dread	$8_{12.13}$		
156	ירושלים/ישראל	Israel/Jerusalem	8_{14} (7_{1})		
157	נפל/כשל	stumble/fall	3_{8} 8_{15} 31_{3}		
158	לכד/נקש/שבר/כשל	stumble/break/snare/take	8_{15} 28_{13}		
159	שבר/נפל	fall/break	(8_{15}) 21_{9} 30_{13}		
160	לכד/נפל	fall/take	8_{15} 24_{18}		
161	תורה/תעודה	testimony/teaching	$8_{16(20)}$		
162	צוקה/צרה	distress/gloom	8_{22} 26_{16} (30_{6})		
163	אפלה/חשך	darkness/thick darkness	8_{22} (29_{18})		(58_{10}) 59_{9}
164	מוצק/יעף	gloom/anguish	(8_{22}) ($9_{1[8.23]}$)		
165	אחרון/ראשון	former/latter	9_{1} (8_{23})	41_{4} (44_{6}) 48_{12}	
166	ישב/הלך	walk/dwell	9_{2} (37_{37})		
167	גדל/רבה	multiply/increase	$9_{3(2)}$ 5_{9}		
168	גיל/שמח	rejoice/rejoice	$9_{3(2)}$ (16_{10}) (25_{9}) 29_{19}		(66_{10})

No.	Hebrew	English	I Isaiah	II Isaiah	III Isaiah
169	שמח/שיש	sing/rejoice	(22_{13}) 24_{11} (35_{10}) $9_{4(3)}$ $10_{5.15.24.26}$ 14_{5} 28_{27} 30_{31-32}	($51_{3.11}$)	65_{13-14} 66_{10}
171	שכם/סבל	burden/shoulder	$9_{4(3)}$ (10_{27}) (14_{25})		
172	בן/ילד	child/son	$9_{6(5)}$		57_{3-4}
173	נתן/ילד	born/give	$9_{6(5)}$ (7_{14})		
174	אכל/זרע	sow/eat	(37_{30})	55_{10}	
175	לחם/זרע	seed/grain	30_{23}	55_{10}	
176	עולם/אין קץ	no end/forever	$9_{7(6)}$	40_{28}	
177	בורא/אלהים	God/creator		40_{28} (45_{18})	
178	בורא/יהוה	Lord/creator	4_{5}	40_{28} 41_{20} 42_{5} $43_{1.15}$ $45_{7.(8)18}$	
179	ישראל/יעקב	Jacob/Israel	$9_{8(7)}$ 14_{1} 27_{6} 10_{20} 29_{23}	40_{27} $41_{8.14}$ 42_{24} $43_{1.22.28}$ $44_{1.5.21.23}$ 45_{4} 46_{3} $48_{1.12}$ $49_{5.6}$	
180	פלט/שאר	remnant/survivor	10_{20} (37_{31})		
181	קדש/אלהים	God/holy one	29_{23}	43_{3} 48_{17} 54_{5} 55_{5} 60_{9}	
182	זנב/ראש	head/tail	($9_{14[13]}$) $9_{15(14)}$ (19_{15})		
183	אגמון/כפה	palm branch/reed	$9_{14(13)}$ (19_{15})		
184	נבלה/חנף	godless/folly	$9_{17(16)}$ 32_{6}		
185	אכל/בער	burn/consume	$9_{18(17)}$ (10_{17}) 30_{27}		
186	אש/בער	burn/fire	($9_{18[17]}$)	50_{11}	
187	בער/אש/אור	light/fire/burn	$9_{18(17)}$ 10_{17} $30_{27.33}$	50_{11} 43_{2}	
188	יצת/אכל	consume/kindle	$9_{18(17).19(18)}$		
189	אש/יצת	burn/fire	$9_{19(18)}$ (33_{12})		
190	עם/ארץ	land/people	8_{9} (9_{2}) $9_{19(18)}$ 10_{14} 13_{14} 14_{20} $18_{2.7}$ 23_{13} 24_{13} (25_{8}) (30_{6})	42_{5} 49_{8} 51_{16} 53_{8}	(60_{21}) (63_{6})

191	שמאול/ימין	right/left	$9_{20\,(19)}$ (30_{21})	(54_{3})	
192	שבע/רעב	hungry/satisfy	$9_{20\,(19)}$		(58_{10})
193	עמל/און	iniquity/oppression	10_{1}		59_{4}
194	כתב/חקק	decree/write	10_{1} 30_{8}		
195	עני/דל	needy/poor	10_{2} 11_{4} 26_{6}		
196	משפט/דין	justice/right	10_{2} 3_{13-14}		
197	בזז/שלל	spoil/prey	$10_{2.6}$ 33_{23}		
198	שלל/חלק	prey/spoil	(9_{3}) (33_{23})	(53_{12})	
199	בזז/חלק	prey/prey	(17_{14}) 33_{23}		
200	זעם/אף	anger/fury	$10_{5.25}$ 30_{27}		66_{14-15}
201	זעם/יד	hand/fury	(10_{5})		66_{14}
202	עבר/חנף	godless/wrath	10_{6} 24_{5}		
203	כרת/שמד	destroy/cut off	10_{7} (14_{22-23})	(48_{19})	
204	שמרון/חמת	Hamath/Samaria	10_{9} (36_{19})		
205	שמרון/ירושלים	Jerusalem/Samaria	(10_{10}) 10_{11}		
206	כח/יד	hand/power	(10_{13})	50_{2}	
207	כרמל/יער	forest/fruitful field	(10_{18}) 29_{17} 32_{15}		
208	יהוה/נכה	smiter/Lord	9_{13} 10_{20}		
209	נשא/וכה	smite/lift up	10_{24}	53_{4}	
210	על/סבל	burden/yoke	10_{27} (9_{4}) 14_{25}		
211	חכם/ידע	know/be wise	11_{2} (33_{6})	44_{25} (47_{10})	
212	ידע/יעץ	counsel/knowledge	11_{2}	(40_{14})	
213	משפט/למד	teach/justice	1_{17} 26_{9}	(40_{14})	
214	בין/למד לקח	instruction/under-standing	29_{24}	(40_{14})	
215	למד/ידע	teach/show	29_{24}	40_{14}	
216	בין/יעץ	counsel/instruct	11_{2} 3_{3}	(40_{14})	
217	ישר/צדק	righteousness/equity	11_{4} $(26_{7a,b})$	$45_{13.19}$ (33_{15})	
218	מות/נכה	smite/slay	11_{4} 37_{36}		
219	שפה/פה	mouth/lip	6_{7} 11_{4} 29_{13}		

No.	Hebrew	English	I Isaiah	II Isaiah	III Isaiah
220	רוח/פה	mouth/breath	11_{4} 34_{16}		
221	אמונה/צדק	righteousness/faith-fulness	11_{5} (26_{2})		59_{4}
222	אמת/צדק	justice/truth	16_{5}	43_{9} (48_{1})	59_{14}
223	בקר/אריה	lion/ox	(11_{7})		(65_{25})
224	ים/ארץ	earth/sea	(5_{30}) 9_{1} 11_{9} (21_{1})	42_{10} 49_{12}	
225	ארץ/גוים	nation/land	5_{26} $14_{9 (12). 26}$ $18_{2.7}$ 26_{15} 11_{12} 34_{1} (36_{18}) 9_{1}	49_{6} 52_{10}	61_{11} 66_{8}
226	קבץ/אסף	assemble/gather	11_{12}	43_{9}	62_{9}
227	יהודה/אפרים	Ephraim/Judah	(7_{17}) (9_{20}) 9_{21} $11_{13a.b}$		
228	צרר/קנא	be jealous/harass	$11_{13a.b}$		
229	שמע/יד שלח	put forth the hand/obey	11_{14} ($37_{4.17}$) (39_{1})	(48_{16})	
230	נהר/ים	sea/river	11_{15} 18_{2} 19_{5}	48_{18} 50_{2}	
231	עז/ישע	salvation/strength	12_{2} 26_{1})		
232	חול/חבל	agony/anguish	13_{8} (26_{17})		66_{7}
233	חול/ציר	pang/childbirth	13_{8} 21_{3}		
234	ילד/חול	anguish/travail	(13_{8}) 21_{3} 23_{4} $26_{17.18}$	45_{10} 54_{1}	$66_{7.8}$
235	אף/עבר	wrath/anger	(13_{9}) 13_{13} 14_{6}		
236	שמש/ירח	sun/moon	13_{10}		$60_{19.20}$
237	עון/רע	evil/iniquity	1_{4} 13_{11}		
238	גאות/גאון	pride/haughtiness	13_{11} 16_{6}		
239	רעש/רגז	tremble/shake	13_{13} 14_{16}		
240	בן/בטן	womb/children	13_{18}	(49_{15})	
241	כשדים/ממלכה	kingdom/Chaldeans	13_{19}	47_{5}	
242	גאון/צבי	glory/pride	4_{2} 13_{19} (23_{9}) 28_{1}		
243	כבד/עבי	glory/honor	(4_{2}) 13_{19}		
244	דור/נצח	forever/generation	13_{20} 34_{10}		
245	שכן/ישב	inhabit/dwell	13_{20} 18_{3} 26_{18-19} 32_{16} 33_{24}		

246	איים/ציים	wild beast/hyenas	13_{21} (34_{14})		
247	שעיר/יענה	ostrich/satyr	13_{21} $(34_{13\text{-}14})$		
248	תנים/איים	hyena/jackal	13_{22} $(34_{13\text{-}14})$		
249	יום/עת	time/day	13_{22}	49_{8}	
250	קום/עור	rouse/raise	14_{9}	51_{17} $52_{1\text{-}2}$	
251	קום/רגז	stir/rise	14_{9} 28_{21}		
252	גדע/נפל	fall/cut	9_{10} $10_{33\text{-}34}$ 14_{12} (22_{25})		
253	רום/עלה	go up/lift up	14_{13}	40_{9}	
254	שמים/כוכב	star/heaven	(13_{10}) 14_{13}	47_{13}	
255	בור/שאול	Sheol/Pit	14_{15} 38_{18}		
256	ממלכה/ארץ	earth/kingdom	14_{16} (23_{17}) $(37_{16.20})$		
257	עיר/תבל	world/city	$14_{17\,(21)}$		
258	בית/כבד	glory/tomb	14_{18} $(22_{23.24})$		
259	חרב/הרג	slay/sword	14_{19} (27_{1})		
260	בוס/ירד	go down/tread	14_{19}		63_{6}
261	תבל/ארץ	earth/world	14_{21} 18_{3} 24_{4} $26_{9.18}$ 34_{1}		
262	שוב/פרר	annul/turn back	14_{27}	44_{25}	
263	אביון/דל	poor/needy	14_{30} 25_{4}		
264	רבץ/רעה	graze/lie down	14_{30} 11_{7} 27_{10}		
265	חרג/מות	kill/slay	14_{30} 22_{13}		
266	שאר/שרש	root/remnant	14_{30} (37_{31}) 37_{32}		
267	עיר/שער	gate/city	14_{31} 24_{12}		
268	זעק/ילל	wail/cry	14_{31} 15_{8}		
269	ילל/בכה	weep/wail	$15_{2\,(3)}$		
270	קרחה/בכה	weep/bald	15_{2} 22_{12}		
271	חגך/בכה	weep/gird on sackcloth	15_{3} 22_{12}		
272	זקן/ראש	head/beard	(7_{20}) $(9_{15\,[14]})$ 15_{2}		
273	שמע/זעק	cry/hear	15_{4} (30_{19})		(65_{19})
274	אלעלה/חשבון	Hesbon/Elealeh	(15_{4}) (16_{9})		
275	זעק/בכה	weep/cry	15_{5} 30_{19}		65_{19}

No.	Hebrew	English	I Isaiah	II Isaiah	III Isaiah
276	ירק/דשא/חציר	grass/new growth/ verdure	15_{6} 37_{27}		
277	פקד/יתר	abundance/lay up	15_{7} (38_{10})		
278	שאר/פלט	escape/remnant	(10_{20}) 15_{9} (37_{31}) 37_{32}		
279	מדבר/ארץ	land/desert	16_{1} 21_{1}	41_{18}	
280	ארץ/נגב	Negeb/land	21_{1} 30_{6}		
281	הר/מדבר	desert/mountain	16_{1}	42_{11}	
282	חמס/שדד	destroy/oppress	16_{4}		60_{18}
283	כלה/אפס	no more/cease	16_{4} 29_{20}		
284	ישב/כון	establish/sit	16_{5}	(45_{18})	
285	גפן/שדדה	field/vine	16_{8} 32_{12}		
286	ים/מדבר	desert/sea	16_{8} (21_{1})		
287	רוע/רנן	sing/shout	16_{10}	44_{23}	
288	רנן/גיל	glad/sing	(16_{10}) (35_{2})	49_{13}	
289	רנן/שמח	joy/song	(16_{10}) 35_{10}	51_{11} 55_{12}	61_{7}
290	מפלה/עיר	city/ruins	17_{1} (25_{2})		
291	עדר/עזב	to desert/for flocks	17_{2} 32_{14}		
292	ישראל/ארס	Syria/Israel	(7_{1}) $9_{12(11)}$ 17_{3}		
293	X/X + 1	numerical	17_{6} 19_{18} 30_{17} 37_{30}	47_{9}	
294	קדש/מעשה	maker/holy one	17_{7}	54_{5}	
295	ראה/שעה	regard/look	$17_{7.8}$ (32_{3})	(41_{23})	
296	אשרה/מזבח	altar/aserim/incense	17_{8} (27_{9})		
297	עזב/עיר	city/deserted place	($17_{2.9}$) (27_{10})		(62_{12})
298	זכר/שכח	forget/remember	17_{10} 23_{16}	54_{4}	65_{16-17}
299	צור/אלהים	God/rock	17_{10}	44_{8}	
300	זרע/נטע	plant/set up	$17_{10.11}$ (37_{30})	40_{24}	
301	קצר/זרע	sow/reap	(37_{30}) 23_{3}		
302	בקר/יום	day/morning	17_{11} 28_{19}		

303	לילה/בקר	morning/night	(21_{12}) 28_{19} 38_{12-13}		
304	לאום/עם	people/nation	17_{12}	51_{4} 55_{4-5}	
305	מים/לאום	nation/water	$17_{12\,(13)}$		
306	מים/ים	sea/water	(11_{9}) 17_{12} 18_{2} (19_{5})	43_{16} 50_{2} 51_{10}	57_{20}
307	נוס/גער	rebuke/flee	17_{13} (30_{17})		
308	רדף/נוס	flee/chase	17_{13} (30_{16})		
309	בקר/עת	time/morning	17_{14} 33_{2}		
310	גורל/חלק	portion/lot	17_{14} 34_{17}		57_{6}
311	בזז/שסה	despoil/plunder	17_{14}	(42_{22a}) $42_{22b.\,24}$	
312	ים/כוש	Ethiopia/Nile	18_{1} (11_{11})		
313	ירא/מרט משך	tall and smooth/fear	$18_{2.\,7}$		
314	בחמה/עיט	bird of prey/beast	$18_{6a.b}$		
315	הר/ארץ	earth/mountain	11_{9} 14_{25} 16_{1} (18_{3}) 18_{6} 27_{13}	40_{12} 44_{23} 49_{13}	57_{13}
316	רעה/אח	brother/neighbor	19_{2}	41_{6}	
317	עצה/רוח	spirit/plan	(11_{2}) 19_{3}	40_{13}	
318	בלע/בקק	to empty/confound	19_{3} (24_{1})		
319	ידענים/אחות	medium/wizard	(8_{19}) (19_{3})		
320	מלך/אדון	master/king	19_{4} (36_{8}) (37_{4})		
321	יבש/חרב	parch/dry	(19_{5})	42_{15} 44_{27}	
322	יאור/נהר	canal/branch	19_{6} (33_{21})		
323	ידע/נגד	tell/make known	(19_{12})	40_{21} $41_{22.\,23.\,26}$ (48_{6})	
324	גבול/ארץ	land/border	19_{19}		60_{18}
325	מנחה/זבח	sacrifice/burnt offering	(19_{21})	43_{23}	57_{6-7}
326	יחף/ערום	naked/barefoot	($20_{2.\,3.\,4}$)		
327	מופת/אות	sign/portent	(20_{3}) (8_{18})		
328	זקן/נער	young/old	(20_{4}) (3_{5})		(65_{20})
329	שדד/בגד	plunder/destroy	21_{2} 33_{1}		
330	שתה/אכל	eat/drink	(21_{5}) (22_{13}) (32_{12}) 32_{16} 29_{8}		62_{9} 65_{13}

No.	Hebrew	English	I Isaiah	II Isaiah	III Isaiah
331	פרש/רכב	rider (chariot)/horseman	$21_{7(9)}$ (22_{6}) 22_{7} 31_{1} (36_{9})		
332	נצב/עמד	to stand/to station	3_{13} 21_{8}		
333	לילה/יום	day/night	4_{5} 21_{8} (28_{19}) (34_{10})		(60_{11})
334	לילה/תמיד	continually/night	21_{8}		60_{11}
335	נגד/שמע	hear/announce	21_{10}	40_{21} $41_{22.26}$ 42_{9} $43_{9(12)}$ $44_{7(8)}$ 45_{21} $48_{3.5.6.14.20}$	66_{19}
336	יצר/עשה	do/plan	22_{11} 27_{11} 29_{16} 37_{26}	(43_{7}) $44_{2.24}$ $45_{7.9(18)}$ (46_{11})	64_{8}
337	בוא/יצר/עשה	do/plan/bring to pass	37_{26}	46_{11}	
338	צאן/בקר	ox/sheep	(22_{13}) (7_{21})		65_{10}
339	סלע/מרום	height/rock	22_{16} 33_{16}		
340	בית/ישב	inhabitant/house	8_{14} 22_{21}	(42_{7})	
341	סגר/פתח	open/shut	(22_{22})	45_{1}	60_{11}
342	קציר/זרע	sow grain/reap harvest	(17_{11}) 23_{3} (37_{30})		
343	מעוז/ים	sea/stronghold	(23_{4}) 23_{11}		
344	בתולה/בחור	young man/virgin	23_{4}		(62_{5})
345	אי/תרשיש	Tarshish/coast	23_{6}		60_{9} (66_{19})
346	ישב/ארץ	earth/inhabitants	(9_{2}) (21_{14}) $24_{1(5)6(17)}$ $26_{9(21)}$	40_{22} (42_{10}) 49_{19} 51_{6}	
347	אדון/עבד	slave/master	(24_{2}) (36_{9})		
348	שפחה/עבד	slave/maid	(14_{2}) 24_{2}		
349	נשה/מכר	sell/credit	24_{2}	(50_{1})	
350	מרום/ארץ	earth/heaven	$24_{4.18}$ 26_{5}		
351	בית/קריה	city/house	24_{10} (32_{13})		
352	עולל/זית	olive tree/gleaning	17_{6} 24_{13}		
353	צחל/רנן	sing/shout	(12_{6}) 24_{14}	54_{1}	
354	צחל/קול	voice/shout	(10_{30}) 24_{14}		

355	רנן/קול	voice/sing	24_{14}	42_{11} (48_{20}) 52_{8}	
356	פה/פחת/פחד	terror/pit/snare	(24_{17}) 24_{18}		
357	חמה/לבוה	moon/sun	24_{23} (30_{26})		
358	ארמון/עיר	city/palace	25_{2} 32_{14}		
359	ירא/כבד	glorify/fear	25_{3} 29_{13}		
360	צל/מחסה	shelter/shade	4_{6} 25_{4}		
361	צל/מעוז	stronghold/shade	25_{4} $30_{2.3}$		
362	חרב/זרם	storm/heat	4_{6} 25_{4}		
363	זרם/רוח	wind/storm	25_{4} 32_{2}		
364	עריץ/זור	alien/stranger	25_{5} 29_{5}		
365	בוא/פתח	open/go in	13_{2} 26_{2}		60_{11}
366	בטח/סמך	have say on/trust in	26_{3} 36_{6}		
367	עולם/עד	forever/forever	26_{4} (30_{8})	45_{17}	
368	שגב/מרום	height/lofty	26_{5} 33_{5}		
369	עפר/ארץ	ground/dust	2_{19} 25_{12} 26_{5} 29_{4} $34_{7.9}$	(40_{12}) 47_{1} 49_{23}	
370	רוח/נפש	soul/spirit	26_{9}	42_{1}	
371	צר/עם	people/adversaries	26_{11}		63_{18}
372	אכל/בוש	ashamed/consumed	26_{11}		(65_{13})
373	מעשה/שלום	peace/works	26_{12} (32_{17})		
374	רפא/מות	dead/shades	26_{14} (19)		
375	סגר/בוא	enter/shut	26_{20}		60_{11}
376	עשה/חזק	lay hold of/do	27_{5}		56_{2}
377	חנן/רחם	have compassion/ show favor	27_{11} 30_{18}		
378	נבל/גאון	proud/fade	14_{11} 28_{1}		
379	אמץ/חזק	strengthen/make firm	(28_{2}) 35_{3}		
380	ברד/זרם	storm/hail	(28_{2}) (30_{30})		
381	שטף/ברד	hail/overflow	(28_{2}) 28_{17}		
382	מים/זרם	storm/water	28_{2} 32_{2}		
383	מים/ברד	hail/water	$28_{2.17}$		

No.	Hebrew	English	I Isaiah	II Isaiah	III Isaiah
384	אש/להב	flame/fire	(29_{6}) (30_{30})		(66_{15})
385	סופה/אש	fire/whirlwind	29_{6}		66_{15}
386	אף/אש	fire/anger	(30_{30})		65_{5} 66_{15}
387	רעש/קול	noise/earthquake	(24_{18}) (29_{6})		
388	פאר/עבי	glory/beauty	(4_{2}) 13_{9} $28_{5(1)(4)}$		
389	נביא/כהן	priest/prophet	(28_{7}) (37_{2})		
390	שד/חלב	milk/breast	28_{9}		60_{16}
391	קו/צו	precept/line	$28_{10.13}$		
392	לשון/שפה	lip/tongue	28_{11} 30_{27} 33_{19}		59_{3}
393	חזות/ברית	convenant/agreement	$28_{15.18}$		
394	שאול/מות	death/Sheol	$28_{15.18}$ 38_{18}		
395	סתר/מחס	take refuge/take shelter	$28_{15.17}$		
396	אבן/יסד	foundation/stone	28_{16}	54_{11}	
397	קום/כפר	annul/stand	28_{18} 27_{9}		
398	נכר/זר	stranger/alien	28_{21}		61_{5}
399	עבד/עשה	deed/work	28_{21} 32_{17}		(65_{8})
400	אמר/קול	voice/speech	28_{23} 29_{4} 32_{9}		
401	כמן/קצח	dill/cumin	$28_{25.27a.b}$		
402	דוש/דקק	crush/thresh	28_{28}	(41_{15})	
403	אמר/דבד	speak/say	29_{4} 32_{17} (19_{18}) (8_{20}) 30_{21} (36_{5}) 36_{21} $38_{4.15}$	40_{27} (44_{26}) 45_{19} (51_{16})	(59_{21}) (66_{5})
404	נוע/שכר	be drunk/stagger	(24_{20}) 29_{9}		
405	חשר/סתר	hide/dark	29_{15} $45_{3.19}$		
406	מעשה/עצה	counsel/deeds	5_{19} 29_{15}		
407	מעשה/חמר	clay/thing	29_{16}		$64_{8(7)}$
408	חמר/יצר	potter/clay	(29_{16})	(41_{25}) (45_{9})	$64_{8(7)}$
409	עור/חרש	deaf/blind	29_{18} 35_{5}	$42_{18.19}$ 43_{8}	
410	עין/עור	blind/eye	(29_{18}) (35_{5})	(42_{7}) (43_{8})	59_{10}

411	אביון/ענו	poor/needy	29_{19} 32_{7}	(41_{17})	
412	ערץ/קדש	sanctify/stand in awe	8_{13} 29_{23}		
413	מצרים/פרעה	Pharaoh/Egypt	$30_{2.3}$ 36_{6}		
414	כלם/בוש	shame/humiliation	30_{3}	(41_{11}) ($45_{16.17}$) 50_{7} 61_{7} 54_{4}	
415	חרף/בוש	shame/disgrace	(30_{5})	54_{4}	
416	בין/עם	people/son	1_{4} 30_{9}	(49_{22})	63_{8}
417	חזה/כאה	see/look	$30_{10a.b}$ $33_{17.20}$		
418	חזה/דבר	speak/prophesy	(29_{11}) 30_{10}		
419	שען/בטח	trust/rely	30_{12} 31_{1}	50_{10}	
420	פתע/פתא	suddenly/instantly	(29_{5}) (30_{13})		
421	נס/תרן	flag staff/signal	30_{17} 33_{23}		
422	בוא/זרע	sow/produce	(23_{3}) 30_{23}		
423	מכה/שבר	hurt/wound	(14_{29}) 30_{26}		
424	נחל/אש	fire/stream	$30_{27-28\,(33)}$		
425	רכב/מצרים	Egypt/chariot	31_{1} (36_{9})		
426	סוס/מצרים	Egypt/horses	$31_{1.3}$		
427	סוס/רכב	chariot/horses	31_{1} (36_{8})	(43_{17})	(66_{20})
428	עצם/רב	many/strong	31_{1}	(40_{29}) (47_{9})	
429	פעל און/מרעים	evildoer/workers of iniquity	31_{2}		59_{7}
430	כפיר/אריה	lion/young lion	(11_{6-7}) (31_{4})		
431	חמין/קול	shout/noise	(13_{4}) 31_{4} (33_{3})		
432	נצל/גנן	protect/deliver	(31_{5}) 38_{6}		
433	מלט/נצל	deliver/rescue	(20_{6}) 31_{5}		
434	שר/מלך	king/prince	(10_{8}) (19_{11}) $32_{1a.b}$	$49_{7.23}$	
435	סתר/חבא	hide/hide	32_{2}	49_{2}	
436	ארץ/ציון	dry place/land	32_{2}	(41_{18})	
437	אמר/קרא	call/say	(6_{3}) (29_{12}) 32_{5} (36_{13})	(40_{6}) (41_{9}) 44_{5} 54_{6}	(58_{9}) 61_{6} 62_{4}
438	עשה/דבר	speak/plot	32_{6} (38_{7}) 38_{15}	(42_{16}) 46_{11} (55_{11})	(65_{12}) ($66_{2.4}$)

No.	Hebrew	English	I Isaiah	II Isaiah	III Isaiah
439	בטח/שאנן	at ease/complacent	$32_{9.11.18}$		
440	כרמל/מדבר	wilderness/fruitful field	$32_{15.16}$		
441	בטח/שקט	quiet/trust	(30_{15}) (32_{17})		
442	שוב/בטח	trust/return	30_{15} 36_{9}	47_{10}	
443	שלום/בטח	trust/peace	$32_{17.18}$ 26_{3}		
444	ישע/זרוע	arm/salvation	32_{2}	51_{5} 52_{10}	59_{16} (63_{5})
445	רום/קול	noise/lift up	(13_{2}) 33_{3} (37_{23})	(40_{9})	(58_{1})
446	אבל/אמלל	mourn/languish	19_{8} (33_{9})		
447	כרמל/שרון	Sharon/Carmel	33_{9} (35_{2})		
448	כרמל/לבנון	Lebanon/Carmel	29_{17} 33_{9} 37_{24}		
449	רום/קום	rise/lift up	(10_{33}) 33_{10}		
450	ילד/הרה	conceive/bring forth	(7_{14}) (8_{3}) $26_{17.18}$ 33_{11}		59_{4}
451	און/שוא	lie/iniquity	(1_{13})		59_{4}
452	און/תהו	empty/iniquity		41_{29}	59_{4}
453	הרה/דבר	speak/conceive			$59_{4.13}$
454	קרב/רחק	far/near	6_{12} 33_{13}	46_{13} 54_{14}	(57_{19})
455	ידע/שמע	hear/know	(6_{9}) 33_{13}	$40_{21.28}$ $41_{22(26)}$ $48_{6.7.8}$ (51_{7})	
456	יקד/אש	fire/burnings	(10_{16}) (30_{14}) 33_{14}		(65_{5})
457	עין/כף	hand/eye	33_{15} 1_{15}		
458	רע/דם	bloodshed/evil	33_{15}		59_{7}
459	עבר/הלך	go/pass	(35_{8}) 33_{21}	43_{2} 45_{14}	
460	פלל/שחה	bow down/make supplication		(44_{17}) 45_{14}	
461	קשב/שמע	hear/hearken	28_{23} (32_{3}) 34_{1}	(42_{23}) 49_{1}	
462	לאום/גוים	nation/people	34_{1}	43_{9}	
463	צבא/גוים	nation/host	13_{4} (29_{7}) 34_{2}		
464	עלה/נבל	fig/leaf	34_{4}		$(64_{6[5]})$

465	תאנה/גפן	vine/fig tree	34_{4} 36_{16}		
466	ירד/רוה	to water/to descend	$34_{5.7}$	55_{10}	
467	תעה/עבר	pass over/err	16_{8} 35_{8}		
468	בוא/שוב	return/come	35_{10} 37_{34}	51_{11}	59_{20} 66_{15}
469	בוא רנן/שוב	return/come with singing	35_{10}	51_{11}	
470	יגון/אנחה	sorrow/sighing	(35_{10})	(51_{11})	
471	נוס/נשג	obtain/flee	35_{10}	51_{11}	
472	בטח/נשא	deceive/rely	$36_{14\text{-}15}$ (37_{10})		
473	תירוש/דגן	grain/wine	36_{17}		62_{8}
474	יאור/מים	water/streams	19_{8} 23_{3} 37_{25}		
475	קדם/רחק	long ago/of old	23_{7} 37_{26}		
476	חתת/בוש	dismay/confound	(20_{5}) (37_{27})		
477	בוא/יצא	go/come	(37_{28})	48_{3}	
478	שאנן/רגז	rage/arrogance	(32_{11}) 37_{29}		
479	שפה/אף	nose/mouth	(30_{27}) 37_{29}		
480	פרי/שרש	root/fruit	14_{29} 37_{31}		
481	לא היה/מות	die/not recover	$26_{14\,(19)}$ (38_{1})		
482	אדום/בצרה	Bozrah/Edom	34_{6}		63_{1}
483	שנה/יום	day/year	(23_{15}) (32_{10}) 34_{8} (38_{5}) 38_{10}		61_{2} 63_{4} 65_{20}
484	עולם/יום	day/forever	34_{10}	(51_{9})	(63_{11})
485	דור/עולם	forever/generation	$34_{10.17}$	$51_{8\,(9)}$	58_{12} 60_{15} 61_{4}
486	שכן/ירש	possess/dwell	$34_{11.17}$		65_{9}
487	חציר/נוח	haunt/abode	34_{13} 35_{7}		
488	יענה/תנים	jackal/ostrich	($13_{21\text{-}22}$) 34_{13}	(43_{20})	
489	שעיר/ציים	wild beast/satyr	(13_{21}) 34_{14}		
490	ערבה/מדבר	wilderness/desert	$35_{1.6}$	40_{3} 41_{19}	51_{3}
491	פרח/גיל	rejoice/blossom	(35_{1}) 35_{2}		
492	גיל/שוש	be glad/rejoice	35_{1}		61_{10} (65_{18a}) $65_{18b.19}$ 66_{10}

No.	Hebrew	English	I Isaiah	II Isaiah	III Isaiah
493	פרח/שוש	be glad/blossom	35_{1}		64_{14}
494	הדר/כבד	glory/majesty	$35_{2a.b}$		
495	רבץ/נוח	haunt/resting place	(27_{10}) (35_{7})		65_{10}
496	דרך/מסלה	highway/way	35_{8}	40_{3} 49_{11}	59_{7-8} 62_{10}
497	טוב/אמת	faithful/gold	38_{3} (39_{8})		
498	הגה/צפף	clamor/moan	(8_{19}) 38_{14}		
499	קרא/דבר	speak/cry		40_{2} 46_{11} (48_{15})	(59_{4}) $65_{12.24}$ 66_{4} 58_{9}
500	ראה/גלה	reveal/see		40_{5} 47_{3}	
501	ציץ/חציר	grass/flower		$40_{6.7.8}$	
502	נבל/יבש	wither/fade		$40_{7.8}$	
503	פעל/שכר	reward/recompense		40_{10}	62_{11}
504	צרף/חרש	workman/goldsmith		40_{19} (41_{7})	
505	ראה/נשא	lift up/see	(18_{3})	(40_{26}) (49_{18}) (52_{8})	$60_{4})$
506	ראה/עין	eye/see	(17_{17}) (29_{18}) (30_{20}) (32_{3}) $(33_{15.17.20})$	(40_{26}) 44_{18} $(52_{8.10})$	59_{15} 60_{4} (64_{4})
507	כח/אונים	might/strength		(40_{26}) 40_{29}	
508	משפט/דרך	way/right		40_{27}	58_{2} (59_{8})
509	יגע/יעף	faint/grow weary		$(40_{28.30})$ 40_{31}	
510	כשל/יעף	faint/fall exhausted	5_{27}	40_{30}	
511	לאום/אי	island/people		41_{1} 49_{1}	
512	קרב/נגש	approach/draw near		$41_{1.21}$	65_{5}
513	קשת/חרב	sword/bow	21_{15} 22_{2-3}	41_{2}	
514	גוים/מלך	nation/king	(14_{9})	41_{2} 45_{1} 52_{15}	$60_{3.11.16}$ 62_{2}
515	בחר/עבד	servant/chosen		$41_{8.9}$ 42_{1} (43_{10}) $44_{1.2}$ 45_{4}	$65_{9.15}$
516	אהב/עבד	servant/friend		41_{8} 56_{6}	
517	קרא/חזק	take/call	(4_{1})	41_{9} 42_{6}	64_{7}
518	אין/אפס	naught/nothing		(41_{12}) $41_{24.29}$ 40_{17} 46_{9}	

519	עזר/ירא	fear/help		$41_{10.13.14}$ 44_{2}	
520	צמא/מים	water/thirst	(21_{14}) (35_{7})	41_{17} (44_{3}) 48_{21} 50_{2} 55_{1}	
521	שים/נתן	put/set		41_{19} 47_{6}	61_{3} 62_{7}
522	ארז/ברוש	cypress/cedar	14_{8} 37_{24}	(41_{19})	
523	עץ/ארז	cedar/olive		(41_{19}) (44_{14})	
524	ארז/אלון	oak/cedar	2_{13}	(44_{14})	
525	בשן/לבנון	Lebanon/Bashan	2_{3} 33_{9}		
526	ברוש/הדס	myrtle/cypress		41_{19} 55_{13}	
527	תאשור/תדהר	plane/pine		(41_{19})	(60_{13})
528	ברוש/לבנון	Lebanon/cypress	14_{8} (37_{24})		60_{13}
529	ידע/ראה	see/know	5_{19} (6_{9}) (29_{15})	(41_{20}) (44_{9}) 44_{18}	58_{3} 61_{9} 66_{14}
530	שים/ראה	see/consider		41_{20}	(66_{19})
531	שכל/ראה	see/understand		41_{20} 44_{18}	
532	שכל/ידע	know/understand		41_{20} (44_{18})	
533	שים/ידע	know/consider		41_{20} $_{22}$ $(42_{16.25})$ (43_{19}) (44_{19}) (50_{7})	
534	ברא/עשה	do/create		41_{20} 43_{7} $45_{7.12.18}$	
535	יצר/ברא	create/form		$43_{1.7}$ (45_{7}) 45_{18} 54_{16}	
536	מלך/יהוה	Lord/king		41_{21} 43_{15} (44_{6})	
537	מלך/צבא	host/king	(6_{5}) 24_{21}	46_{6}	
538	צבא/גאל	redeemer/host		(44_{6}) (47_{4}) 54_{5}	
539	ברא/יהוה	Lord/creator		40_{28} 43_{15}	
540	גאל/יהוה	Lord/redeemer		$44_{6\,(24)}$ (49_{7})	(60_{16})
541	בוא/ראשון	former things/things to come	35_{10}	41_{22} (42_{9}) 48_{3}	
542	רמס/בוא	come/tread	1_{12}	41_{25}	
543	אמר/ידע	know/say	9_{9} (12_{4}) (29_{15})	41_{26} (48_{7})	
544	כהה/רצץ	bruse/burn dimly		$42_{3\,(4)}$	
545	משפט/אמת	faithful/justice	16_{5}	(42_{3})	$59_{14.15}$ 61_{8}
546	תורה/משפט	justice/law		42_{4} 51_{4}	

No.	Hebrew	English	I Isaiah	II Isaiah	III Isaiah
547	אי/ארץ	earth/coastland		41_{5} 42_{4}	
548	נטה/ברא	create/stretch		(42_{5}) 45_{12}	
549	רקע/נטה	stretch/spread		42_{5} 44_{24}	
550	רוח/נשמה	breath/spirit		42_{5}	57_{16}
551	חשך/אסר	prisoner/those in darkness		42_{7} 49_{9}	
552	תהלה/כבד	glory/praise		$42_{8.12}$	
553	חדש/ראשון	former/new		42_{9}	65_{17}
554	אי/ים	sea/coast	(11_{11} (23_{2}) (24_{15})	42_{10}	
555	עיר/מדבר	desert/city		(42_{11})	(64_{10})
556	אפק/חשה	be silent/restrain		(42_{14})	64_{12}
557	אגם/נהר	river/pool		41_{18} 42_{15}	
558	דרך/הלך	lead/guide	2_{3} 8_{11} 30_{21} 35_{8}	42_{16} $_{(24)}$ 48_{17}	(57_{17}) (65_{2})
559	נתיבה/דרך	way/path		42_{16} 43_{16}	59_{8}
560	עזב/עשה	do/forsake	10_{3}	42_{16}	58_{2}
561	מסכה/פסל	graven image/molten image	(30_{21})	42_{17}	
562	נבט/שמע	hear/look		42_{18} 51_{1}	
563	מלאך/עבד	servant/messenger		42_{19} 44_{26}	
564	תורה/צדק	righteousness/law		42_{21} 51_{7}	
565	שוב/נצל	rescue/restore		42_{23} 43_{13}	
566	שמע/הלך	walk/obey		42_{24} 50_{10} 55_{3}	
567	אף/חמה	heat/anger		(42_{25})	$63_{3.6}$ (66_{15})
568	קרא/גאל	redeem/call		43_{1} (54_{5})	(62_{12})
569	נהר/מים	water/river	8_{7} 18_{2} 19_{5}	41_{18} $43_{2.20}$ 50_{2}	
570	ישע/יהוה	Lord/savior	(19_{20})	$43_{3.11}$ (45_{15}) 45_{21} 49_{26}	60_{16}
571	כוש/מצרים	Egypt/Ethiopia	(11_{11}) ($20_{3.4.5}$)	43_{3}	
572	סבא/כוש/מצרים	Egypt/Ethiopia/Sabia		43_{3} 45_{14}	
573	צפון/מזרה	east/north		43_{5-6} 41_{25}	

574	מערב/מזרה	east/west		43_{5} 45_{6}	59_{19}
575	קבץ/בוא	bring/gather		43_{5} (45_{20}) (49_{18})	(60_{4}) (66_{18})
576	בת/בן	son/daughter		43_{6} 49_{22}	(56_{5}) 60_{4}
577	כבד/שם	name/glory	24_{15}	42_{8} 43_{7}	59_{19} 62_{2}
578	אמר/שמע	hear/say	(6_{8}) 28_{12} (30_{21}) (37_{9})	(41_{26}) (43_{9}) (47_{8}) (48_{7}) 48_{20} 52_{7}	62_{11} (66_{5})
579	אמר/בשר	bring/say		40_{9} 52_{7}	
580	שמע/ישע	save/proclaim		(43_{12}) (52_{7})	59_{1}
581	כשדים/בבלה	Babylonian/Chaldean		43_{14} 47_{1} $48_{14.20}$	
582	בין/זכר	remember/consider		43_{18} (46_{8})	
583	קדם/ראש	former/of old		43_{18} 46_{10}	
584	ישימון/מדבר	wilderness/desert		$43_{19.20}$	
585	בחר/עם	people/chosen		(43_{20})	65_{22}
586	יגע/עבד	burden/weary		$43_{23.24}$	
587	לבונה/מנחה	offering/frankincense		43_{23}	63_{3}
588	נזל/מים	water/streams		44_{3} (48_{21})	
589	צאצא/זרע	descendant/offspring		44_{3} 48_{19}	61_{9} 65_{23}
590	יבל/סים	water/stream	(30_{25})	44_{4}	
591	כתב/אמר	say/write	4_{3}	44_{5}	
592	כנה/קרא	call/surname		44_{5} 45_{4}	
593	נגד/קרא	proclaim/declare		44_{7}	58_{1}
594	בוא/אתה	things to come/to be		41_{25} 44_{7}	
595	ירא/פחד	fear/be afraid		(44_{8})	60_{5}
596	יצר/פעל	work/shape		44_{12} 45_{11}	
597	שתה/רעב	hungry/thirsty	29_{8}	44_{12}	65_{13}
598	יעף/אין כח	strength fails/faint		$40_{29.31}$ 44_{12}	
599	עץ/ברזל	bronze/wood		44_{12-13}	
600	ישראל/עבד	servant/Israel		(41_{8}) $44_{1 (21)}$ 45_{4} $49_{3 (5) (6)}$	
601	פצה/רנן	sing/break forth into singing	(14_{7})	44_{23} 49_{13} (52_{9}) 54_{1} (55_{12})	

No.	Hebrew	English	I Isaiah	II Isaiah	III Isaiah
602	גיל/רנה	sing/exult	(35_{2})	49_{13}	
603	יער/הר	mountain/forest	37_{24}	44_{23}	
604	יער/עץ	tree/forest	(7_{2}) (10_{19})	($44_{14.23}$)	
605	עץ/הר	mountain/tree		44_{23} 55_{12}	
606	ביה/ישב	inhabit/build		44_{26}	(58_{12}) ($65_{21.22}$)
607	קום/בנה	build/raise up		44_{26}	58_{12} 61_{4}
608	בריח/נהושה	bronze/iron		45_{2} 48_{4}	$60_{17a.b}$
609	רעע/שלם	weal/woe		45_{7}	57_{1-2}
610	צדק/ישע	salvation/righteousness		$45_{8(21)}$ 46_{13} $51_{5.6.8}$	56_{1} $59_{16.17}$ 61_{10} 62_{1} 63_{1}
611	חרש/יצר	maker/potter	30_{14}	45_{9}	
612	צבא/שמים	heaven/host	(34_{4})	45_{12}	
613	סחר/יגע	labor/traffic in		45_{14} 47_{15}	
614	אלהים/אל	God/God		$45_{14.15}$ 46_{9}	
615	אל/פסל	idol/god		($44_{10.17}$) 44_{15} 45_{20}	
616	נגש/נגד	declare/present case		(41_{22}) (45_{21})	
617	יעץ/נגד	declare/take council	19_{12}	45_{21}	
618	שוב/יצא	go forth/return		45_{23} 55_{11}	
619	קרס/כרע	to bow/to stoop		$46_{1(2)}$	
620	שבה/מלט	burden/captivity		46_{2} ($49_{24.25}$)	
621	נשא/עמס	bear/carry		$46_{1.3}$	
622	רחם/בטן	birth/womb	(13_{18})	46_{3} (49_{15})	
623	סבל/נשא	bear/carry		$46_{4(7)}$ $53_{4(11-12)}$	
624	שוה/דמה	liken/make equal		40_{25} 46_{5}	
625	נחל/עם	people/heritage	19_{25}	47_{6} 49_{8}	
626	זכר/לב שים	lay to heart/remember		46_{8} 47_{7}	57_{11} 65_{17}
627	שכול/אלמנה	widow/loss of children		$47_{8(9)}$	
628	יום/רגע	moment/day	27_{3}	(47_{9})	
629	חבר/כשף	sorcery/enchantment		$47_{9.12}$	

630	שוב/בטח	be secure/lead astray	30_{15}	47_{10}	
631	נפל/בוא	come/fall upon	30_{13}	47_{11}	
632	יצא/קרא	call/come forth		40_{26} 48_{1}	
633	נסך/פסל	graven image/molten image		(40_{19}) (44_{10}) (48_{5})	
634	צוה/עשה	do/command		45_{12} 48_{5}	
635	תהלה/שם	name/praise		42_{8} 48_{9}	
636	קרא/שמע	hearken/call		48_{12} (49_{1})	60_{18}
637	עת/ראש	beginning/time	(9_{1})	48_{16}	
638	צדק/שלם	peace/righteousness	(9_{7}) (32_{17})	48_{18}	60_{17}
639	יד/פה	mouth/hand	9_{12} 10_{14}	49_{2} 51_{16}	
640	הבל/ריק	vain/vanity	(30_{7})	49_{4}	
641	פעל/משפט	right/recompense		49_{4}	61_{8}
642	עז/כבד	honor/strength	(25_{3})	49_{5}	
643	שוב/קום	raise up/restore		49_{6}	58_{12}
644	נתן/נצר	keep/give		42_{6} (49_{8})	
645	נחלה/ארץ	land/heritage		49_{8}	58_{14}
646	שמם/ארץ	land/desolate	(13_{9})	$(49_{8.19})$	(62_{4})
647	הרס/חרב	waste/devastate		$49_{17\,(19)}$	
648	גלה/יצא	come forth/appear	26_{21}	49_{9}	
649	צפון/רחק	afar/north		(43_{6}) 49_{12}	
650	עזב/שכח	forsake/forget		49_{14}	65_{11}
651	כלה/עדה	ornament/bride		49_{18}	(61_{10})
652	גדל/ילד	bear/bring up	23_{4}	49_{21} 51_{18}	
653	נשא/בוא	bring/carry		49_{22}	$60_{4\,(6)}$
654	שבי/מלקות	prey/captive		$49_{24.25}$	
655	מלט/לקח	take/rescue		$49_{24.25}$	
656	ערץ/גבור	mighty/tyrant		$49_{24.25}$	
657	גאל/ישע	savior/redeemer		49_{26}	63_{9} (60_{16})
658	מכר/שלח	put away/sell		$50_{1a.b}$	
659	פשע/עון	iniquity/transgression		50_{1} 53_{5} (43_{24-25})	59_{12}

No.	Hebrew	English	I Isaiah	II Isaiah	III Isaiah
660	קרא/בוא	come/call		41_{25} 48_{15} 50_{2}	
661	שים מדבר/חרב	dry up/make desert		50_{2} 51_{3}	64_{10-11} $_{(9-10)}$
662	שמע/ירא	fear/obey	(37_{6})	50_{10} 51_{7}	
663	עבד/יהוה	Lord/servant	(20_{3})	(42_{19}) (43_{10}) (44_{2}) (48_{20}) (49_{5}) 50_{10}	(56_{6}) (63_{17}) (65_{8}) (66_{14})
664	נגה/חשך	darkness/night	(9_{2}) 13_{10}	50_{10}	(59_{9}) (60_{2-3})
665	גדף/חרף	reproach/revile	(37_{23})	51_{7}	
666	ים/תנין	dragon/sea	(27_{1})	51_{9-10}	
667	יסד/נטע	plant/lay foundation		$51_{13.16}$	
668	קבע/רעל	wrath/stagger		$51_{17.22}$	
669	חמה/יד	hand/wrath		$51_{17\,(22)}$	
670	שבר/שדד	devastate/destroy		(51_{19})	(59_{7}) (60_{18})
671	גער/חמת	wrath/rebuke		51_{20}	(66_{15})
672	חוץ/ערץ	ground/street	(24_{11})	51_{23}	
673	טוב/שלם	peace/good	39_{8}	52_{7}	
674	ירושלים/עם	people/Jerusalem	(28_{14}) (30_{19})	52_{9}	$65_{18.19}$
675	אסף/לפני הלך	go before/be rear guard		52_{12} 58_{8}	
676	תאר/מראה	appearance/form		52_{14} 53_{2}	
677	חמד/ראה	look/desire		(44_{9}) 53_{2}	
678	חשב/כאב	sorrow/esteem not		$53_{3\,(4)}$	
679	חול/כאב	sorrow/grief		$53_{3.4}$	
680	חשב/חדל	forsake/esteem not	2_{22}	53_{3}	
681	רפא/שלם	be whole/heal		53_{5}	(57_{18}) 57_{19}
682	החל/דכא	bruse/make sick		$53_{5.10}$	
683	סבל עון/צדק	make righteous/ bear iniquities		53_{11}	64_{6}
684	בעל/שמם	desolate/marry		54_{1}	62_{4}
685	עזב/שמם	desolate/forsake	(17_{9})		62_{4}

686	חפץ/עזב	forsake/delight			(58_{2}) (62_{4})
687	מאס/עזב	forsake/cast off	(7_{16})	54_{6}	
688	רחם/חסד	love/compassion		$(54_{8.10})$	63_{7}
689	ברית/חסד	love/covenant		54_{10} 55_{3}	
690	מוס/מוש	depart/remove		$54_{10a.b}$	
691	נחם/עניה	afflict/comfort		(49_{13}) (54_{11})	
692	גבול/שער	gate/wall		54_{12}	60_{18}
693	קרב/ירא	fear/come near		41_{5} 54_{14}	
694	ענג/אכל	eat/delight		55_{2}	58_{14}
695	קרא/דרש	seek/call	(34_{16})	55_{6}	(62_{12}) (65_{1})
696	חשב/דרך	way/thought		$55_{7.8.9}$	65_{2}
697	עולם/שם	name/everlasting		55_{13}	(56_{5}) $(63_{12.16.19})$
698	גלה/בוא	come/reveal	(23_{1})		56_{1}
699	שמר/חזק	hold/keep			$56_{2.4.6}$
700	עשה/שמר	keep/do			$56_{1.2}$
701	חלל/שמר	keep/profane			$(56_{2.6})$
702	סרים/נכר	foreigner/eunuch			$56_{3.4-6}$
703	שם/יד	monument/name	(29_{23})	(44_{5})	(56_{5})
704	עבד/אהב	love/serve		41_{8}	56_{6}
705	עבד/לוה	join/serve	24_{2}		56_{6}
706	ברית/שבת	sabbath/covenant			$56_{4.6}$
707	ידע/עור	blind/without knowledge		42_{16}	56_{10}
708	שבע/נפש	appetite/satisfy		(53_{11}) (55_{2})	56_{11} (58_{11})
709	בצע/דרך	way/gain			56_{11} 57_{17}
710	חסד/צדק	righteous/devout	(16_{5})		57_{1}
711	בוא/אסף	take away/go	(32_{10})		57_{1-2} 60_{20}
712	ארך/רחב	open/put out		54_{2}	57_{4}
713	זרע/ילד	children/offspring			57_{4} 65_{23}
714	שקר/פשע	transgression/deceit			57_{4} 59_{13}
715	נשא/גבה	high/lofty	30_{25}	(53_{13})	(57_{7})

No.	Hebrew	English	I Isaiah	II Isaiah	III Isaiah
716	מעשה/צדק	righteousness/doing	(32_{17})		(57_{12})
717	פנה/סלה	build up/prepare			57_{14} 62_{10}
718	שפל/דכא	contrite/humble			$57_{15a.b}$
719	לב/רוח	spirit/heart			57_{15} 65_{14}
720	נצח/עולם	forever/always	34_{10}		57_{16}
721	סתר/קצף	angry/hide		(54_{8})	57_{17}
722	נכה/קצף	angry/smite			57_{17} (60_{10})
723	סתר/נכה	smite/hide		(50_{6})	(57_{17})
724	ענה/צום	fast/humble			$58_{3.5}$
725	בית/לחם	bread/house	(3_{7})		58_{7}
726	כבד/צדק	righteousness/glory			58_{8} 62_{2}
727	אמר/ענה	answer/say	14_{10} (21_{9}) (36_{21})		58_{9}
728	אפלה/אור	light/gloom			58_{10} (59_{9})
729	קדש/שבת	sabbath/holy day			$58_{13a.b}$
730	כבד/ענג	delight/honor			58_{13} (66_{11})
731	חפץ/דרך	way/pleasure			(58_{2}) 58_{13} (66_{3})
732	עון/דם	blood/iniquity	26_{21}		59_{3}
733	הגה/דבר	speak/mutter			$59_{3.13}$
734	הרה/דבר	speak/conceive			$59_{4.13}$
735	משפט/שלם	peace/justice	9_{7}		59_{8}
736	נגה/אור	light/brightness	(9_{2}) (13_{10})		59_{9} $60_{3.19}$
737	הגה/המה	growl/moan	31_{4}		59_{11}
738	ישע/משפט	justice/salvation			(56_{1}) 59_{11}
739	צדק/זרע	arm/justice		51_{5}	59_{16}
740	סמך/ישע	bring victory/uphold			59_{16} 63_{5}
741	עטה/לבש	put on/wrap self			59_{17} 61_{10}
742	מעיל/לבש	clothing/mantle			59_{17} (61_{10})
743	שלם/גמלה	deed/repay			59_{18} 66_{6}

744	דבר/רוח	spirit/word			59_{21} 66_{2}
745	לאום/ארץ	earth/people	(34_{1})		60_{2}
746	בית/מזבח	altar/house			56_{7} 60_{7}
747	אבן/עץ	wood/stone	(37_{19})		60_{17}
748	מעשה/נטע	plant/work			60_{21} (65_{22})
749	ראש/עולם	ancient/former	(35_{10})	(46_{9}) (51_{11})	61_{4}
750	שמם/חרב	ruin/devastate			$61_{4a.b}$
751	גזל/משפט	justice/robbery	(10_{2})		61_{8}
752	מעיל/בגד	garment/robe			61_{10} 59_{17}
753	כלה/חתן	bridegroom/bride			61_{10} (62_{5})
754	צמח/זרע	shoot/sow		(55_{10})	61_{11}
755	יד/כף	hand/hand	1_{15}		62_{3}
756	אלהים/חתן	bridegroom/God			(61_{10}) 62_{5}
757	זרוע/ימין	right hand/arm			62_{8} 63_{12}
758	גאל/קדש	be holy/redeem		(41_{14}) (43_{14}) (47_{4}) (48_{17}) (49_{7}) (54_{5})	62_{12}
759	עזב/דרש	seek out/forsake			58_{2} 62_{12}
760	כגד/לבש	apparel/garment		(52_{1})	$63_{2.3}$ (59_{17}) (61_{10})
761	בקעה/מדבר	desert/valley		40_{3-4} 41_{18}	63_{13-14}
762	פאר/קדש	holy/glorious		(55_{5})	(60_{9}) (63_{15}) (64_{11})
763	גבור/קנא	zeal/might		42_{13}	(63_{15})
764	ישראל/אברהם	Abraham/Israel		41_{8}	63_{16}
765	נכר/ידע	know/acknowledge			61_{9} 63_{16}
766	שבט/עבד	servant/tribe		(49_{6})	63_{17}
767	נחלה/עבד	servant/heritage		(54_{17})	63_{17}
768	זלל/ירד	come down/quake			$64_{1.3}$
769	הר/שמים	heavens/mountain	14_{13}	40_{12} 44_{23} 49_{13}	64_{1}
770	רגז/ידע	make known/tremble	(37_{28})		64_{2}
771	דרך/צדק	righteousness/way		45_{13}	58_{2} 64_{5}
772	עון/קצף	angry/iniquity			(57_{17}) 64_{9}

No.	Hebrew	English	I Isaiah	II Isaiah	III Isaiah
773	לבונה/זבח	sacrifice/frankincense		43_{23}	65_{3}
774	אש/עשן	smoke/fire	(4_{5}) (9_{18})		65_{5}
775	אש/אף	nostril/fire	($30_{27.30}$)		(65_{5})
776	ירש/זרע	descendant/inheritor		(54_{3})	65_{9}
777	יהודה/יעקב	Jacob/Judah		48_{1}	65_{9}
778	שמע/ענה	answer/listen	(30_{19})		$65_{12.24}$ 66_{4}
779	בחר/עשה	do/choose		44_{2}	65_{12} 66_{4}
780	חפץ/רעע	evil/delight			65_{12} 66_{4}
781	בוש/שמח	rejoice/shame			65_{13} 66_{5}
782	אתם/עבד	servant/you			$65_{13.14}$
783	נטע/בנה	build/plant			$65_{21.22}$
784	כרם/בית	house/vineyard	(3_{14}) (5_{7})		65_{21}
785	אכל/ישב	inhabit/eat			$65_{21.22}$
786	עם/עץ	tree/people	(7_{2})		56_{3} (65_{22})
787	אריה/זאב	wolf/lion	11_{6-7}		65_{25}
788	מקום/בית	house/place	22_{23}		66_{1}
789	נכה/עני	humble/contrite	(11_{4})		(66_{2})
790	שה/שור	ox/lamb	7_{25}		66_{3}
791	חפץ/בחר	choose/delight			$66_{3(4)}$ (56_{4})
792	קול/שאון	uproar/voice	(13_{4})		66_{6}
793	ענג/שבע	satisfy/delight		(55_{2})	66_{11}
794	נחל/נהר	river/stream	11_{15} (27_{12})		66_{12}
795	אש/להב	flame/fire	(26_{9}) (30_{30})		(66_{15})
796	שקץ/חזיר	swine/abomination			($66_{3.17}$)
797	שם/זרע	descendant/name		48_{19}	66_{22}

PHRASES

No.	Hebrew	English	I Isaiah	II Isaiah	III Isaiah
1	נטה אזן	incline the ear	37_{17}	55_{3}	
2	מרעים זרע	offspring of evildoers	1_{4} 14_{20}		
3	קדוש ישראל	holy one of Israel	1_{4} $5_{16.24}$ 10_{20} 17_{7} 29_{19} $30_{11.12.15}$ 31_{1}	$41_{14.16.20}$ $43_{3.14}$ 45_{11} 47_{4} 48_{17} 49_{7} 54_{5} 55_{5}	$60_{9.14}$
4	בת ציון	daughter of Zion	1_{8} $3_{16.17}$ 4_{4} 10_{32} 16_{1} 37_{22}	52_{2}	62_{11}
5	כף פרש	spread forth the hand	1_{15} 19_{8} 25_{11}		65_{2}
6	דבר פה	mouth has spoken	1_{20}	40_{5}	58_{14}
7	אביר ישראל	mighty one of Israel	1_{24}	49_{26}	60_{16}
8	קריה נאמנה	faithful city	$1_{21.26}$		
9	נבל עלה	leaf withers	1_{30} 34_{4}		$64_{6(5)}$
10	בית תפלה	house of prayer			$56_{7a.b}$
11	הר יהוה	mountain of the Lord	$2_{2.3}$ 30_{29}		
12	הר קדוש	holy mountain	11_{9} 27_{13}		56_{7} 57_{13} $65_{11.25}$ 66_{20}
13	ושגב יהוה	Lord will be exalted	$2_{11.17}$ $9_{11(10)}$ 33_{5}		
14	אניות תרשיש	ships of Tarshish	2_{16} $23_{1.14}$		60_{9}
15	ארץ ערץ קום	rise to terrify the earth	$2_{19.21}$		
16	נשא פנים	honored man	3_{3} $9_{15(14)}$		
17	רעה איש	one to another	13_{8}	41_{6}	
18	נדח קבץ	gather the outcasts	11_{12}		56_{8}
19	יד נכה	stretch out the hand	5_{25} $9_{12.17.21}$ 10_{4} $14_{26.27}$ 23_{11} 31_{3}	45_{12}	
20	רגז הר	mountains quake	5_{25} 13_{13} 14_{16} 23_{11}		
21	נס נשא	raise a signal	5_{26} 11_{2} 13_{2} 18_{3}		
22	תקע שופר	trumpet blows	18_{3} 27_{13}		
23	נס רום	raise a signal		49_{22}	62_{10}

No.	Hebrew	English	I Isaiah	II Isaiah	III Isaiah
24	ארץ קצה	ends of the earth	5_{26} 26_{15}	40_{28} $41_{5.9}$ 42_{10} 43_{6} 48_{20} 49_{6}	62_{11}
25	יער סבך	thickets of the forest	9_{18} 10_{34}		
26	ארץ חיים	land of the living	38_{11}	53_{8}	
27	עזר נוס	flee for help	10_{3} 20_{6}		
28	מצא יד	hand has found	$10_{10.14}$		
29	נהג נער	child shall lead	10_{19} 11_{6}		
30	יום יהוה	day of the Lord	$13_{6.9}$ 34_{8}		
31	חרב נפל	fall by the sword	3_{25} 13_{15} 31_{8} 37_{7}		
32	ירד בור	go down to the pit	$14_{11.15.19}$		
33	שק חגר	gird on sackcloth	15_{3} 22_{12} 32_{11}		
34	בכי בכה	weep with weeping	16_{9} 38_{3}		
35	ישע	God of salvation	12_{2} 17_{10}	52_{10}	
36	בזא נהר ארץ	land the rivers divide	$18_{2.7}$		
37	בכי מרר	weep bitter tears	22_{4} 38_{17}		
38	ישבי אי	inhabitants of the coast	20_{6} $23_{2.6}$	42_{10}	
39	כבד ארץ	honored of the earth	$23_{8.9}$		
40	יה	Lord	12_{2} 26_{4} 38_{11}		
41	אפרים שכר	drunkards of Ephraim	$28_{1.3}$		
42	עטרה גאות	proud crown	$28_{1.3.5}$		
43	משפט רוח	spirit of justice	4_{4} 28_{6}		
44	חנה קריה דוד	city where David encamped	29_{1}		
45	ספה . . .	add year to year	29_{1} 30_{1}		
46	יד מעשה	work of the hands	2_{8} 5_{12} 17_{8} 19_{25} 29_{23} 37_{19}		$64_{8(7)}$ 60_{21} 65_{22}
47	אש אכל	devouring fire	$30_{27.30}$ 29_{6} 33_{14}		
48	צואר חצה	reach the neck	8_{8} 30_{28}		

49	חית השדה	wild beasts		43_{20}	56_{9}
50	שרב	burning sand	35_{7}	49_{10}	
51	יער כרמל	densest forest	10_{18} 37_{24}		
52	עיר בצרה	fortified city	25_{2} 27_{10} 36_{1} 37_{26}		
53	שלם . . .	bring to an end	$38_{12.13}$		60_{20}
54	רוח יהוה	breath of the Lord	11_{2}	$40_{7.13}$	59_{19} 61_{1} 63_{14}
55	כח חלף	renew strength		40_{31} 41_{1}	
56	אפס ארץ	end of the earth		45_{22} 52_{10}	
57	אין . . .	no other besides me		$45_{5.6.21}$ $47_{8.10}$ 43_{11} 44_{6} 46_{9}	
58	מורג חרוץ	threshing sledge	28_{27}	41_{15}	
59	מים מוצא	springs of water		41_{18}	58_{11}
60	אני יהוה . . .	I am with you		$43_{2.5.11.13.25}$ $45_{3.6.5.7}$ 46_{9}	65_{1}
61	בטן יצר	formed from the womb		$44_{2.24}$ 49_{5}	
62	קו נטה	stretch out a line	34_{11}	44_{13}	
63	פצח רנן	break forth in song	14_{7}	44_{23} 49_{13} 52_{9} 54_{1} 55_{12}	
64	אני יהוה	I am the Lord		$43_{2.5.11.13.\ 25}$ $45_{3.6.5.7.18.21}$ 46_{9} 48_{15}	
65	פה יצא	go forth from the mouth		45_{23} 48_{3} 55_{11}	
66	רשע שלם	no peace for the wicked		48_{22}	57_{21}
67	יד צל	shadow of the hand		49_{2} 51_{16}	
68	מבוע מים	springs of water	35_{7}	49_{10}	
69	אחור סוג	turn back		50_{5} 42_{17}	
70	אכל עש	moth will eat		50_{9} 51_{8}	
71	מעשה יהוה	Lord your maker	17_{7}	(44_{24}) (51_{13}) (54_{5})	
72	בגד בלה	wear out like a garment		50_{9} 51_{6}	
73	עם אור	light to the peoples		42_{6} 49_{6} 51_{4}	
74	זרוע יהוה	arm of the Lord		51_{9} 53_{1}	
75	כרת עות	cut off the sign		55_{13}	56_{5}

No.	Hebrew	English	I Isaiah	II Isaiah	III Isaiah
76	יום ראון	acceptable day		49_{8}	58_{5} 61_{2}
77	אור עולם	everlasting light			$60_{19.20}$
78	ברית עולם	everlasting convenant	24_{5}	55_{3}	61_{8}
79	עשה שם	make a name			$63_{12.14}$
80	דבר חרד	tremble at the word			$66_{2.5}$

3. *Job*

WORD PAIRS

No.	Hebrew	English	Job	Elsewhere
1	שוב/יצא	come forth/return	1_{21} 15_{13} (39_{4}) 39_{21-22}	(Ec 5_{15})
2	הלך/משט	go to and fro/walk up and down	(1_{7}) (2_{2})	
3	ישר/תם	blameless/upright	($1_{1.8}$) (2_{3})	Ps 37_{37} (Pr 29_{10})
4	סור רע/ירא אלהים	fear God/turn from evil	($1_{1.8}$) (2_{3})	
5	בשר/עצם	bone/flesh	(2_{5}) (19_{20})	(Ge 29_{14}) (Ju 9_{2}) (II Sa 5_{1} 19_{13}) (I Ch 11_{1})
6	קדקד/כף רגל	sole of foot/crown	(2_{7})	(I Sa 1_{6}) (De 28_{35}) (II Sa 14_{25})
7	דע/טוב	good/evil	2_{10} (30_{26})	(Nu 13_{19}) Ps 34_{14} (35_{12}) 37_{27}
8	נחם/נוד	condole/comfort	(2_{11}) (42_{11})	Ps $69_{20(21)}$ Is 51_{19} Na 3_{7}
9	הרה/ילד	born/conceive	3_{3} 15_{35}	Nu 11_{12} (Ju 13_{3}) Ps $7_{14(15)}$ Is 26_{18} 33_{11} 59_{4} (8_{3}) (Ho 1_{3}) etc.
10	אור/חשך	dark/light	3_{4} $12_{22(25)}$ 24_{16} 38_{19}	Ps 139_{11} (Ec 11_{7-8}) Mi 7_{8} Ek $32_{7.8}$ (La 3_{2}) Is $9_{2(1)}$ 45_{7} 59_{9}
11	צלמות/חשך	gloom/deep darkness	(3_{5}) ($10_{21.22}$) (28_{3}) (34_{22})	Je 13_{16} (Ps 107_{10})
12	אפל/חשך	darkness/thick darkness	23_{17} 28_{3}	(Is 29_{18})
13	גוע/מות	die/expire	3_{11} 14_{10}	
14	בטן/רחם	womb/belly	3_{11} 10_{18-19} 31_{15}	Ps $22_{10(11)}$ $58_{3(4)}$ Je 1_{5} (Ho 9_{11})
15	ישן/שכב	lay down/sleep	3_{13}	(Ps $3_{5[6]}$ $4_{8[9]}$)
16	נוח/שקט	quiet/rest	$3_{13.26}$	(Is 14_{7}) Ek 16_{42} (II Ch 20_{30})
17	שר/עצי	counselor/prince	3_{14-15} 12_{17-19}	Ps 119_{23-24} Is 19_{11} (Da 3_{2} 6_{7})
18	כסף/זהב	gold/silver	3_{15} 28_{1}	(Ps 105_{37} 115_{4}) Is 13_{17} 40_{19} 46_{6} Je 10_{19}
19	יגיע/רשע	wicked/weary	3_{17} (10_{3})	
20	שמע/שאן	at ease/hear	3_{18}	(Pr 1_{33})

No.	Hebrew	English	Job	Elsewhere
21	חיים/אור	light/life	3_{20}	Ps 27_{1} 36_{9} Pr 6_{23}
22	שיש/שמח	rejoice/glad	3_{22}	Is 66_{10} (Ps $40_{16[17]}$ $68_{3(4)}$ ($70_{4[5]}$)
23	מים/לחם	bread/water	3_{24} 22_{7}	Ps 78_{20} Pr 9_{17} 25_{21}
24	מלין/דבר	speak/word	4_{2} 15_{13} 16_{4} 18_{2} 29_{22} 32_{11} 33_{1}	(Ps $19_{3-4[4-5]}$) Pr 23_{9}
25	חזק/יסר	instruct/strengthen	4_{3}	(Ho 7_{15})
26	ברך/כשל	stumble/knees	(4_{4})	(Ps 109_{24}) (Is 35_{3})
27	נגע/בוא	come/touch	(1_{19}) 4_{5}	
28	תקוה/כסלה	confidence/hope	4_{6} 8_{13-14}	(Pr 26_{12})
29	ישר/נקי	innocent/upright	4_{7} 17_{8}	
30	עמל/און	iniquity/trouble	4_{8} 5_{6} 15_{35}	Ps $7_{14(15)}$ (10_{7}) ($55_{10[11]}$) (90_{10}) Is 10_{1} 59_{4}
31	און/מרמה	deceit/mischief	15_{35}	Ps 10_{7} (36_{3})
32	עמל/מרמה	deceit/evil	15_{35}	Ps 10_{7} $55_{10-11(11-12)}$
33	רוח/נשמה	breath/blast	4_{9} 27_{3} 32_{8} 33_{4} 34_{14}	(Ps $18_{15[16]}$) Is 42_{5} 57_{16}
34	קול/שאג	roar/voice	4_{10} (37_{4})	
35	כפיר/אריה	lion/young lions	4_{10} 38_{39}	Is 5_{29} 11_{6-7} (31_{4}) Je 51_{88} Ek $19_{2.6}$ Am 3_{4} Mi 5_{8} Na 2_{11}
36	שחל/אריה	lion/fierce lion	4_{10}	Pr 26_{13}
37	כפיר/שחל	fierce lion/young lion	4_{10}	Ps 91_{13} Ho 5_{14}
38	לביש/ליש	strong lion/lioness	4_{11}	(Is 30_{6})
39	תרדמה/לילה	night/deep sleep	4_{13} 33_{15}	
40	רעד/פחד	dread/tremble	(4_{14})	Is 33_{14}
41	גבר/אנוש	man/man	4_{17} 10_{5} 33_{16-17} (34_{8-9}) 34_{34}	
42	מעשה/אלוה	God/maker	4_{17} (35_{10}) 36_{2-3}	(Is 17_{7} 51_{13}) Pr 14_{31} 17_{5}
43	מלאך/עבד	servant/messenger	4_{18}	Is 42_{19} 44_{2e}
44	עפר/חמר	clay/dust	4_{19} 10_{9} 27_{16} 30_{19}	
45	חמר/אפר	ashes/clay	13_{12} 30_{19}	

46	עפר/אפר	ashes/dust	(30_{19}) (42_{6})	(Ge 18_{27})
47	שער/ישע	safety/gate	5_{4}	(Is 60_{18})
48	חקר/גדל	great/unsearchable	5_{9} 9_{10}	(Ps 131_{1} 136_{4})
49	פלא/מספר	marvelous/without number	5_{9} 27_{2}	
50	מים/מטר	rain/water	5_{10} (28_{25-26}) 36_{27}	Je 10_{13} 51_{16}
51	חוץ/ארץ	earth/field	5_{10} 18_{17}	(Pr 8_{26}) Is 24_{11} 51_{23} (Je 7_{34})
52	צהרים/יומם	daytide/noonday	5_{14}	Ps 91_{5-6} Je 6_{4} (Am 8_{9})
53	יד/חרב	sword/hand	5_{15}	Ps 17_{13-14} $22_{20(21)}$ (63_{10}) (149_{6}) Je 19_{7} 20_{4}
54	יד/פה	mouth/hand	5_{15} (21_{5}) (31_{27}) (40_{4})	
55	שדי/אלוה	God/almighty	5_{17} 6_{4} 11_{7} 22_{26} 27_{10} 31_{2} 40_{2}	
56	מוסר/יכח	reprove/chasten	5_{17}	Ps 94_{10} $6_{1(2)}$ Pr 3_{11} 9_{7}
57	רפא/חבש	bind/heal	5_{18}	Ek 34_{4} Is 30_{26} Ho 6_{1}
58	רע/צרה	trouble/evil	5_{19}	(Ps 71_{20}) 78_{49} (Pr 12_{13}) (Je 15_{11})
59	מלחמה/רעב	famine/war	5_{20}	(Je 18_{21})
60	יד חרב/מות	death/hand of the sword	5_{20}	Je 15_{2} 18_{21} (43_{11}) La 1_{20}
61	ירא/שחק	laugh/fear not	5_{22}	Ps $52_{6(8)}$
62	שלם/ברית	league/peace	5_{23}	(Is 54_{10}) (Ek 34_{25})
63	פקד/ידע	know/inspect	5_{24} 35_{15}	
64	נוה/אהל	tent/fold	5_{24} 18_{15}	Is 33_{20}
65	צאצא/זרע	descendant/offspring	5_{25} 21_{8}	Is 44_{3} 48_{19} 61_{9} 65_{23}
66	עשב ארץ/רב	many/grass of the earth	5_{25}	Mi $5_{7(6)}$
67	נשא אזן/שקל	to weigh/lay in the balance	6_{2} (31_{6})	(Is 40_{12}) (Je 32_{10})
68	שור/פרא	wild ass/ox	6_{5} 21_{10}	
69	נחש/אבן	stone/bronze	6_{12} (28_{2})	(Is 60_{17})
70	ישע/עזר	help/save	6_{13}	Ps $60_{11(13)}$ $108_{12(13)}$
71	אפיק/וחל	torrent bed/freshet	6_{15}	Jl 3_{18}
72	שלג/קרח	snow/ice	6_{16}	Ps 147_{16-17}

No.	Hebrew	English	Job	Elsewhere
73	חפר/בוש	disappoint/confound	6_{20}	Ps 35_{4} ($40_{14[15]}$) ($70_{2[3]}$) ($83_{17.18}$) Is 1_{29} 54_{4} Je 50_{12} (15_{9})
74	עריץ/צר	adversary/oppressor	6_{23}	(Is 25_{4})
75	יכח/ישר	honest/reproof	6_{25} (23_{7})	
76	אמר/מלה	word/speech	6_{26} 32_{14}	
77	כרה/נפל	cast lots/bargain	6_{27}	Ps 7_{15} 57_{7}
78	חך/לשון	tongue/taste	6_{30} (29_{10}) 33_{2}	(Ps 137_{6}) (La 4_{4}) (Ek 3_{26})
79	לילה/ירח	month/night	7_{3}	(Ps 121_{6}) (Je 31_{35})
80	קום/שכב	lie down/arise	7_{4} (14_{12})	(Is 43_{17})
81	נשף/ערב	night/dawn	7_{4}	Pr 7_{9} (I Sa 30_{17})
82	עור/בשר	flesh/skin	7_{5} (10_{11}) (19_{20}) 19_{26}	(Le 4_{11} 8_{17} 9_{11}) (La 3_{4}) Ek $37_{6.8}$ Mi 3_{3}
83	רמה/עפר	dust/worms	(7_{5}) 21_{26}	
84	עין/חי	life/eye	7_{7} (28_{21})	(Is 49_{18})
85	עין/עין	eyes/eyes	7_{8} 24_{15}	Ps 123_{2}
86	מקום/בית	house/place	7_{10}	Ps 26_{8} (Is 5_{8}) 22_{23} 66_{1} Je 7_{14} 28_{3} (Ek 45_{4}) Hg 2_{9}
87	דבר/חשך	restrain/speak	7_{11} (16_{6})	
88	נפש/רוח	spirit/soul	7_{11} 12_{10}	Is 42_{1}
89	משכב/ערש	bed/couch	7_{13}	Pr 7_{16-17}
90	חזיון/חלום	dream/vision	7_{14} 20_{8} (33_{15})	Jl 2_{28} (3_{1}) (Is 29_{7})
91	בחן/פקד	visit/test	7_{18}	Ps 17_{3}
92	רגע/בקר	morning/monument	7_{18}	(Ps $30_{5[6]}$)
93	עון/פשע	transgression/iniquity	7_{21} 14_{17} 31_{33}	Ps $59_{3-4(4-5)}$ $36_{1-2(2-3)}$ $51_{1-2(2-4)}$ ($65_{3[4]}$) $89_{32(33)}$ 107_{17} Is 50_{1} 53_{5} 59_{12} (Ek 18_{30}) 21_{24} etc.
94	שדי/אל	God/almighty	$8_{3.5}$ 13_{3} 15_{25} (21_{14-15}) (22_{2-3}) 22_{17} 23_{16} $27_{2.11.13}$ 33_{4} $34_{10.12}$ 35_{13}	(Ek 10_{5})
95	צדק/משפט	justice/righteousness	8_{3} 9_{15} 13_{18} 29_{14} $34_{5.17}$ 35_{2} 37_{23} 40_{8}	(Ps $9_{4[5]}$) 17_{1-2} 72_{2} Je 22_{13} 23_{5-6} Ec 3_{16} Is $1_{21.27}$ 5_{7} 16_{5} Ho $2_{19(21)}$ Zp 2_{3} Pr $1_{3.29}$ 8_{20} etc.

96	אחר/ראש	beginning/later	8_{7} (42_{12})	(Ec 7_{8}) (Is 46_{10})
97	אב/דר	age/father	8_{8}	(Ps $95_{9.10}$ 109_{13-14}) (Pr 30_{11}) (Jl 1_{2-3})
98	בטח/כסל	confidence/trust	8_{14} 31_{24}	
99	קום/עמד	stand/endure	8_{15} (29_{8})	
100	אבן/גל	stoneheap/rock	(8_{17})	(Ge 31_{46}) (Jo 7_{26}) (II Sa 18_{17})
101	שפה/פה	mouth/lips	(8_{21}) (15_{6}) (16_{5}) (23_{12}) 33_{2-3}	(Ps17_{3-4}) $51_{15(17)}$ $59_{7(8).12(13)}$ ($63_{5[6]}$) 66_{14} 119_{13} 141_{3} Pr 4_{24} 10_{32} 13_{3} 14_{3} (Is 6_{7}) 11_{4} etc.
102	לבב/חכם	wise/heart	9_{4} 34_{34}	
103	כח/לב	heart/strength	9_{4} (36_{5})	(Da. 11_{25})
104	עמוד/ארץ	earth/pillar	9_{6}	Ps $75_{3(4)}$
105	כימה/כסיל	Orion/Pleiades	9_{9} 38_{31}	(Am 5_{8})
106	חלף/עבר	pass by/move on	9_{11}	SS 2_{11} Is 8_{8} 24_{5}
107	חנן/ענה	answer/appeal for mercy	$9_{15.16}$	Ps $4_{1(2)}$ (27_{7})
108	חנם/שערה	hairs/without cause	9_{17}	Ps $69_{4(5)}$
109	משפט/כח	strength/justice	9_{19} (37_{23})	Is 41_{1} (49_{4}) Mi 3_{8}
110	תמם/צדק	innocent/blameless	9_{20} 22_{3} 27_{5} 31_{6}	
111	חי/נפש	self/life	(3_{20}) 9_{21} 10_{1} (12_{10}) $33_{18.20.22.28.30}$ 36_{14}	Ps $7_{5(6)}$ 26_{9} ($49_{18[19]}$) (66_{9}) 74_{19} 78_{50} $88_{3(4)}$ 143_{3} (Pr 3_{22}) La 3_{58}
112	עזב/שכח	forget/put off	9_{27}	Is 49_{14}
113	זכך/רחץ	wash/cleanse	9_{30}	Ps 73_{13} Is $1_{.16}$
114	ריב/רשע	condemn/contend	10_{2}	(Is 50_{8-9})
115	שנה/יום	day/year	(3_{6}) 10_{5} 15_{20} 32_{7} 36_{11}	Ps $61_{6(7)}$ 77_{5} 78_{33} $90_{4.9(10).15}$ $102_{24(25)}$ (Pr 3_{2}) 9_{11} 10_{27} (Ec 6_{3} 11_{8}) 12_{1} Is 63_{4} 65_{20} 34_{8} etc.
116	דרש/בקש	seek/search	10_{6}	Is 65_{1} Ps 105_{4} 24_{6} $38_{12(13)}$
117	חטא/עון	iniquity/sin	10_{6} (13_{23}) 14_{16-17} (7_{20-21})	Ps 32_{5} $51_{2(4)}$ $85_{2(3)}$ 109_{14} Pr 5_{22} Is 6_{7} 27_{9} 43_{24} 40_{2} 59_{2} Je 5_{25} 14_{10} 16_{10} 30_{14} Ho 4_{8} etc.
118	עצב/עשה	make/fashion	(10_{8})	(Je 44_{19})
119	עצם/עור	skin/bone	10_{11} (19_{20}) 30_{30}	La 3_{4} (4_{8}) Mi $3_{2.3}$
120	גיד/בשר	flesh/sinew	10_{11}	(Ek $37_{6.8}$)
121	גיד/עור	skin/sinew	10_{11}	(Ek $37_{6.8}$)

No.	Hebrew	English	Job	Elsewhere
122	עצם/בשר	flesh/bone	10_{11} (2_{5}) 4_{14-15} (19_{20}) 33_{21}	Ps $38_{3\,(4)}$ $(102_{5\,[6]})$ Pr 14_{30} La 3_{4} Mi 3_{3}
123	רוח/חיים	life/spirit	(7_{7}) 10_{12} 12_{10}	Pr 15_{4}
124	חסד/חיים	life/love	(10_{12})	(Ps $63_{3\,[4]}$) 103_{4}
125	צדק/רשע	wicked/righteous	(9_{20}) 10_{15} 35_{8}	(De 25_{1}) (Ps $45_{7\,[8]}$) (Ec 3_{16}) Pr 10_{2} 11_{5} 16_{12} (13_{6}) Ek 33_{12} $18_{20\,(27)}$
126	שפה/דבר	speak/lips	$11_{2.\,5}$ (27_{4}) 32_{20}	(Pr 10_{19}) Ec 10_{12}
127	תושיה/חכמה	wisdom/understanding	11_{6} 26_{3}	(Pr 2_{6-7})
128	שאול/שמים	heaven/Sheol	11_{8}	Ps 139_{8} Am 9_{2}
129	רחבה/ארכה	longer/broader	11_{9}	(Ek $40_{7.\,11.\,20.\,21.\,25.\,29.\,30}$)
130	ים/ארץ	earth/sea	11_{9} 12_{8}	Ps $46_{2\,(3)}$ $65_{5\,(6)}$ $69_{34\,(35)}$ 72_{8} Pr 8_{29} Is 9_{1} 11_{9}
131	און/שוא	worthless/iniquity	11_{11}	Ps $41_{6\,(7)}$ Is 59_{4} Ho $12_{11\,(12)}$ Zc 10_{2}
132	און/מתים	men/iniquity	11_{11} (22_{15})	
133	אדם/איש	man/man	11_{12} 38_{26} 32_{21} 34_{11} 35_{8}	Ps $22_{6\,(7)}$ $39_{11\,(12)}$ $(49_{2\,[3]})$ 62_{9} 80_{17} $140_{1\,(2)}$ Is 2_{9} 5_{15} (44_{13}) 52_{14} Je 2_{6}
134	כף/לב	heart/hand	11_{13} 31_{7}	La 2_{19}
135	עולה/און	iniquity/wickedness	11_{14} 31_{3}	(Pr 22_{8})
136	אהל/יד	hand/tent	11_{14}	Je 6_{3}
137	זכר/שכח	forget/remember	11_{16} 24_{20}	
138	בקר/צהרים	noon/morning	11_{17}	(Ps $55_{17\,[18]}$) Je 20_{16}
139	חכמה/דעת	knowledge/wisdom	12_{2}	(Da 1_{4}) Ec 8_{1}
140	עוף/בהמה	beast/bird	12_{7} 35_{11}	(Ge 1_{26} 2_{20}) (Je 7_{33} $9_{10\,(9)}$ 12_{4} 15_{3} 16_{4} 34_{20}) (Ek 44_{31}) Zp 1_{3}
141	בשר/חי	life/flesh	12_{10}	(Pr 14_{30})
142	נפש/בשר	flesh/life	(12_{10}) 13_{14} 14_{22}	(Ps 16_{9-10}) $63_{1\,(2)}$ $84_{2\,(3)}$ (Is 10_{18}) Je 45_{5}
143	חך/אזן	ear/palate	12_{11} 34_{3}	
144	אכל/מלין	words/food	12_{11} 34_{3}	
145	טעם/בחן	try/taste	12_{11} 34_{3}	

146	תבונה/חכמה	wisdom/understanding	$12_{12.13}$	(Ex 31_{3} 35_{31} 36_{1}) (I Ki 4_{29} 7_{14}) Pr 2_{2} $3_{13.19}$ 5_{1} 8_{1} (10_{23} 21_{30}) 24_{3} Je 10_{12} 51_{15} etc.
147	גבורה/חכמה	wisdom/might	(12_{13})	(Ec 9_{16})
148	עצה/חכמה	wisdom/council	12_{13}	(Pr 21_{30}) Is 11_{2} Je 49_{7}
149	עצה/גבורה	might/council	12_{13}	Pr 8_{14} (Is 11_{2} 36_{5})
150	תבונה/עצה	council/understanding	(12_{13})	Pr 20_{5} (21_{30})
151	שלח/עצר	withhold/send out	12_{15}	(II Ch 7_{13})
152	אזן/עין	eye/ear	13_{1} 29_{11} 42_{5}	Ps $34_{15(16)}$ $92_{11(12)}$ 94_{9} 115_{5-6} 135_{16-17} (Pr 20_{12}) Ec 1_{8} Is 6_{10} 11_{3} 32_{3} 33_{15} 35_{5} 37_{17} 43_{8} Da 9_{18} Je 5_{12} Ek 8_{18} 12_{2} 40_{4}
153	שמע/ראה	see/hear	13_{1} 29_{11} 42_{5}	Ps $48_{8(9)}$ $45_{10(1)1}$ Is 6_{9} 21_{3} 33_{15} 37_{17} 52_{15} $64_{4(3)}$ $66_{8.19}$ Ek 12_{2} La 1_{18} Ek 40_{4} 44_{5} Da 9_{18}
154	בין/ראה	see/understand	9_{11} 11_{11} 13_{1}	Is $6_{9.10}$ 44_{18}
155	בין/שמא	hear/understand	(13_{1}) (15_{8-9}) 26_{14}	
156	חכמה/חרש	keep silent/wisdom	13_{5} (33_{33})	
157	קשב/שמע	hear/listen	13_{6} (33_{31})	I Sa 15_{22} (Zc 7_{11}) Ps 17_{1} 61_{1} Pr 4_{1} 7_{24} Is 28_{23} (42_{23}) 49_{1} Je 18_{19} (Da 9_{19}) Ho 5_{1} Mi 1_{2} (Ma 3_{16})
158	רמיה/עולה	falsely/deceitfully	13_{7} 27_{4}	
159	פחד/שאת	majesty/dread	13_{11} 31_{23}	
160	נפל/בעת	terrify/fall	13_{11}	(Da 8_{17})
161	ענה/קרא	call/answer	(13_{22}) (14_{15})	
162	שמר/סדשים	put in stocks/watch	13_{27} 33_{11}	
163	ארחלה/רגל	feet/path	13_{27} (30_{12}) 33_{11}	Ps 119_{101}
164	אכל עש/רקב	rotten/moth eaten	13_{28}	Ho 5_{12}
165	בוא משפט/פקח עין	open eye/bring judgment	14_{3}	Ps 146_{7-8}
166	טמא/טהור	clean/unclean	(14_{4})	(Ec 9_{2}) (Ek 22_{26} 44_{23}) (De $12_{15.22}$ 15_{22})
167	חק/יום	days/bounds	14_{5}	(Mi 7_{11}) (Ma 3_{7})
168	יום/ירח	month/day	3_{6} 14_{5} 29_{2}	Ps 72_{7}
169	מספר/יום	day/number	3_{6} 14_{5}	
170	גזע/שרש	root/stump	14_{8}	Is 11_{1}

No.	Hebrew	English	Job	Elsewhere
171	עפר/ארץ	earth/ground	$14_{8(19)}$ 39_{14}	Ps $7_{5(6)}$ $22_{29(30)}$ $44_{25(26)}$ Pr 8_{26} (Ec 12_{7}) Is $34_{7.9}$ (25_{12}) $26_{5.19}$ 29_{4} $34_{7.9}$ (40_{12}) (47_{1}) 49_{23} La 2_{10} (Ek 24_{7}) (Am 2_{7}) Mi 7_{17}
172	נטע/פרח	bud/plant	14_{9}	Is 17_{11}
173	אדם/גבר	man/man	14_{10} 16_{21} 33_{17}	Pr 20_{24} (Je 17_{5}) La 3_{39}
174	יבש/חרב	waste away/dry up	14_{11}	Ge 8_{13-14} (Is 19_{5}) 42_{15}
175	נהר/ים	lake/river	14_{11}	Ps 24_{2} 66_{6} 72_{8} $80_{11(12)}$ 89_{25} Is 11_{15} 19_{5} 48_{18} 50_{2} Ek 32_{2} Mi 7_{12} Na 1_{4} Hb 3_{8} Zc 9_{10}
176	סתר/צפן	hide/conceal	14_{13}	Ps $31_{20(21)}$ 27_{5}
177	צור/הר	mountain/rock	14_{18} 24_{8} (28_{9-10})	Is 30_{29}
178	עפר/אבן	stone/soil	14_{19} $28_{2.6}$	Ps $102_{14(15)}$ (Ek 26_{12})
179	צער/כבד	honor/bring low	14_{21}	(Je 30_{19})
180	בין/ידע	know/perceive	11_{11} 14_{21} 15_{9} 23_{5} 28_{23} 38_{18} 42_{13}	(Ps 82_{5}) $92_{6(7)}$ Pr 24_{12} Is 44_{18}
181	קדים/רוח	wind/east wind	15_{2}	(Ex 10_{13} 14_{21}) (Ps $48_{7[8]}$) (Is 27_{8}) (Je 18_{17}) (Ek 17_{10}) (Jn 4_{8}) Ho $12_{1(2)}$ (13_{15})
182	יעל/סכן	unprofitable/do no good	15_{3} 35_{3}	
183	לשון/פה	mouth/tongue	15_{5} 20_{12} 33_{2}	Ps $5_{9(10)}$ 10_{7} 37_{30} $39_{1(2)}$ 50_{19} 66_{17} 73_{9} 78_{36} 109_{2} 126_{2} Pr 10_{31} 15_{2} (21_{23}) 26_{28} 31_{26} Is 57_{4} Je $9_{8(7)}$ (Mi 6_{12}) Zp 3_{13} (Zc 14_{12})
184	חול/ילד	born/bring forth	15_{7} 39_{1}	(Is 23_{4}) 26_{18} 54_{1} 66_{8}
185	עין/לב	heart/eyes	15_{12} (31_{7})	Ps $19_{8(9)}$ 131_{1} $36_{1(2)}$ $38_{10(11)}$ Pr 15_{30} (21_{4}) $23_{26.33}$ Ec 2_{10} (8_{16}) (11_{9}) Is 6_{10} (38_{3}) (Je 22_{17}) La 2_{18} 5_{17} Ek 6_{9} 40_{4}
186	מלין/רוח	spirit/word	15_{13} 32_{18}	II Sa 23_{2}
187	אשה/אנוש	man/woman	15_{14} 25_{4}	
188	צדק/זכה	clean/righteous	(8_{6}) 15_{14} 25_{4}	Ps $51_{4(6)}$
189	חרה/שמע	hear/show	(15_{17}) 32_{10}	

190	עריץ/רשע	wicked/ruthless	15_{20} 27_{13}	(Ps 37_{25})
191	מצוקה/צר	distress/anguish	(15_{24})	(Ps 119_{143}) $107_{6.19.28}$ 25_{17} (Zp 1_{15})
192	בית/עיר	city/house	15_{28}	Ps 127_{1} Is 6_{11} 14_{17} (Je 33_{4}) $26_{6.9(12)}$ 38_{17} Jl 2_{9} (Zc 14_{2})
193	חיל/עשר	rich/wealth	15_{29}	Ps $49_{6(7)}$
194	נצה/בטר	unripe grape/blossom	15_{33}	(Is 18_{5})
195	זית/גפן	vine/olive tree	15_{33}	(De 8_{8}) Ps 128_{3} Hb 3_{17} (Hg 2_{19})
196	עין/אף	wrath/eyes	16_{9} 40_{24}	Pr 24_{18}
197	שן/אף	wrath/teeth	16_{9}	SS $7_{4(5)}$
198	רשע/עול	ungodly/wicked	16_{11} 27_{7}	Ps 82_{2} Pr 29_{27} (Ek 18_{24} 33_{15})
199	תפלה/כף	hand/prayer	16_{17}	Ps 141_{2}
200	מרום/שמים	heaven/on high	16_{19}	Ps $102_{19(20)}$ 148_{1} Je 51_{53}
201	עין/רע	friend/eye	16_{20} (17_{5})	(Pr 21_{10})
202	רע/אלה	God/neighbor	(16_{20}) 16_{21} (19_{21}) 12_{4}	
203	תקע/ערב	pledge/give surety	17_{3}	Pr 17_{18} 22_{26}
204	טהר/צדק	righteousness/clean	17_{9}	(Ec 9_{2})
205	לילה/יום	day/night	(2_{13}) $3_{3(6)}$ (17_{12})	
206	לילה/אור	light/night	(17_{12}) 24_{14}	(Ps 78_{14}) (Je 31_{35}) (Zc 14_{7})
207	חשך/לילה	night/dark	5_{14} 17_{12}	(Ps 104_{20}) $139_{11.12}$
208	חשך/אור	light/dark	(12_{25}) (17_{12}) (18_{18}) (12_{22}) (26_{10}) (29_{3}) 24_{16} 38_{19}	(Ps 112_{4}) 139_{11} (Ec 2_{13} 11_{7-8}) Is $5_{20(30)}$ 9_{2} 13_{10} (42_{16}) 42_{6-7} 45_{7} (58_{10}) 59_{9} 60_{2-3} (La 3_{2} (Ek 32_{8}) (Am $5_{.18.20}$) Mi 7_{8}
209	מקום/שכן	dwelling/place	18_{21} 38_{19}	(De 12_{5}) Ps 26_{8} 132_{5} Is 54_{2}
210	יום/חשך	dark/day	(3_{4}) (5_{14}) (15_{23}) (17_{12}) 24_{16}	Ps 139_{12} (Ec $5_{17[16]}$) (Is 29_{18}) (Jl 2_{2}) Am $5_{18(20)}$ (Zp 1_{15})
211	יצועי/בית	house/couch	17_{13}	Ps 132_{3}
212	אם/אב	mother/father	17_{14} 31_{18}	(Ps 27_{10}) 109_{14} Pr 4_{3} 6_{20} 10_{1} 15_{20} 19_{26} (20_{20}) $23_{22(25)}$ $30_{11.17}$ (28_{24}) (Is 8_{4}) Je $16_{3(7)}$ La 5_{3} Ek 16_{3} (22_{7}) Mi 7_{6} etc.
213	אחה/אם/אב	father/mother/sister	17_{14}	(Ek 44_{25})

No.	Hebrew	English	Job	Elsewhere
214	טמא/בהמה	cattle/unclean	18_{3}	(Le 5_{2} 7_{21} 11_{26} 20_{25} $27_{11.27}$)
215	נר/אור	light/lamp	18_{6} 29_{3}	Ps 119_{105} (Pr 6_{23}) 13_{9} (Je 25_{10})
216	דעך/חשך	dark/pull out	18_{6}	(Pr 20_{20})
217	איד/און	strength/calamity	18_{12} 31_{3}	
218	קציר/שרש	root/branch	18_{16} 29_{19}	
219	שם/זכר	memory/name	18_{17}	Ex 3_{15} Ps 135_{13} Pr 10_{7} (Is 26_{8})
220	נכר/נין	offspring/descendant	(18_{19})	(Ge 21_{23}) (Is 14_{22})
221	קדמן/אחרן	west/east	18_{20}	(Zc 14_{18}) Jl 2_{20}
222	שער/שמם	appall/horror	18_{20}	Ek 27_{35} 32_{10} Je 2_{12}
223	נתיבה/ארח	way/path	19_{8}	(Ju 5_{6}) Ps $142_{3(4)}$ Pr 8_{20} 12_{28}
224	ירע/אח	brother/acquaintance	19_{13} 42_{11}	
225	נכר/זור	stranger/alien	19_{15}	Ps $81_{9(10)}$ Pr 2_{16} $5_{10.20}$ 7_{5} 20_{16} $27_{2.13}$ Is 61_{5} 28_{21} (Je 5_{19}) La 5_{2}
226	חנן/קרא	call/beseech	19_{16}	(Ex 33_{19})
227	בן/אשה	wife/son	19_{17}	Ps 109_{9} 128_{3} (Is 49_{15}) (Je 16_{2}) Am 7_{17}
228	בטן/רוח	spirit/belly	15_{2} 19_{17} 32_{18}	(Ec 11_{5})
229	ספר/כתב	write/book	19_{23} (31_{35})	(Je 3_{8} 32_{10} 45_{1} 51_{60}) Ma 3_{16}
230	עפר/ברזל	iron/lead	(19_{24}) (28_{2})	
231	ראה/חזה	see/behold	19_{27} 23_{9}	Is 30_{10} 33_{17}
232	שמח/רנן	exult/joy	20_{5}	Ps $5_{11(12)}$ ($67_{4[5]}$) (90_{14}) 100_{2} 35_{27} (Zc $2_{10[14]}$) Zp 3_{14}
233	חנף/רשע	wicked/godless	20_{5}	Pr $11_{8\text{-}9\text{-}10}$
234	עב/שמים	heavens/cloud	20_{6} 22_{14}	(Ps $104_{2\text{-}3}$) (147_{8})
235	מקום/עין	eye/place	20_{9}	(Pr 15_{3})
236	קרב/מעים	stomach/inside	20_{14}	Is 16_{11} (La 1_{20})
237	נהר/פלג	river/stream	20_{17}	(Ps $46_{4[5]}$)
238	חמאה/דבש	honey/curds	(20_{17})	De $32_{13\text{-}14}$ (II Sa 17_{29}) (Is $7_{15.22}$)
239	מטר/שלח	to rain/to send	20_{23}	

240	נחושה/ברזל	iron/bronze	20_{24} 28_{2} 40_{18} $41_{27(19)}$	Le 26_{19} Is 45_{2} 48_{4} Mi 4_{13}
241	קשת/נשק	weapon/arrow	20_{24}	(Ek 39_{9})
242	יצא/שלף	draw forth/come out	(20_{25})	(Ju 3_{22})
243	ארץ/שמים	heaven/earth	$11_{8\text{-}9}$ 20_{27} 28_{24} 35_{11} 37_{3} 38_{33}	Ps $8_{1(2)}$ 50_{4} $57_{5(6).11(12)}$ $68_{8(9)}$ $69_{34(35)}$ $73_{9.25}$ $76_{8(9)}$ etc.
244	נגר/גלה	carry away/drag off	20_{28}	Mi 1_{6}
245	נחלה/חלק	portion/heritage	20_{29} 27_{13} 31_{2}	Je 10_{16} 51_{19}
246	אל/אלהים	God/God	5_{8} 20_{29}	Ps $7_{11(12)}$ $42_{2(3)}$ 43_{4} 50_{1} 55_{19} $57_{2(3)}$ ($63_{1[2]}$) etc.
247	פלץ/בחל	dismay/shudder	21_{6}	Is $21_{3\text{-}4}$
248	עין/פנים	presence/eyes	21_{8} 24_{15}	Pr 17_{24} Je 40_{4} 42_{2} Is 5_{21} (38_{3}) Da $8_{3.5}$ 9_{18} 10_{6} (Zc 3_{9})
249	שלם/פחד	fear/peace	(15_{21}) (21_{9}) 25_{2}	(Je 30_{5} 33_{9})
250	שמח/שיש	sing/rejoice	21_{12}	(Ps 40_{16}) $68_{3(4)}$ ($70_{4[5]}$) Is 66_{10} ($65_{13\text{-}14}$)
251	עוגב/כנור	lyre/pipe	21_{12} 30_{31}	(Ge 4_{21})
252	תף/עוגב/כנור	tambourine/lyre/pipe	21_{12}	Ps $150_{3\text{-}4}$
253	סופה/רוח	wind/storm	21_{18}	Is 17_{13} Ho 8_{7}
254	חמה/יד	hand/wrath	21_{20}	Is 51_{17} (Je 21_{5}) Ek 3_{14} (20_{33}) (25_{14})
255	אהל/בית	house/tent	21_{28}	Ps $84_{10(11)}$ (132_{3}) Pr 14_{11} (Je 35_{7}) Zc 12_{7}
256	רשע/נדיב	prince/wicked	21_{28} (34_{18})	
257	לפני/אחר	after/before	21_{33}	Is 43_{10} Je 25_{26} 49_{37} 17_{16} Jl 2_{3}
258	משפט/יכח	reprove/judgment	($9_{32\text{-}33}$) 22_{4}	
259	עון/רעה	wickedness/iniquity	22_{5}	Ps $40_{12(13)}$ $49_{5(6)}$ Pr 16_{6} Is 13_{11} (Je 16_{10} $36_{3.31}$); (Ek 36_{31}) (Da 9_{13}) Ho 7_{1}
260	אין קץ/רבה	great/no end	22_{5} $16_{2\text{-}3}$	
261	רעב/עיף	weary/hungry	22_{7}	(II Sa 17_{29}) (Is 29_{8})
262	יתום/אלמנה	widow/fatherless	22_{9} 24_{3} $29_{12\text{-}13}$ $31_{16\text{-}17}$	Ps $68_{5(6)}$ 94_{6} 109_{9} (146_{9}) Is $1_{17.23}$ (9_{17}) 10_{2} (Je 7_{6}) 49_{11} etc.
263	פהד/פח	snare/terror	22_{10}	(Is 24_{17}) 24_{18} Je $48_{43.44}$
264	בוכב/אלוה	God/star	22_{12} 38_{7}	(Is 14_{13})
265	רום/גבה	high/lofty	22_{12} 39_{27}	(Is 52_{13}) (Je 49_{16})

No.	Hebrew	English	Job	Elsewhere
266	נקי/צדק	righteous/innocent	22_{19} 17_{8-9} 27_{17}	Ps 94_{21}
267	אמר/תורה	instruction/word	22_{22}	Ps 78_{1}
268	לבב/פה	mouth/heart	22_{22}	Ps 17_{3} $19_{14(15)}$ $49_{3(4)}$ 55_{21} (Pr 16_{23}) Is 29_{13} Ek 33_{31}
269	נחל/עפר	dust/torrent	22_{24} 30_{6}	Is 34_{9}
270	ישע/שפל	abase/save	22_{29}	Ps $18_{27(28)}$
271	אחור/קדם	forward/backward	23_{8}	(Ps 139_{5}) Is $9_{12(11)}$
272	ימין/שמאול	left hand/right hand	23_{9}	(Ec 10_{2}) Pr 3_{16} (4_{27}) Is $9_{20(19)}$ (54_{3}) (Ek 1_{10} 16_{46}) 39_{3} etc.
273	דרך/רגל	step/way	23_{11}	Ps 119_{59} Pr 1_{15} 3_{23} 4_{26}
274	אמר/מצוה	commandment/word	23_{12}	Pr 2_{1} 7_{1}
275	יום/עת	time/day	24_{1} 38_{23}	Ps 37_{19} Pr 8_{30} Is 13_{22} 49_{8} Je 30_{7} (33_{15}) (50_{4}) 50_{27} (Ek 7_{7}) etc.
276	מלהמה/קרב	battle/war	38_{23}	Ps 144_{1} (Zc 14_{2-3})
277	שור/חמור	ass/ox	24_{3}	Is 1_{3} (32_{20}) Ge $32_{5(6)}$ (Ex 20_{17}) $22_{4(3).9(8)}$ (21_{33}) (I Sa 12_{3}) 15_{3} etc.
278	עני/אביון	poor/needy	$24_{4(14)}$	(De 15_{11} 24_{14}) Ps $9_{18(19)}$ $12_{5(6)}$ (35_{10}) (37_{14}) ($70_{5[6]}$) $72_{4.12}$ etc.
279	ערבה/מדבר	desert/wilderness	24_{5}	Is $35_{1.6}$ 40_{3} 41_{19} 51_{3} Je 2_{6} 17_{6} (50_{12})
280	לקט/קצר	gather/glean	24_{6}	(Ru $2_{3.7}$)
281	כרם/שדה	field/vineyard	24_{6}	Ps 107_{37} Pr 24_{30} 31_{16} Je 32_{15} (35_{9}) Mi 1_{6}
282	לבוש/ערום	naked/without clothing	($24_{7.10}$)	
283	רעב/ערום	naked/hungry	24_{10}	Is 58_{7}
284	כסות/ערום	naked/without covering	24_{7} 26_{6}	
285	כסות/לבוש	clothing/covering	24_{7} 31_{19}	
286	עני/יתום	fatherless/poor	24_{9} 29_{12}	Ps 82_{3} (Is 10_{2}) (Zc 7_{10})
287	צמא/רעב	hungry/thirst	24_{10-11}	(Is 49_{10}) 65_{13} (De 28_{48}) (II Ch 32_{11}) Ne 9_{15} Am 8_{11} (II Sa 17_{29}) (Ps 107_{5}) etc.
288	חלל/מתים	dying/wounded	24_{12}	(Nu $19_{16.18}$) Ps $88_{5(6)}$ Is 22_{2}

289	שוע/נאק	groan/cry	24_{12}	(Ex 2_{23-24})
290	התיבה/דרך	way/path	24_{13}	Pr 1_{15} 7_{25} 8_{2} 12_{28} Is 42_{16} 43_{16} 59_{8} Je 6_{16} 18_{15} La 3_{9} Ho $2_{6(8)}$
291	נאף/גנב	thief/adulterer	24_{14-15}	Ps 50_{18}
292	נשף/לילה	night/twilight	24_{14-15}	Pr 7_{9}
293	ארץ/מים	water/land	24_{18}	Ps $63_{1(2)}$ (107_{35}) (136_{6}) (Is 54_{9})
294	שם/מקום	place/name	24_{20}	(Is 18_{7}) Je 7_{12}
295	כוכב/ירח	moon/stars	25_{5}	Ge 37_{9} De 4_{19} (Ps $8_{3[4]}$) (136_{9}) 148_{3}(Ec 12_{2}) Is 13_{10} Je 31_{35} Ek 32_{7} Jl 2_{10} 3_{15} (4_{15})
296	אדם/אנוש	man/man	16_{21} 25_{6} 35_{8} 36_{25} 37_{7}	Ps $8_{4(5)}$ 73_{5} 90_{3} 144_{3} Is $2_{11.17}$ 13_{12} 51_{12} 56_{2} 52_{14} (Ek 14_{3}) 23_{42} Je $49_{18.33}$; 50_{40} 51_{43} 32_{19}
297	תולעה/רמה	maggot/worm	25_{6}	Is 14_{11}
298	ישע/עזר	help/save	26_{2}	(Jo 10_{6}) Ps 109_{26} 37_{40}
299	עז/כח	power/strength	26_{2}	Pr 24_{5}
300	אבדון/שאול	Sheol/Abaddon	26_{6}	(Pr 15_{11}) (27_{20})
301	ארץ/צפון	north/earth	26_{7}	Ge 28_{14} Ps 107_{3} Ec 11_{3} Is 43_{6} Je 6_{22} 47_{2} (1_{14}) (16_{15}) (23_{8}) (25_{9}) 31_{8}
302	ענן/עב	thick cloud/cloud	26_{8} $37_{11.15-16}$	Is 44_{22} (Ex 19_{9})
303	רהב/ים	sea/Rahab	26_{12}	(Ps 89_{9-10}) (Is 51_{9-10})
304	יד/רוח	wind/hand	26_{13}	Ps $31_{5(6)}$ Is 11_{15} (Ek 3_{14}) (8_{3}) $21_{7(12)}$ 37_{1}
305	לשון/שפה	lip/tongue	27_{4}	Ps $12_{3(4).4(5)}$ $34_{13(14)}$ $119_{171-172}$ 120_{2} $140_{3(4)}$ Pr 12_{19} 17_{4} SS 4_{11} etc.
306	קום/איב	enemy/he who rises against	27_{7}	(De 28_{7}) (II Sa 18_{31-32})
307	קרא/ענג	delight in/call	27_{10}	(Is 58_{13})
308	מלבוש/כסף	silver/clothing	27_{16}	Je 10_{9} (Ek 16_{13})
309	סכה/בית	house/booth	27_{18}	(II Sa 11_{11}) (Ge 33_{17})
310	סופה/מים	flood/whirlwind	27_{20}	(Is 17_{13})
311	זהב/ספיר	sapphire/gold	28_{6}	SS 5_{14} Ek 28_{13}
312	נהר/צור	rock/stream	28_{10-11}	Ps 105_{41}
313	בינה/חכמה	wisdom/understanding	$28_{12.20.28}$ 38_{36} 39_{17}	(Pr 1_{2}) $4_{5.7}$ 9_{10} 16_{16} 23_{23} (Is 11_{2}) 29_{14} (Da 1_{20})

No.	Hebrew	English	Job	Elsewhere
314	ים/תהום	the deep/sea	28_{14} 38_{16}	Ps 33_{7} 106_{9} (135_{6}) Is 51_{10}
315	ספיר/שהם	onyx/sapphire	(28_{16})	(Ek 28_{13})
316	כתם/זהב	gold/fine gold	28_{16-17} 31_{24}	(Pr 25_{12}) La 4_{1}
317	פז/זהב	gold/fine gold	28_{17}	Ps $19_{10 (11)}$ (119_{127})
318	סתר/עלם	hide/conceal	28_{21}	(Nu 5_{13})
319	עוף/חי	living/bird	28_{21}	Ek. $31_{6.13}$ $32._{4}$ ($38._{20}$) (Ho. $2._{18}$) $4._{3}$
320	מקום/דרך	way/place	28_{23} 38_{19}	(Je 7_{3})
321	ראה/נבט	look/see	28_{24} (35_{5})	Is 5_{12} $22_{8-9.11}$ (La $1_{11.12}$ 5_{1}) Is 65_{15} 43_{18} 38_{11}
322	מדה/משקל	weight/measure	28_{25}	(Le 19_{35})
323	מים/ריח	wind/water	28_{25}	(Ps 147_{18}) 104_{3} Is 17_{13} (32_{2}) 44_{3} Je 10_{13} 51_{16}
324	דרך/חק	decree/way	28_{26}	Ps $119_{5 (33)}$
325	ספר/ראה	see/declare	(28_{27}) 31_{4}	
326	נגיד/שר	prince/noble	29_{9-10}	(II Ch 32_{31}) (35_{8}) I Ch 13_{1}
327	צניף/לבש	clothe/turban	29_{14}	(Zc 3_{5})
328	מעיל/לבש	clothe/robe	29_{14}	(Ps 109_{29}) (Is 59_{17}) (61_{10}) (Ek 26_{16})
329	רגל/עין	eye/foot	29_{15}	Is 3_{16}
330	פסח/עור	blind/lame	29_{15}	(Le 21_{18}) (De 15_{21}) (II Sa $5_{6.8}$) Is 35_{5-6} (Je 31_{8}) Ma 1_{8}
331	שן/מתלעה	fang/tooth	29_{17}	Pr 30_{14} Jl 1_{6}
332	טל/מים	water/dew	29_{19}	(Ju 6_{38})
333	קשת/כבוד	glory/bow	29_{20}	(Ek 1_{28})
334	מלקוש/מטר	rain/spring rain	29_{23}	(De 11_{14}) Zc 10_{1}
335	שכן/ישב	sit/dwell	15_{28} 29_{25}	Is 13_{20} 32_{16} 33_{24} Je 17_{6} 49_{31} (50_{39})
336	מלך/ראש	chief/king	29_{25}	SS $7_{5 (6)}$ (Je $21_{21 [26]}$) (Da 1_{10}) Mi 2_{3}
337	משל/נגינה	song/byword	30_{9}	Ps $69_{11-12 (12-13)}$
338	שלח/פתח	loose/cast off	30_{11} 39_{5}	
339	עב/רוח	wind/cloud	30_{15}	Ps 104_{3} Ec 11_{4}
340	יחל/קוה	look for/wait for	30_{26}	Ps 130_{5} Is 51_{5}

341	אור/טוב	good/light	30_{26}	Ps $4_{6(7)}$ (Ec 11_{7}) Is 5_{20}
342	רע/אח	brother/companion	30_{29}	(Ps 35_{14}) (122_{8}) Pr 17_{17} 18_{24} 27_{10} Is 19_{2} 41_{6} Je 9_{4} (23_{35}) (31_{34}) (34_{17})
343	יענה/תנים	jackal/ostrich	30_{29}	(Is 13_{21-22}) (43_{20}) 34_{13} Mi 1_{8}
344	בכה/אבל	mourning/weep	30_{31}	(De 34_{8})
345	צעד/דרך	way/step	31_{4} 34_{21}	Pr 16_{9} (Je 10_{23})
346	מרמה/שוא	falsehood/deceit	31_{5}	Ps 24_{4}
347	לב/אשר	step/heart	31_{7}	Ps 37_{31} $44_{18(19)}$
348	כף/עין	eye/hand	31_{7}	Ps $88_{9(10)}$ Is 1_{15} 33_{15}
349	שרש/זרע	sow/root out	31_{8}	Is 40_{24}
350	ריב/משפט	cause/complaint	31_{13}	(Ex 23_{6}) (De 17_{8}) (25_{1}) (II Ch 19_{10}) Ps 35_{23} (Ek 44_{24}) Mi 7_{9}
351	אלמנה/דל	poor/widow	31_{16}	Is 10_{2}
352	כביר/רב	great/much	31_{25}	Is 17_{12}
353	יד/חיל	wealth/hand	31_{25}	(Ps $76_{5[6]}$) (Is 10_{14}) (Je 34_{21}) (38_{3})
354	ירח/אור	light/moon	31_{26}	(Ps 148_{3}) (Ec 12_{2}) (Is 13_{10}) ($60_{19.20}$) (Je 31_{35}) (Ek 32_{7}) Hb 3_{11}
355	פה/לב	heart/mouth	31_{27}	Ps 17_{3} $19_{14(15)}$ $55_{21(22)}$
356	חתת/ערץ	stand in fear/terrify	31_{34}	(Jo 1_{9})
357	בכה/זעק	cry out/weep	31_{38}	Je 48_{31-32} Ek 27_{30-31}
358	שערה/חטה	wheat/barley	31_{40}	(De 8_{8}) (Ru 2_{23}) (II Sa 17_{28}) (II Ch $2_{10[9].15[14]}$) Is 28_{25} (Je 41_{8}) (Ek 4_{9}) (45_{13}) (Jl 1_{11})
359	משפט/חכם	wise/right	32_{9}	(Ps 37_{30})
360	ענה/יכח	confute/answer	32_{12} (40_{2})	
361	שוב/ערך	direct/return	32_{14} 33_{5}	
362	ענה/דבר	speak/answer	32_{16} (40_{5})	(Je 7_{27})
363	אזן/שמע	hear/give ear	13_{17} 33_{1} $34_{2.16}$	Is 32_{9} 42_{23} 28_{23} $64_{4(3)}$ $1_{2.10}$ 28_{23} Ps 17_{1} $39_{12(13)}$ $49_{1(2)}$ etc.
364	שפה/אמר	word/lip	(23_{12}) 33_{3}	
365	כף/אימה	fear/hand	13_{21} 33_{7}	

No.	Hebrew	English	Job	Elsewhere
366	שים/אחד	numerical	5_{19} 33_{14} 40_{5}	Ps $62_{11(12)}$ (Ec 4_{9}) $4_{11.12}$ 11_{6} Je 3_{14} Ek 41_{24} 43_{14} Pr 6_{16}
367	מאכל תאות/לחם	bread/dainty food	33_{20}	(I Ch 12_{40}) Pr 6_{8} (Hg 2_{12})
368	אור/שחת	pit/light	$33_{28.30}$	
369	ירע/חכם	wise/know	34_{2}	(Ec 2_{19}) 8_{1} (9_{11})
370	טוב/משפט	right/good	34_{4}	(Ps 112_{5}) (119_{39}) (Pr 2_{9}) (24_{23}) (Ek 20_{25}) Am 5_{15} Mi 6_{8}
371	רשע/פלע און	evil doers/wicked	34_{8}	Ps 28_{3} $92_{7(8)}$ 101_{8} 141_{4}
372	עול/רשע	do wickedness/wrong	27_{7} 34_{10}	Ps 71_{4} 82_{2} Pr 29_{27} (Ek 18_{24} 33_{15})
373	תבל/ארץ	earth/world	34_{13} (37_{12})	Ps $19_{4(5)}$ 24_{1} 33_{8} (90_{2}) 96_{13} $77_{18(19)}$ $89_{11(12)}$ 97_{4} 98_{9} Na 1_{5} etc.
374	אדם/בשר	flesh/man	34_{15}	Is 31_{3} Je 17_{5}
375	עפר שוב/גוע	perish/return to dust	34_{15}	Ps 104_{29}
376	רשע/בליעל	worthless/wicked	34_{18}	Pr 19_{28}
377	עני/דל	poor/afflicted	34_{28}	Ps 82_{3} Pr 22_{22} Is 10_{2} 26_{6} (Zp 3_{12})
378	השכיל/דעת	knowledge/insight	34_{35}	(Pr 21_{11})
379	שחק/שמים	heavens/cloud	35_{5} 38_{37}	De 33_{26} (Ps $36_{5(6)}$ $57_{10(11)}$ 78_{23} $108_{4(5)}$ (Pr 8_{27-28} Is 45_{8} Je 51_{9}
380	פשע/חטא	sin/transgression	8_{4} (13_{23}) (34_{37}) 35_{6}	
381	עשה/פעל	accomplish/do	35_{6}	(Is 41_{4}) (44_{15})
382	שוע/זעק	cry out/call for help	35_{9}	(La 3_{8})
383	דעת/מלה	word/knowledge	(35_{16}) 36_{4} (38_{2})	
384	דעת/הבל	empty talk/knowledge	35_{16}	Ps 94_{10-11}
385	עני/רשע	wicked/afflicted	36_{6}	(Ps 10_{2}) (37_{14})
386	מלך/צדק	righteous/king	36_{7}	(Je 23_{5}) (Zc 9_{9})
387	נעים/טוב	prosperity/pleasantness	36_{11}	(Ps 133_{1}) 135_{3} 147_{1}
388	לחץ/עני	affliction/adversity	36_{15}	(De 26_{7}) Ps $44_{24(25)}$
389	רעף/נזל	pour down/drop	36_{28}	Is 45_{8}

390	סכה/עב	cloud/pavilion	36_{39}	(II Sa 22_{12}) (Ps $18_{11\,[12]}$)
391	כסה/פרש	scatter/cover	36_{30}	Ek 16_{8}
392	ים/אור	light/sea	36_{30}	Je 31_{35}
393	פה/קול	voice/mouth	37_{2}	(Ec $5_{6\,[5]}$) (Je 7_{28}) Ek $21_{22\,(27)}$
394	מטר/שלג	snow/rain	37_{6}	Pr 26_{1}
395	אור/ברך	moisture/light	37_{11}	(Hb 3_{11})
396	ירה/טבע	sink/lay	38_{6}	Ex 15_{4}
397	רוע/רנן	sing/shout for joy	38_{7}	Ps 98_{4} 95_{1}
398	ערפל/ענן	cloud/thick darkness	38_{9}	(De 4_{11}) (5_{22}) (Ps 97_{2}) (Ek 34_{12}) (Jl 2_{2}) (Zp 1_{15})
399	דלת/בריח	bar/door	(38_{10})	(De 3_{5}) (Ju 16_{3}) (I Sa 23_{7}) II Ch 8_{5} $14_{7\,(6)}$ Ne $3_{3.6.13.14.15}$ Ps 107_{16} Is 45_{2} etc.
400	זרוע/אור	light/arm	38_{15}	Ps $44_{3\,(4)}$
401	ראה/גלה	reveal/see	38_{17}	Is 40_{5} (53_{1-2})
402	בית/גבול	territory/home	38_{20}	Pr 15_{25}
403	ברד/שלג	snow/hail	38_{22}	(Ps 148_{8})
404	מדבר/ארץ	land/desert	38_{26}	Ps 107_{35} (Pr 21_{19}) Is 16_{1} 21_{1} 41_{18} Je $2_{2.6.31}$ 3_{2} ($9_{12\,[11]}$) 12_{12} etc.
405	משאה/שאה	waste/desolate	(30_{3}) (38_{27})	(Zp 1_{15})
406	טל אגל/מטר	rain/drops of dew	38_{28}	(I Ki 17_{1}) (II Sa 1_{21}) De 32_{2}
407	תחום/מים	waters/deep	38_{30}	Ps 33_{7} $77_{16\,(17)}$ 104_{6} Pr 8_{24} Ek 26_{19} $31_{4\,(15)}$ Jn $2_{5\,(6)}$ Hb 3_{10}
408	מלחה/ערבה	steppe/salt land	39_{6}	Je 17_{6}
409	שכן/בית	home/dwelling	(21_{28}) 39_{6}	Ps 26_{8} $49_{11\,(12)}$
410	דרש/תור	range/search	39_{8}	(Ec 1_{13})
411	אברה/כנף	wing/pinion	$39_{13\,(26)}$	De 32_{11} Ps $68_{13\,(14)}$ 91_{4}
412	נצה/כנף	wing/plumage	39_{13}	(Le 1_{16-17}) (Ek $17_{3.7}$)
413	היה/רגל	foot/beast	39_{15}	Ps 66_{9} ($56_{13\,[14]}$)
414	רעם/גבר	might/strength	(26_{14}) 39_{19}	
415	חרב/פחד	fear/sword	39_{22}	SS 3_{8}
416	כידון/להב	spear/sword	(39_{23})	(I Sa 17_{45})

No.	Hebrew	English	Job	Elsewhere
417	פה/בינה	wisdom/command	39_{26-27}	Pr 4_{5}
418	חללים/דם	blood/fat	39_{30}	Is 1_{11} 34_{6}
419	רשע/משפט	wrong/condemn	$34_{12(17)}$ 40_{8}	(Is 54_{17})
420	קול/זרוע	arm/voice	40_{9}	Is 30_{30} (Da 10_{6})
421	לבש/עדע	deck/clothe	40_{10}	(Ek 16_{10-11}) Is 61_{10} Je 4_{30}
422	הדר/גאון	majesty/splendor	40_{10}	(Is $2_{10.19.21}$)
423	גבה/גאון	majesty/dignity	(40_{10})	Pr 16_{18} Je 48_{29}
424	הדר/הוד	glory/splendor	(40_{10})	(I Ch 16_{27}) (Ps $21_{5[6]}$) ($45_{3[4]}$) (96_{6}) (104_{1}) (111_{3}) (145_{5})
425	בקר/בהמה	Behemoth/ox	40_{15}	Jl 1_{18} (Jn 3_{7})
426	און/כח	strength/power	40_{16}	Ge 49_{3} (Is 40_{26}) 40_{29}
427	שדה/הר	mountain/field	40_{20}	Is 55_{12} (Je 26_{18}) (32_{44}) (Mi 3_{12})
428	אש/לפיד	torch/fire	41_{19} (41_{11})	(Ge 15_{17}) (Ju 15_{5}) (Ek 1_{13}) (Da 10_{6}) (Zc 12_{6})
429	פה/נפש	breath/mouth	7_{11} $41_{21(13)}$	Ps $63_{5(6)}$ Pr $13_{2(3)}$ 16_{26} 21_{23} (Ec 6_{7}) Is 5_{14} Ek 4_{14}
430	להב/גחל	coals/flame	$41_{21(13)}$	Is 47_{14}
431	חנית/חרב	sword/spear	(39_{22-23}) $41_{26(18)}$	Ps $57_{4(5)}$ Is 2_{4} Mi 4_{3} (Na 3_{3})
432	אבן קלע/קשת	bow/slingstones	$41_{28(20)}$	(II Ch 26_{14})
433	ים/מצולה	the deep/sea	41_{31}	(Ne 9_{11}) (Ps $68_{22[23]}$) Jn $2_{3(4)}$ (Mi 7_{19}) Zc 10_{11}
434	בין/ידע	know/understand	42_{3}	

No.	Hebrew	English	Job	Elsewhere
1	עצת רשע	counsel of the wicked	10_{3} 21_{16} 22_{18}	Ek 11_{2}
2	חפש עבד	slave is free	3_{19}	Je $34_{9.10.11.16}$
3	מר נפש	bitter in soul	3_{20} 7_{11} 10_{1} 21_{25} 27_{2}	Pr 31_{6} Ju 18_{25} Is 38_{15} ISa 22_{2} 1_{10}
4	אריה שאג	roaring lion	4_{10}	Is 5_{29} Zc 11_{3}
5	חול ימים	sand of the sea	6_{3}	Ge $32_{12(13)}$ Ps 78_{27} Is 10_{22} Je 15_{8} Ho 1_{10} (2_{1})
6	קלל מן . . .	swifter than . . .	7_{6} 9_{25}	IISa 1_{23} Je 4_{13} Hb 1_{8}
7	ירד שאול	go down to Sheol	7_{9} 17_{16} 21_{13}	Ps $55_{15(16)}$ Ek $31_{15.17}$
8	אמרי פה	words of the mouth	8_{2} 23_{12}	De 32_{1} Ps $19_{14(15)}$ $54_{2(4)}$ 138_{4}
9	חנף	godless man	17_{8} 20_{5} 27_{8} 34_{30} 8_{13} 15_{34} 36_{13}	
10	ובוז שפך	pour out contempt	12_{21}	Ps 107_{40}
11	דרך תהו תעה	wander in pathless waste	12_{24}	Ps 107_{40}
12	עם ראש	chief of the people	12_{24}	De 33_{21} Nu 25_{4}
13	שקר טפל	whitewash with lies	13_{4}	Ps 119_{69}
14	אויב חשב	count as an enemy	13_{24} 19_{11}	33_{10}
15	מספר . . .	number of . . .	3_{6} 15_{20} 21_{21} 14_{5} 16_{22} 31_{37} 36_{26} 38_{21}	
16	אלוה סוד	council of God	15_{8} 29_{4}	
17	ילד	he that is born of woman	15_{14} 25_{4}	
18	חשך . . .	darkness . . .	10_{21} 15_{22} 23_{30} 17_{13} 23_{17} 28_{3}	
19	ראש נוע	shake the hand	16_{4}	Ps $22_{7(8)}$ 109_{25} La 2_{15} Zp 2_{15} Is 37_{22}
20	מקום עתק	remove from place	18_{4} 14_{18}	
21	ריקם שלח	send away empty	22_{9}	ISa 6_{3}
22	כסה שפעת	flood of water covers	22_{11} 38_{34}	
23	נדר שלם	pay your vow	22_{27}	Ps $22_{25(26)}$ Ec $5_{5(4)}$ Pr 7_{14} Jn $2_{9(10)}$ Ps 66_{13}

No.	Hebrew	English	Job	Elsewhere
24	כף ביר	cleanness of hands	9_{30} 22_{30}	II Sa 22_{21} Ps $18_{20(21).24(25)}$
25	לב רכך	make the heart faint	23_{16}	Is 7_{4} Je 51_{46} II Ki 22_{19}
26	מדבר פרא	wild ass in the desert	24_{5}	Je 2_{24}
27	פעל יצא	go to toil	24_{5}	Ps 104_{23}
28	יקב דרך	tread the wine press	24_{11}	Is 63_{3} 16_{10} Am 9_{13}
29	נחש בריח	fleeing serpent	26_{13}	Is 27_{1}
30	בכה אלמנה	widows make no lament	27_{15}	Ps 78_{64}
31	מקום אי . . .	where is the place of . . .	$28_{12.20}$	
32	חיים ארץ	land of the living	28_{13}	Ps 27_{13} $52_{5(7)}$ 116_{9} $142_{5(6)}$ Is 38_{11} 53_{8} Je 11_{19} Ek 32_{23} etc.
33	אופר כתם	gold of Ophir	28_{16}	Ps $45_{9(10)}$ Is 13_{12}
34	קלות חזיז	lightning of thunder	28_{26} 38_{25}	Ex 9_{34}
35	יראת אדני	fear of the Lord	28_{28}	Ps $19_{9(10)}$ 111_{10} $34_{11(12)}$ Pr $1._{7.29}$ etc.
36	רע סור	depart from evil	28_{28}	Is 1_{16}
37	פה פער	open the mouth	29_{23}	Ps 119_{131} Is 5_{14}
38	פני אור	light of his countenance	29_{24}	Ps $4_{6(7)}$ $44_{3(4)}$ $89_{15(16)}$ Pr 16_{15}
39	קדר	go about blackened	30_{28}	Je 8_{21} Ps 35_{14} $38_{6(7)}$ $42_{9(10)}$ 43_{2} Ek 31_{15}
40	פלל עון	iniquity to be punished	$31_{11.28}$	
41	אל ממעל	God above	3_{4} $31_{2.28}$	De 4_{39} Jo 2_{11}
42	נשא פני	show partiality	11_{15} $13_{8.10}$ $22_{8.26}$ 32_{21} 34_{19}	
43	לב ישר	uprightness of heart	33_{3}	Ps 119_{7}
44	חזינות לילה	vision of the night	4_{13} 20_{8} 33_{15}	
45	אלף אחד	one of a thousand	9_{3} 33_{23}	
46	ירד פדה שחת	redeem from going down to the pit	$33_{24.28}$	
47	פעלי און	evil doers	31_{3} $34_{8.22}$	Ps $5_{5(6)}$ Ho 6_{8} Pr 10_{29} 21_{15} etc.
48	אזן גלה	open the ears	33_{16} $36_{10.15}$	

49	שלח עבר	perish by the sword	33_{18} 36_{12}	
50	חלץ אזר	gird up the loins	38_{3} 40_{7}	Je 1_{17} Is 32_{11}
51	יסדי ארץ	foundation of the earth	38_{4}	Ps 104_{5} Pr 3_{19} Is $61_{13.15}$ Zc 12_{1}
52	קו נטה	stretch a line	38_{5}	II Ki 21_{13} Is 34_{11} 44_{13} La 2_{8} Zc 1_{16}
53	ארץ כנפה	skirts of the earth	37_{3} 38_{13}	Is 11_{12} 24_{16}
54	להב חנית	flashing spear	39_{23}	Na 3_{3}
55	חית השדה	wild beasts	5_{23} 39_{15} 40_{20}	Is 43_{20} Je 12_{9} 28_{14} 27_{6} Ek 31_{6}
56	נחל ערב	willows of the brook	40_{22}	Le 23_{40}
57	טיט חרוץ	threshing sledge on the mire	41_{30}	Zc 9_{3}

4. Lamentations

WORD PAIRS

No.	Hebrew	English	Lamentations	Elsewhere
1	רע/אהב	lover/friend	1_{2}	(Ps $38_{11\,[12]}$) ($88_{18\,[19]}$) Pr 14_{20} 17_{17} 18_{24} 22_{11} Ho 3_{1}
2	איב/רע	friend/enemy	1_{2}	Je 19_{9} (Mi $7_{5\text{-}6}$)
3	עבדה/עני	affliction/servitude	1_{3}	(De 26_{6})
4	בתולה/כהן	priest/maiden	1_{4} $1_{18\text{-}19}$	(Ps $78_{63\text{-}64}$) (Je $31_{13\text{-}14}$) (Ek 44_{22})
5	שעך/דרך	road/gate	1_{4}	Pr $8_{2\text{-}3}$ Je 15_{7}
6	איב/צר	foe/enemy	1_{5} $2_{4.17}$ (4_{12})	Ps $13_{4\,(5)}$ (27_{2}) 74_{10} $81_{14\,(15)}$ $89_{42\,(43)}$ Is 1_{24} $9_{11\,(10)}$ 59_{18} Mi $5_{9\,(8)}$ Na 1_{2}
7	שבי צר/עולל	children/captive before foes	1_{5}	Na 3_{10}
8	שחק/ראה	gloat/mock at	1_{7}	Ps 37_{13}
9	מרוד/עני	bitterness/affliction	(1_{7}) (3_{19})	
10	ראש/לענה	wormwood/gall	(3_{19})	(De $29_{18\,[17]}$) Je 9_{15} 23_{15} Am 6_{12}
11	נבט/ראה	look/see	($1_{11.12}$) 2_{20} (4_{16}) (5_{1})	Is 5_{12} $22_{8\text{-}9.11}$ 38_{11} (42_{18}) (63_{15}) Jb 28_{24} (35_{5}) (Hb 1_{5})
12	ירד עין/בכה	weep/eyes flow with tears	1_{16} (2_{11}) ($3_{48.49}$)	Je 9_{1} 13_{17}
13	לב/מעים	heart/soul	1_{20}	Je 4_{19} Ps $22_{14\,(15)}$
14	בית/חוץ	street/house	1_{20}	Ek 7_{15} (40_{5}) $41_{9.17}$ (43_{21}) Pr 24_{27}
15	מות/חרב	sword/death	1_{20}	Je 15_{2} (18_{21}) 43_{11} Jb 5_{20}
16	פשע/רע	evil/transgression	1_{22}	
17	בת ציון/בת ירושלים	daughter of Jerusalem/ daughter of Zion	2_{13}	Mi 4_{8} Zp 3_{14}
18	חלל/חמל	mercy/dishonor	2_{2}	Ek 36_{21}
19	ממלכה/מבצר	stronghold/kingdom	2_{2}	Is 17_{3}
20	ישראל/יעקב	Israel/Jacob	2_{3}	Je 2_{4} 10_{16} 30_{10} Ek 28_{25} 39_{25} Mi 1_{5} 2_{12} $3_{1.8.9}$

21	חץ/קשת	bow/arrow	3$_{12}$	Ps 11$_{2}$ Is 5$_{28}$ (7$_{24}$) (Je 50$_{14}$) Ek 39$_{3}$ (39$_{9}$)
22	אש/איב	enemy/fire	2$_{4}$ (2$_{3}$)	Je 15$_{14}$ 17$_{4}$
23	אש/צר	foe/fire	2$_{4}$	Ek 30$_{16}$
24	שחת/בלע	destroy/lay in ruins	2$_{5.8}$	
25	אניה/תאניה	mourning/lamentation	(2$_{5}$)	(Is 29$_{2}$)
26	ישראל/יהודה	Israel/Judah	2$_{5}$	Je 3$_{11}$ etc.
27	מבצר/ארמנה	place/stronghold	2$_{5}$	Is 34$_{13}$
28	מועד/שך	booth/appointed feast	2$_{6}$	De 31$_{10}$
29	שבת/מועד	appointed feast/sabbath	2$_{6}$	Ek 44$_{24}$ 45$_{17}$ (Ho 2$_{11\,[13]}$) (I Ch 23$_{31}$)
30	כהן/מלך	king/priest	2$_{6}$	(Je 1$_{18}$) (2$_{26}$) 4$_{9}$ (8$_{1}$) (13$_{13}$) (32$_{32}$) Ho 5$_{1}$
31	נאר/זנח	scorn/disown	2$_{7}$	Ps 89$_{38-39\,(39-40)}$
32	בית/מקדש	sanctuary/house	2$_{7}$	(Je 51$_{51}$) (Ek 8$_{6}$) 9$_{6}$ 23$_{39}$ 43$_{21}$ (25$_{3}$) Am 7$_{.9.13}$
33	אמלל/אבל	lament/languish	2$_{8}$	Is 19$_{8}$ 24$_{4}$ (33$_{9}$) Je 14$_{2}$ Jl 1$_{10}$
34	חומה/חל	rampart/wall	(2$_{8}$)	(II Sa 20$_{15}$) (Is 26$_{1}$) Na 3$_{8}$
35	נביא/תורה	law/prophets	(2$_{9}$)	(Je 2$_{8}$) (18$_{18}$) (Ek 7$_{26}$) (Da 9$_{10}$) (Zp 3$_{4}$) (Zc 7$_{12}$)
36	בריח/שער	gate/bar	2$_{9}$	Ne 3$_{3.6.13.14.15}$ (Ps 147$_{13}$) Na 3$_{13}$
37	שר/מלך	king/prince	(2$_{9}$)	Ps 148$_{11}$ Ec 10$_{16.17}$ (Is 10$_{8}$) 32$_{1}$ 49$_{7}$ (Je 1$_{18}$ 2$_{26}$ 4$_{9}$ 8$_{1}$ 17$_{25}$) etc.
38	בתולה/זקן	elder/maiden	2$_{10.21}$	(Ek 9$_{6}$) (Je 51$_{22}$) (Ps 148$_{12}$)
39	בחור/בתולה	maiden/young man	(1$_{18}$) (2$_{21}$)	(Ek 9$_{6}$) (Am 8$_{13}$) Zc 9$_{17}$ Je 31$_{13}$ (51$_{22}$) Is 23$_{4}$ (62$_{5}$) (Ps 148$_{12}$) (II Ch 36$_{17}$) (De 32$_{25}$) Ps 78$_{63}$
40	זקן/נער	young/old	(2$_{21}$)	(Ps 148$_{12}$) (Is 3$_{5}$) (20$_{4}$) 65$_{20}$ (Je 51$_{22}$)
41	בחור/נער	young/young man	2$_{21}$ 5$_{13}$	(Je 51$_{22}$) Is 40$_{30}$ (Ps 148$_{12}$)
42	חרפה שבע/מכח לחי	cheek to smiter/fill with insults	3$_{30}$	(Jb 16$_{10}$)
43	שק/עפר	dust/sackcloth	2$_{10}$	Jb 16$_{5}$ (Ek 27$_{30-31}$)
44	יונק/עולל	infant/babe	4$_{4}$ (2$_{11}$)	(I Sa 15$_{3}$) (22$_{19}$) (Ps 8$_{2\,[3]}$) (Je 44$_{7}$) (Jl 2$_{16}$)
45	יין/דגן	bread/wine	(2$_{12}$)	(Ho 14$_{7\,[8]}$)
46	נוע/שרק	hiss/wag	(2$_{15}$)	(Zp 2$_{15}$)

No.	Hebrew	English	Lamentations	Elsewhere
47	ראש/כף	hand/head	2_{15}	Is 1_{6}
48	צוה/זמם	propose/ordain	2_{17}	Zc 1_{6}
49	עין/לב	heart/eyes	2_{18} 5_{17}	
50	יום/לילה	day/night	(2_{18})	(Ps 1_{2}) $22_{2(3)}$ (32_{4}) ($42_{3[4]}$) $42_{8(9)}$ ($55_{10[11]}$) 78_{14} 91_{5} 121_{6} Jb 5_{14} Is 4_{5} 21_{8} (34_{10}) (60_{11}) (Je 9_{1}) etc.
51	נביא/כהן	priest/prophet	4_{13} (2_{20})	(Is 28_{7}) Je $2_{8(26)}$ 4_{9} 5_{31} (6_{13}) ($8_{1.10}$) (13_{13}) (14_{18}) 18_{18} etc.
52	עצם/עור/בשר	flesh/skin/bones	3_{4} 4_{8}	Jb 7_{5} 10_{11} (19_{20}) 19_{26} Ek $37_{6.8}$ Mi 3_{3}
53	נתיבה/דרך	way/path	3_{9}	Jb 24_{13} Pr 1_{15} 3_{17} 7_{25} (8_{2}) 12_{28} Is 42_{16} 43_{16} 59_{8} Je 6_{16} 18_{15} Ho 2_{6}
54	אריה/דב	bear/lion	3_{10}	Is 17_{37} ($17_{34.36}$) (11_{7}) (Pr 28_{15}) Am 5_{19}
55	סתר/ארב	lie in wait/hide	3_{10}	Ps 10_{9}
56	רוח/שבע	fill/state	3_{15}	(Je 46_{10}) $31_{14(13)}$
57	טוב/שלום	peace/happiness	3_{17}	(Zc 8_{19}) Ps $34_{14(15)}$ Is 39_{8} 52_{7} (Je 8_{15} 14_{19} 33_{9})
58	דרש/קוה	wait/seek	3_{25}	(Ps 119_{94-95})
59	יגה/ענה	afflict/grieve	3_{33}	(Zp 3_{18-19})
60	חסד/רחם	compassion/steadfast love	3_{22} (3_{32})	(Is $54_{8.10}$) (63_{7}) (Je 16_{5}) (Da 1_{9}) Ho 2_{19} (Zc 7_{9}) (Ps 25_{6}) $40_{11(12)}$ $51_{1(3)}$ $69_{16(17)}$ (103_{4})
61	ריב/משפט	right of man/cause	$3_{35-36.58-60}$	(Ek 44_{24}) Mi 7_{9} Ps 35_{23}
62	אדם/גבר	man/man	$3_{35-36.39}$	(Je 17_{5}) Pr 20_{24} Jb 14_{10} 16_{21} 33_{17}
63	אדון/עליון	most high/Lord	$3_{35-36.37-38}$	
64	טוב/רע	good/evil	(3_{38})	(Je 18_{20}) (Pr 31_{12})
65	כף/לבב	heart/hands	(3_{41})	(Ps 24_{4}) 73_{13} 78_{72}
66	אל/יהוה	Lord/God	3_{40-41}	(Je 32_{18}) (51_{56}) (Da 9_{4}) Na 1_{2}
67	פחד/איב	enemy/panic	3_{46-47}	(Ps $64_{1[2]}$)
68	פחת/פחד	panic/pitfall	3_{47}	(Je $48_{43.44}$) Is 24_{18} (24_{17})
69	ראה/שקף	look down/see	(3_{50})	Ps 14_{2} $53_{2(3)}$
70	גאל/ריב	take up cause/redeem	3_{58}	Je 50_{34}

71	חיי/נפש	soul/life	3$_{58}$	(Ek 47$_{9}$) (Jn 4$_{3.8}$) Jb 9$_{21}$ 10$_{1}$ (3$_{20}$) (12$_{10}$)
72	שמד/רדף	pursue/destroy	(3$_{66}$)	II Sa 22$_{38}$
73	כתם/זהב	gold/pure gold	4$_{1}$	(Jb 28$_{16-17}$) 31$_{24}$ (Pr 25$_{12}$)
74	חטאה/עון	iniquity/sin	4$_{6.13.22}$ 5$_{7}$	Jb 10$_{6}$ (13$_{23}$) Ps 32$_{5}$ 38$_{18}$ Pr 5$_{22}$ Is 6$_{7}$ 27$_{9}$ 40$_{2}$
75	עון/עון	punishment/iniquity	(4$_{22}$)	Ps 32$_{5}$ Ek 44$_{12}$
76	תפל/שוה	false/deceptive	(2$_{14}$)	(Ek 22$_{28}$)
77	אדם/צחח	white/ruddy	4$_{7}$	(SS 5$_{10}$)
78	רעב/חרב	sword/hunger	4$_{9}$ 5$_{9-10}$	(Jb 5$_{20}$) Ek 5$_{12.17}$ (6$_{11.12}$) 7$_{15}$ (12$_{16}$) (14$_{21}$) Je 11$_{22}$ (5$_{12}$) (14$_{12}$) (14$_{15.16.18}$) (16$_{14}$) 18$_{21}$ etc.
79	שפך/כלה	give vent/pour out	4$_{11}$ 2$_{11}$	Ek 20$_{8.13}$
80	אף/חמה	wrath/anger	4$_{11}$	Ps 61$_{(2)}$ 37$_{8}$ 78$_{38}$ 90$_{7}$ Pr 15$_{1.18}$ 21$_{14}$ 22$_{24}$ 27$_{4}$ 29$_{22}$ (Is 42$_{25}$) (66$_{15}$) Ek 7$_{8}$ 13$_{13}$ (Je 7$_{20}$) (21$_{5}$) etc.
81	תבל/ארץ	earth/world	4$_{12}$	Jb 34$_{13}$ (37$_{12}$) Ps 19$_{4(5)}$ 24$_{1}$ 33$_{8}$ 77$_{18(19)}$ 89$_{11(12)}$ (90$_{2}$) 96$_{13}$ 97$_{4}$ 98$_{9}$ Pr 8$_{26}$ Is 14$_{21}$ 18$_{3}$ 24$_{4}$ etc.
82	סור/נגע/טמא	unclean/touch/away	4$_{15}$	Is 52$_{11}$
83	זקן/כהן	priest/elder	4$_{16}$ (1$_{19}$)	Ek 7$_{26}$ (Je 29$_{1}$) (19$_{1}$) Jb 12$_{19-20}$
84	מדבר/הר	mountain/wilderness	4$_{19}$	Je 9$_{10(9)}$ Is 16$_{1}$ 42$_{11}$ (Ps 75$_{6[7]}$)
85	אף/רוח	breath/nostril	(4$_{20}$)	Jb 4$_{9}$ 27$_{3}$ (Ps 18$_{15[16]}$) (Is 2$_{22}$)
86	שמח/שיש	rejoice/be glad	(4$_{21}$)	Ps 35$_{9}$ (40$_{16[17]}$) 68$_{3(4)}$ (70$_{4[5]}$)
87	עוץ/אדום	Edom/Uz	4$_{21}$	(Je 25$_{20-21}$)
88	שכר/כוס	cup/be drunk	4$_{21}$	(Is 51$_{21-22}$) (Hb 2$_{15-16}$) Je 51$_{7}$
88	שכר/כוס	cup/be drunk	4$_{21}$	(Is 51$_{21-22}$) (Hb 2$_{15-16}$) Je 51$_{7}$
90	נכר/זור	stranger/alien	5$_{2}$	Ps 81$_{9(10)}$ Is 61$_{5}$ Je 5$_{19}$ Jb 19$_{15}$ Pr 2$_{16}$ 5$_{10.20}$ 7$_{5}$ 20$_{16}$ 27$_{2.13}$ Ob 11 Is 28$_{21}$
91	אלמנה/יתום	orphan/widow	5$_{3}$	(Ex 22$_{22(21)24[23]}$) (De 10$_{18}$) Jb 22$_{9}$ 24$_{3}$ 29$_{12-13}$ 31$_{16-17}$ Ps 94$_{6}$ 109$_{9}$ Is 1$_{17.23}$ (9$_{17}$) 10$_{2}$ etc.
92	אם/אב	father/mother	5$_{3}$	Jb 17$_{14}$ 31$_{18}$ (Ps 27$_{10}$) 109$_{14}$ Pr 1$_{8}$ 4$_{3}$ 6$_{20}$ 10$_{1}$ 15$_{20}$ 19$_{26}$ etc.
93	עץ/מים	water/wood	5$_{4}$	(Ps 1$_{3}$) (Ec 2$_{6}$) (Je 17$_{8}$) (Ez 31$_{14}$)
94	אשור/מצרים	Assyria/Egypt	5$_{6}$	(Is 11$_{11}$) (19$_{23}$) Je 2$_{18.36}$ Ho 9$_{3}$

No.	Hebrew	English	Lamentations	Elsewhere
95	בתולה/אשה	woman/virgin	5_{11}	(Ek 9_{6}) (44_{22})
96	זקן/שר	prince/elder	5_{12}	Ps 105_{22} (148_{11-12})
97	דוד ודור/עולם	forever/all generations	5_{19}	Jl 2_{2} 3_{20} Pr 27_{24} Ec 1_{4} Is 34_{10} 34_{17} 51_{8} 58_{12} 60_{15} 61_{4} (Ps $12_{7[8]}$) 33_{11} 45_{17} $49_{11(12)}$ 79_{13} etc.

PHRASES

No.	Hebrew	English	Lamentations	Elsewhere
1	יד פרש	stretch out the hand	$1_{10.17}$	I Ki 3_{38}
2	יום אף חרון	day of fierce anger	1_{12} $2_{3.6}$ 4_{11} 1_{21} 2_{22} 4_{20} $3_{43.66}$ 2_{1}	Is 13_{13}
3	רשת פרש	spread a net	1_{13}	Ps $140_{5(6)}$ Ek 12_{13} 17_{20} 19_{8} 32_{3} Ho 7_{12} 5_{1}
4	גת דרך	tread as a wine press	1_{15}	Is 63_{2}
5	פה מרר	rebel against word	1_{18}	Nu 20_{24} 27_{14} I Sa 12_{15} 12_{14} I Ki $13_{21.26}$ De $1_{26.43}$ 9_{23} Jo 1_{18}
6	בקש אכל נפש שוב	seek food to revive strength	$1_{11.19}$	
7	בת ציון	daughter of Zion	$2_{1.4.8.10.13}$ 4_{22} 2_{18}	
8	בתולה בת יהודה	virgin daughter of Judah	1_{15} 2_{13}	II Ki 19_{21} Is 37_{22} Je 46_{11}
9	בת עמי	daughter of my people	2_{11} 3_{48} $4_{3.10}$	Je 4_{11} $6_{26.14}$ $8_{11.19.21.22}$ 9_{7} 14_{17} Ek 13_{17} Is 22_{4}
10	חדם רגל	footstool	2_{1}	Is 66_{1} Ps 99_{5} 110_{1} 132_{7}
11	קשת דרך	bend the bow	2_{4} 3_{12}	Ps $7_{12(13)}$ 37_{14} $64_{3(4)}$ 11_{2} Je 51_{3} Is 5_{28} 21_{15} I Ch 5_{18} 8_{40}
12	דמם ישב	sit in silence	2_{10} 3_{28}	
13	עפר עלה	cast dust	2_{10}	Ek 27_{30}
14	שק חגר	put on sackcloth	2_{10}	Is 15_{3} 22_{12} Ek 7_{18} 27_{31}
15	רחוב עטף	faint in the streets	$2_{11.12.19}$	
16	ירד דמעה	tears stream down	2_{18}	Je $9_{18(17)}$ 13_{17} 14_{17}
17	נגינה	song	3_{14} 5_{14}	Is 38_{20} Ps $69_{12(13)}$
18	שפך לב . . .	pour out the heart, blood, fury, etc.	$2_{4.11.12.19}$ $4_{11.13}$	
19	צפור צוד	hunt like a bird	3_{52} 4_{18}	Jb 10_{16}
20	תנובה שדי	fruits of the field	4_{9}	De 32_{13} Ek 36_{30}

5. *Ruth*

WORD PAIRS

No.	Hebrew	English	Ruth	Elsewhere
1	שוב/הלך	go/return	1$_{8\,(11).\,12.\,15.\,21\,(7)}$	(Ex 4$_{19}$) Jo 18$_{8}$ (Pr 3$_{28}$) Je 40$_{5}$
2	בית/מנוחה	home/house	1$_{9}$	(I Ch 28$_{2}$) Is 66$_{1}$
3	בכה/נשק	kiss/weep	(1$_{9}$)	(Ge 33$_{4}$) (29$_{11}$) (50$_{1}$) (45$_{14\text{-}15}$) (I Sa 20$_{41}$)
4	בכה/קול נשא	lift up voice/weep	(1$_{9}$)	(Ge 21$_{16}$) (27$_{38}$) (Ju 2$_{4}$) (21$_{2}$) (I Sa 30$_{4}$) (II Sa 3$_{2}$) (13$_{36}$) (Jb 2$_{12}$)
5	אנוש/בך	son/husband	1$_{11}$	Jb 25$_{6}$ Ps 8$_{4\,(5)}$ (90$_{3}$) 144$_{3}$ Is 51$_{12}$ 56$_{2}$ Je 18$_{21}$ Mi 7$_{6}$
6	קבר/מות	die/bury	1$_{17}$	(Ju 8$_{32}$) (10$_{2.\,5}$) (12$_{5.\,7.\,10.\,12}$) (Je 20$_{6}$) Jb 3$_{21\text{-}22}$ Is 53$_{9}$
7	שדי/יהוה	Lord/Almighty	1$_{21}$	Is 13$_{6}$ Jl 1$_{15}$ Ex 6$_{3}$
8	שתה/צמא	thirsty/drink	(2$_{9}$)	Is 65$_{13}$ (29$_{8}$)
9	נכר/חן מצא	find favor/take notice	2$_{10}$ (2$_{13.\,19}$) (3$_{14}$)	(Pr 3$_{4}$) (28$_{23}$) De 16$_{19}$
10	ארץ מולדה/אם/אב	father/mother/native land	(2$_{11}$)	(Pr 28$_{24}$) Ek 44$_{25}$ Zc 13$_{3}$ (Je 22$_{10}$) (46$_{16}$)
11	פת/לחם	bread/morsel	2$_{14}$	(Ge 18$_{5}$) (Ju 19$_{5}$) (I Sa 2$_{36}$) (28$_{22}$)
12	חבט/לקט	glean/beat out	2$_{17}$	Is 27$_{12}$
13	עשה/לקט	glean/work	2$_{19}$	Ex 16$_{17}$
14	מתים/חיים	living/dead	(2$_{20}$)	Ec 3$_{5}$ 4$_{2}$ 9$_{4}$ Ps 143$_{3}$ (Is 8$_{19}$)
15	שמלה/סוך/רחץ	wash/anoint/clothe	(3$_{3}$)	(II Sa 12$_{20}$)
16	שתה/אכל	eat/drink	(3$_{3}$) (3$_{7}$)	(Ex 34$_{28}$) (De 9$_{9.\,18}$) (I Sa 30$_{12}$) (Ez 10$_{6}$) (Ec 2$_{24}$ 3$_{13}$ 5$_{18\,[17]}$) (Je 22$_{15}$) (Ek 39$_{17}$) (Is 21$_{5}$) Pr 9$_{5}$ SS 5$_{1}$
17	שכב/גלה	uncover/lie down	(3$_{4}$)	(De 27$_{20}$)
18	ראשון/אחרון	last/first	(3$_{10}$)	Is 41$_{4}$ (44$_{6}$) 48$_{12}$ 9$_{1}$ (8$_{23}$) Ec 1$_{11}$ Je 50$_{17}$ (Da 11$_{29}$) (Hg 2$_{9}$)
19	עשיר/דל	poor/rich	(3$_{10}$)	Ex 30$_{15}$ Pr 10$_{15}$ 22$_{16}$ 28$_{11}$
20	בקר/לילה	night/morning	(3$_{13}$)	(I Sa 14$_{36}$) Ps 92$_{2\,(3)}$ (Is 21$_{12}$) 28$_{19}$ Ho 7$_{6}$ Am 5$_{8}$

21	שכב/לין	remain/lie down	(3_{13})	(Ge 28_{11})
22	ישב/שער עלה	go up to the gate/sit down	(4_{1})	(Jb 29_{7})
23	לאה/רחל	Rachel/Leah	(4_{11})	Ge $29_{16.17\,(25)\,(30)\,31}$ (30_{14}) ($31_{4.14.33}$) ($33_{1.2.7}$)
24	בית לחם/אפרתה	Ephrathah/Bethlehem	(4_{11})	(Ge 35_{19}) (48_{7}) (Mi $5_{2\,[1]}$)
25	ילד/הרה	give conception/bare	(4_{13})	Ge 3_{16} (29_{34}) Nu 11_{12} (Ju 13_{3}) (Ho 9_{11}) Is 26_{18} 33_{11}
26	אמוה/חיק שים	set in bosom/become a nurse	(4_{16})	Nu 11_{12}

PHRASES

No.	Hebrew	English	Ruth	Elsewhere
1	יד יהוה	hand of the Lord	1_{13}	ISa 5_{6} 7_{13} Jb 12_{9}
2	קציר שערים	beginning of the barley harvest	2_{23}	IISa $21_{9.10}$
3	יהוה עמכם	Lord be with you	2_{4}	
4	יהוה ברך	Lord bless you	$2_{19.20}$ 3_{10} 4_{14}	ISa 23_{21} Zc 11_{5} Ps 144_{1} 124_{6} $68_{19\,(20)}$
5	חסה בוא כנף	under whose wing you have come to take refuge	2_{12}	Ps $57_{1\,(2)}$ $61_{4\,(5)}$ 94_{1}
6	כנף פרש	spread your skirt	3_{9}	Je 48_{40} 49_{22} De 32_{11} IKi 6_{27} Jb 39_{26} Ek 16_{8}
7	אשת חיל	woman of value	3_{11} 2_{1}	Pr 12_{4} 31_{10}
8	חי יהוה	as the Lord lives	3_{13}	IISa 15_{21} IKi 1_{29} IIKi $2_{2.4.6}$ IICh 18_{13} (Ps $18_{46\,[47]}$) Je 4_{2} 5_{2} 12_{16} 16_{14} $23_{7.8}$ 44_{26}

Bibliography

A. TEXTS, DICTIONARIES, GRAMMARS, SOURCE MATERIALS

Cunliffe, Richard J., Lexicon of the Homeric Dialect, 1963.

Gordon, Cyrus, Ugaritic Manual, 1965.

Holm-Nielsen, Svend, Hodayot Psalms from Qumran, 1960.

Homer, Homeri Opera. The Oxford Classical Texts. 2 volumes. Edited by David B. Monro and Thomas W. Allen, 1966.

van der Hooght, Edvard, ed. Biblia Hebraica. Second edition, 1867.

Kennicott, Benjamin, ed. Vetus Testamentum Hebraicum cum variis lectionibus. 2 volumes, 1776–1780.

Kittel, Rudolf, ed. Biblia Hebraica. Third edition, 1962.

Lattimore, Richard, The Iliad of Homer: Translated with an Introduction, 1951.

Levy, Kurt, Zur masoretischen Grammatik: Text und Untersuchungen, 1936.

Loewenstamm, Samuel, and Joshua Blau, eds. Thesaurus of the Language of the Bible: Complete Concordance, Hebrew Bible Dictionary, Hebrew-English Bible Dictionary, 1957.

Lord, A.B., ed. Serbocroatian Heroic Songs, Volume I: Novi Pazar: English Translation. Collected by Milman Parry, edited and translated by A.B. Lord, 1954

Mandelkern, Solomon, Veteris Testamenti Concordantiae Hebraicae atque Chaldaicae. 2 volumes, 1955.

May, Herbert G., and Bruce M. Metzger, eds. The Oxford Annotated Bible, 1962.

von Pauly, August Friedrich, and Wilhelm Wissowa, and Wilhelm Kroll, eds. Paulys Real-encyclopädie der classischen Altertumswissenschaft, 1894.

Prendergast, Guy Lushington, A Complete Concordance to the Iliad of Homer, 1875.

Schmidt, Carl Edward, Parallel-Homer: Index aller homerischen Iterati in lexikalischer Anordnung, 1965 (1885).

Craig, Hardin, ed. The Complete Works of Shakespeare, 1961.

Sperber, Alexander, A Historical Grammar of Biblical Hebrew: A Presentation of Problems with Suggestions to their Solution, 1966.

B. BOOKS AND COMMENTARIES

Albright, William Foxwell, From the Stone Age to Christianity. Second edition, 1957.

Allis, Oswald T., The Unity of Isaiah: A Study in Prophecy, 1950.

Auerbach, Erich, Mimesis: The Representation of Reality in Western Literature. Translated by Willard R. Trask, 1957.

Barr, James, The Semantics of Biblical Language, 1961.

—, Comparative Philology and the Text of the Old Testament, 1968.

Ben-Hayyim, Zeev, The Literary and Oral Tradition of Hebrew and Aramaic Amongst the Samaritans. (Hebrew) 2 volumes, 1957.

—, Studies in the Traditions of the Hebrew Language, 1954.
Birkeland, Harris, Zum hebräischen Traditionswesen: Die Komposition der prophetischen Bücher des Alten Testaments, 1938.
Boman, Thorlief, Hebrew Thought Compared with Greek. Translated by J. Moreau, 1960.
Bowra, C.M., Heroic Poetry, 1952.
Bright, John, Jeremiah: Introduction, Translation, and Notes, 1965.
Bruno, Arvid, Der Rhythmus der alttestamentlichen Dichtung: eine Untersuchung über die Psalmen I–LXXII, 1930.
Cassuto, Umberto, A Commentary on the Book of Genesis: From Adam to Noah; From Noah to Abraham. 2 volumes. Translated by Israel Abrahams, 1961.
—, The Goddess Anath. Translated by Israel Abrahams, 1971 (1953).
Chadwick, H.M. and N.K., The Growth of Literature. 3 volumes, 1932–1940.
Cheyne, Thomas Kelly, The Lamentations of Jeremiah, 1885.
Cobb, William H., A Criticism of Systems of Hebrew Metre, 1905.
Condamin, Albert, Poèmes de la Bible, avec une introduction sur la strophie hebraïque, 1933.
Crüsemann, Frank, Studien zur Formgeschichte von Hymnus und Danklied in Israel, 1969.
Culley, Robert C., Oral Formulaic Language in the Biblical Psalms, 1967.
Dahood, Mitchell, Ugaritic-Hebrew Philology, 1965.
—, Psalms One: One to Fifty, 1966.
—, Psalms Two: Fifty-One to One Hundred, 1968.
—, Psalms Three: One Hundred One to One Hundred Fifty, 1970.
Dhorme, Edouard Paul, O.P., A Commentary on the Book of Job. Translated by Harold Knight, 1967 (1926).
—, L'Emploi Metaphorique des Noms de Parties du Corps en Hebreu et en Akkadien, 1963 (1923).
Döderlein, Johann C., Esaias, 1775.
Driver, S.R., and G.B. Gray, A Critical and Exegetical Commentary on the Book of Job; together with a New Translation. 2 volumes, 1921.
Eissfeldt, Otto, The Old Testament: An Introduction. Translated by Peter Ackroyd, 1965.
Engnell, Karl Ivan, The Call of Isaiah: an Exegetical and Comparative Study, 1949.
Finkelstein, Louis, The Pharisees: The Sociological Background of Their Faith. 2 volumes, 1946.
Fohrer, Georg, Introduction to the Old Testament. Initiated by Ernst Sellin, translated by D.E. Green, 1968.
Ginsberg, Christian David, Introduction to the Massoretico-Critical Edition of the Hebrew Bible, 1966 (1894).
Gordis, Robert, The Book of God and Man: A Study of Job, 1965.
—, Poets, Prophets, and Sages: Essays in Biblical Interpretation, 1971.
Gray, George B., The Forms of Hebrew Poetry, 1915.
Gunkel, Hermann, and Joachim Begrich, Einleitung in die Psalmen: Die Gattungen der religiösen Lyrik Israels, 1928.
—, The Psalms: A Form Critical Introduction. Translated by T.M. Horner, 1967.
Hahn, Herbert F., The Old Testament in Modern Research, 1966.

Harrison, R.K., Introduction to the Old Testament; with a Comprehensive Review of Old Testament Studies and a Special Supplement on the Apocrypha, 1969.
Hillers, Delbert, Lamentations, 1968.
Johnson, A.R., Sacral Kingship in Ancient Israel, 1955.
Kahle, Paul, Masoreten des Ostens, 1966 (1913).
Kraft, Charles F., The Strophic Structure of Hebrew Poetry as Illustrated in the First Book of the Psalter, 1938.
Lesky, Albin, Die Homerforschung in der Gegenwart, 1952.
—, A History of Greek Literature. Translated by James Willis and Cornelis de Heer, 1966.
Ley, Julius, Leitfaden der Metrik der hebräischen Poesie nebst dem ersten Buch der Psalmen nach rhythmischer Vers- und Strophenabteilung mit metrischer Analyse, 1887.
Lieberman, Saul, Hellenism in Jewish Palestine: Studies in the Literary Transmission, Beliefs, and Manners of Palestine in the I Century B.C.E.—IV Century C.E., 1950.
Lord, A.B., The Singer of Tales. Harvard Studies in Comparative Literature 24, 1960 (1954).
Lowth, Robert, De Sacra Poesi Hebraeorum Praelectiones, 1753.
—, Lectures on the Sacred Poetry of the Hebrews. Translated by G. Gregory, notes by Calvin Stowe, 1829.
—, Isaiah, A New Translation: with a Preliminary Dissertation, 1778.
Maimonides, Moses, The Guide of the Perplexed. Translated with an Introduction by Shlomo Pines, 1969.
Morag, Shelomo, The Vocalization Systems of Arabic, Hebrew, and Aramaic: Their Phonetic and Phonemic Principles, 1962.
Mowinckel, Sigmund, Psalmenstudien I–IV. 2 volumes, 1961 (1933).
—, Das Thronbesteigungsfest Jahwäs und der Ursprung der Eschatologie, 1922.
Myers, Jacob M., The Linguistic and Literary Forms of the Book of Ruth, 1955.
Newman, L.I., and William Popper, Studies in Biblical Parallelism. 2 volumes, 1918.
Nyberg, Henrik S., Studien zum Hoseabuche: zugleich ein Beitrag zur Klärung des Problems der alttestamentlichen Textkritik, 1935.
Oettli, Samuel, Die Klagelieder, 1889.
Osterley, W.O.E., and T.H. Robinson, An Introduction to the Books of the Old Testament, 1963 (1934).
Palache, J.L., Semantic Notes on the Hebrew Lexicon. Translated and edited by R.J. Zwi Werblowsky, 1959.
Parry, Adam, ed. The Making of Homeric Verse; the Collected Papers of Milman Parry, 1971.
Parry, Milman, L'Epithete traditionelle dans Homere; Essai sur un probleme de style Homerique, 1928.
Pedersen, Johannes P., Israel: Its Life and Culture I–IV, 1926–1947.
Pfeiffer, Robert H., Introduction to the Old Testament, 1963.
Robinson, Theodore H., The Poetry of the Old Testament, 1947.
Rowley, Harold H., ed. The Old Testament and Modern Study: A Generation of Discovery and Research, 1961.
Rückert, R., Hebräische Propheten, 1831.
Rudolph, Wilhelm, Die Klagelieder übersetzt und erklärt, 1939.

Saalschütz, J.L., Form und Geist der biblisch-hebräischen Poesie, 1853.

Sievers, Edvard, Metrische Studien: I Studien zur hebräischen Metrik, 1901; II Die hebräische Genesis, 1904–1905; III Studien zur hebräischen Metrik, 1907.

Streane, Annesley W., Jeremiah and Lamentations, 1913.

Swete, Henry B., Introduction to the Old Testament in Greek, 1907 (1902).

Trachtenberg, Joshua, Jewish Magic and Superstition: A Study in Folk Religion, 1970 (1939).

Tur-Sinai, Naphtali H. (H. Torczyner), The Book of Job: A New Commentary, 1957.

Westermann, Claus, Isaiah 40–66: A Commentary. Translated by D.M.G. Stalker, 1969.

de Wette, Wilhelm M.L., A Critical and Historical Introduction to the Canonical Scriptures of the Old Testament. Translated by Theodore Praker, 1859.

Whallon, William, Formula, Character, and Context: Studies in Homeric, Old English, and Old Testament Poetry, 1969.

C. ARTICLES AND PERIODICALS

Albright, William Foxwell, The Old Testament and Canaanite Language and Literature, CBO 7, 1945, 5–31.

—, Some Oriental Glosses on the Homeric Problem, AJA 54, 1950, 162–176.

—, Two Little Understood Amarna Letters from the Middle Jordan Valley, BASOR 89, 1943, 7–21.

Alt, Albrecht, The God of the Fathers, Essays on Old Testament History and Religion. Translated by R.A. Wilson, 1967, 1–100.

Anderson, George W., Israel: Amphictyony: 'AM; KĀHĀL; 'ĒDÂH, Translating and Understanding the Old Testament: Essays in Honor of H.G. May. Edited by H.T. Frank and W.L. Reed, 1970, 135–151.

Baumgartner, Walter I., The Wisdom Literature, The Old Testament and Modern Study: A Generation of Discovery and Research. Edited by H.H. Rowley, 1961, 210–237.

Bea, Augustin, Der Zahlenspruch im Hebräischen und Ugaritischen, Biblica 21, 1940, 196–198.

—, Ras Shamra und das Alte Testament, Biblica 19, 1938, 435–453.

—, Archäologisches und Religionsgeschichtliches aus Ugarit-Ras Shamra, Biblica 20, 1939, 436–453.

Begrich, Joachim, Zur hebräischen Metrik, ThRv 4, 1932, 67–89.

—, Der Satzstil im Fünfter, ZS 9, 1934, 169–209.

Bentzen, Aage, Skandinavische Literatur zum Alten Testament, 1939–1948, ThRv 17, 1948–1949, 272–328.

Beyerlin, Walter, Die *tôdā* der Heilsvergegenwärtigung in den Klageliedern des Einzelnen, ZAW 79, 1967, 208–224.

Blenkinsopp, Joseph, Structure and Style in Judges 13–16, JBL 82, 1963, 65–76.

Boling, Robert G., Synonymous Parallelisms in the Psalms, JSSt 5, 1960, 221–255.

Bowra, Cecil M., Style, A Companion to Homer. Edited by A.J.B. Wace and F.H. Stubbings, 1962, 26–37.

Brown, Francis, The Measurements of Hebrew Poetry as an Aid to Literary Analysis, JBL 9, 1890, 71–106.

Budde, Karl, Das hebräische Klagelied, ZAW 2, 1882, 1–52.

Byington, Steven T., A Mathematical Approach to Hebrew Meters, JBL 66, 1947, 63–77.

Casanowicz, I. M., Jewish Amulets in the United States National Museum, JAOS 36, 1917, 154–167.

Cassuto, Umberto (Moshe David), The Seven Wives of King Keret, BASOR 119, 1950, 18–20.

—, Word Pairs in Hebrew and Ugaritic, Leshonenu 15, 1947, 97–102. (In Hebrew.)

—, Biblical Literature and Canaanite Literature, Tarbiz 13, 1942, 197–212. (In Hebrew.)

—, Biblical Literature and Canaanite Literature (Conclusion), Tarbiz 14, 1942, 1–10. (In Hebrew.)

Condamin, Albert, Symmetrical Repetitions in Lamentations Chapters I and II, JTS 7, 1906, 137–140.

Creed, Robert P., The Making of an Anglo-Saxon Poem, ELH 26, 1959, 445–454.

—, The Singer Looks at his Sources, CL 14, 1962, 44–52.

Culley, Robert C., An Approach to the Problem of Oral Tradition, VT 13, 1963, 113–125.

Cummins, Patrick, Rhythm, Hebrew, and English, CBQ 3, 1941, 27–42.

Dahood, Mitchell, A New Metrical Pattern in Biblical Poetry, CBQ 29, 1967, 574–579.

Davison, J. A., The Homeric Question, A Companion to Homer. Edited by A. J. B. Wace and F. H. Stubbings, 1962, 234–265.

Driver, Godfrey Rolles, Notes on Isaiah, Von Ugarit nach Qumran: Festschrift für Otto Eissfeldt. Beiträge zur alttestamentlichen und altorientalischen Forschung. Edited by J. Hempel and Leonhard Rost, 1958, 42–48.

—, Abbreviations in the Massoretic Text, Textus 1, 1960, 112–131.

—, Hebrew Poetic Diction, SVT 1, 1953, 26–39.

Dussaud, René, La Poesie phénicienne et son rhythme, RP 44, 1937, 208–216.

Eissfeldt, Otto, The Prophetic Literature, The Old Testament and Modern Study: A Generation of Discovery and Research. Edited by H. H. Rowley, 1961, 115–161.

Elliger, Karl, Der Prophet Tritojesaja, ZAW 8, 1931, 112–140.

Engnell, Karl Ivan A., Profetia och tradition, SEÅ 12, 1947, 110–139.

Finkelstein, Louis, The Transmission of Early Rabbinic Tradition, HUCA 16, 1941, 115–135.

Freedman, David Noel, Archaic Forms in Early Hebrew Poetry, ZAW 72, 1960, 101–107.

Fück, Johann W., Bemerkungen zur arabischen Metrik, ZDMG 111, 1962, 464–469.

Gaster, Theodore H., Prolegomenon, Great Men and Movements in Israel. By Rudolf Kittel, 1968 (1929), xv–lii.

Gehman, Henry S., Adventures in Septuagint Lexicography, Textus 5, 1966, 125–132.

Gerleman, Gillis, Studies in the Septuagint, LUÅ Aud. 1, 52:3, 1956, 16–33.

Gevirtz, Stanley, The Ugaritic Parallel to Jeremiah 8:23, JNES 20, 1961, 41–46.

Ginsberg, Harold L., Rebellion and Death of Ba'lu, Orientalia 5, 1936, 171–172.

Goetze, Albrecht, Is Ugaritic a Canaanite Dialect? Language 17, 1941, 127–138.

Gordis, Robert, Democratic Origins of Ancient Israel: the Biblical 'Ēdāh', Alexander Marx Jubilee Volume on the Occasion of his Seventieth Birthday, 1950, 369–388. English section.

—, Qoheleth and Qumran—A Study in Style, Biblica 41, 1960, 395–410.

Goshen-Gottstein, Moshe H., The Psalms Scroll (11QPs[a]): A Problem of Canon and Text, Textus 5, 1966, 22–33.

Gunkel, Hermann, Klagelieder Jeremiae, RGG 3, cols. 1499–1504, 1927–1931.

Held, Moshe, Still More Word Pairs in the Poetry and the Prose of Ugarit, Leshonenu 18, 1953, 144–160. (In Hebrew.)

—, The YQTL-QTL (QTL-YQTL) Sequence of Identical Verbs in Biblical Hebrew and in Ugaritic, Studies and Essays in Honor of Abraham A. Neuman. Edited by Meir Ben-Horin, Bernard D. Weinryb, and Solomon Zeitlin, 1962, 281–290.

Hölscher, Gustav, Elemente arabischer, syrischer, und hebräischer Metrik, BZAW 34, 1920, 93–101.

Horst, Friedrich, Die Kennzeichen der hebräischen Poesie, ThRv 21, 1953, 97–121.

Johnson, Aubrey R., The Psalms, The Old Testament and Modern Study: A Generation of Discovery and Research. Edited by H.H. Rowley, 1961, 162–207.

König, Eduard, Metrum als Mittel der Textkritik in der althebräischen Poesie, JBL 46, 1927, 331–343.

Kosmala, Hans, Form and Structure in Ancient Hebrew Poetry (a New Approach), VT 14, 1964, 423–445.

—, Form and Structure in Ancient Hebrew Poetry (Continued), VT 16, 1966, 152–180.

Kösters, F.B., Die Strophen, TSK 4, 1931, 40–114.

Kraft, Charles F., Some Further Observations Concerning the Strophic Structure of Hebrew Poetry, A Stubborn Faith: Papers on Old Testament and Related Subjects Presented to Honor William A. Irwin, 1956, 62–89.

de Langhe, Robert, Le Bible et la Literature ugaritique, OBL 1, 1957, 67–87.

Lesky, Albin, Homeros, II. Oral Poetry, and Homeros, III. Mündlichkeit und Schriftlichkeit, Paulys Realencyclopädie der classischen Altertumswissenschaft. Begun by A.F. Pauly, and edited by W. Wissowa and W. Kroll, 1894.

—, Die homerische Frage, Geschichte der griechischen Literatur, 1958, 49–58.

Lias, J.J., The Unity of Isaiah, BS 72, 1915, 560–591.

—, The Unity of Isaiah, BS 75, 1918, 267–274.

Löhr, Max, Der Sprachgebrauch des Buches der Klagelieder, ZAW 14, 1894, 31–50.

—, Threni III und die jeremianische Autorschaft des Buches der Klagelieder, ZAW 24, 1904, 1–16.

—, Alphabetische und alphabetisierende Lieder im Alten Testament, ZAW 25, 1905, 173–198.

Lord, A.B., Homer, Parry, and Huso, AJA 102, 1948, 34–44.

—, Homer and Other Epic Poetry, A Companion to Homer. Edited by A.J.B. Wace and F.H. Stubbings, 1962, 179–214.

—, Composition by theme in Homer and Southslavic Epos, TPAPA 82, 1951, 71–80.

Lund, Eimar, Eine metrische Form im Alten Testament, AcOr(L) 17, 1939, 249–303.

Maecklenburg, Albert, Einführung in die Probleme der hebräischen Metrik, WZKM 46, 1939, 1–46.

Magoun, Jr. F. P., The Theme of the Beasts of Battle in Anglo-Saxon Poetry, NM 56, 1955, 81–89.

—, Oral-Formulaic Character of Anglo-Saxon Narrative Poetry, Speculum 28, 1953, 446–467.

Marcus, Ralph, Jewish and Greek Elements in the Septuagint, Louis Ginzberg Jubilee Volume on the Occasion of his Seventieth Birthday. 2 volumes. 1945, volume 1, 227–245. English section.

—, Alphabetic Acrostics in the Hellenistic and Roman Periods, JNES 6, 1947, 109–115.

Meek, Theophile J., Hebrew Poetic Structure as a Translation Guide, JBL 59, 1940, 1–9.

Möller, Hans, Der Strophenbau der Psalmen, ZAW 50, 1932, 240–256.

Montgomery, James A., Stanza Formation in Hebrew Poetry, JBL 64, 1945, 379–384.

Morawe, Günther, Vergleich des Aufbaus der Danklieder und hymnischen Bekenntnislieder (1 QH) von Qumran mit dem Aufbau der Psalmen im Alten Testament und im Spätjudentum, RQ 4, 1963–1964, 323–356.

Mowinckel, Sigmund, "שחל", Hebrew and Semitic Studies Presented to G. R. Driver in Celebration of his Seventieth Birthday. Edited by D. W. Thomas and W. D. McHardy, 1963, 95–103.

—, Neuere Forschungen zu Deuterojesaja, AO 16, 1938, 1–40.

—, Zum Problem der hebräischen Metrik, Festschrift Alfred Bertholet zum 80 Geburtstag gewidmet von Kollegen und Freunden. Edited by W. Baumgartner, O. Eissfeldt, K. Elliger, and L. Rost, 1950, 379–394.

—, Die Metrik bei Jesus ben Sirach, StTh 9, 1955, 137– 165.

—, Zur hebräischen Metrik, II, ST 7, 1954, 54–85, 166.

—, Marginalien zur hebräischen Metrik, ZAW 68, 1956, 97–123.

Muilenburg, James, Form Criticism, and Beyond, JBL 88, 1969, 1–18.

—, A Study in Hebrew Rhetoric: Repetition and Style, SVT 1, 1953, 97–111.

Munch, Peter A., Die alphabetische Akrostische in der jüdischen Psalmendichtung, ZDMG 90, 1936, 703–710.

Notopoulos, James A., The Homeric Hymns as Oral Poetry: A Study of Post Homeric Oral Tradition, AJP 83, 1962, 337–368.

—, Homer, Hesiod, and the Achaean Heritage of Oral Poetry, Hesperia 29, 1960, 177–197.

O'Callaghan, Robert T., Echoes of Canaanite Literature in the Psalms, VT 4, 1954, 164–176.

Orlinsky, Harry M., The Tribal System of Israel and Related Groups in the Period of the Judges, Studies and Essays in Honor of Abraham A. Neuman. Edited by Meir Ben-Horin, B.D. Weinryb, and S. Zeitlin, 1962, 375–387.

Parry, Milman, Whole Formulaic Verses in Greek and Southslavic Heroic Songs, TPAPA 64, 1933, 179–197.

—, Studies in the Epic Technique of Oral Verse-Making I: Homer and the Homeric Style, HSCP 41, 1930, 73–147.

—, Studies in the Epic Technique of Oral Verse-Making II: Homeric Language as the Language of an Oral Poetry, HSCP 43, 1932, 1–50.

Piatti, P. T., I carmi alfabetici della Bibbia chiave della metrica ebraica, Biblica 31, 281–315, 427–458.

van der Ploeg, Jean, Le Role de la tradition orale dans la transmission du texte de l'Ancien Testament, RB 54, 1947, 5–21.

Rankin, Oliver S., Alliteration in Hebrew Poetry, JTS 31, 1930, 285–291.

Robinson, Theodore H., Some Principles of Hebrew Metrics, ZAW 54, 1936, 28–43.

—, Hebrew Poetic Form: The English Tradition, SVT 1, 1953, 128–149.

—, Basic Principles of Hebrew Poetic Form, Festschrift Alfred Bertholet zum 80. Geburtstag gewidmet von Kollegen und Freunden. Edited by W. Baumgartner, O. Eissfeldt, K. Elliger, and L. Rost, 1950, 438–450.

—, Anacrusis in Hebrew Poetry, Sonderabdruck aus Werden und Wesen des Alten Testaments, 1936, 37–40.

Ross, J., Formulaic Composition in Gaelic Oral Literature, MP 57, 1959, 1–12.

Roth, Wolfgang M. W., The Numerical Sequence x/x + 1 in the Old Testament, VT 12, 1962, 300–311.

Rowley, Harold H., The Book of Job and its Meaning, BJRL 41, 1958–1959, 167–207.

Ruben, Paul, Strophic Forms in the Bible, JQR 11, 1899, 431–479.

Sachsse, E., Untersuchungen zur hebräischen Metrik, ZAW 43, 1925, 173–192.

Schirmann, J., Hebrew Liturgical Poetry and Christian Hymnology, JQR 44, 1953, 123–161.

Schlesinger, K., Zur Wortfolge im hebräischen Verbalsatz, VT 3, 1953, 381–390.

Segert, Stanislav, Vorarbeiten zur hebräischen Metrik I–II, ArOr 21, 1953, 481–542.

—, Vorarbeiten zur hebräischen Metrik III, ArOr 25, 1957, 190–200.

—, Problems of Hebrew Prosody, SVT 7, 1960, 283–291.

—, Die Methoden der althebräischen Metrik, CV 1, 1958, 233–241.

Skehan, Patrick W., Le travail d'Edition des Fragments Manuscrits de Qumrân, RB 63, 1956, 49–67.

Slotki, Israel W., Antiphony in Ancient Hebrew Poetry, JQR 26, 1935–1936, 199–219.

Sperber, Alexander, Hebrew Grammar: A New Approach, JBL 62, 1943, 137–262.

—, Hebrew Based upon Greek and Latin Translations, HUCA 12–13, 1937–1938, 26–67.

—, Problems of the Masora, HUCA 17, 1942–1943, 293–394.

Talmon, Shemaryahu, Pisqah Be'emsa 'Pasuq and 11QPS[a], Textus 5, 1966, 11–21.

Tur-Sinai, Naphtali H. (Torczyner), Some Ideas on the Place of Ugaritic among the Semitic Languages, Tarbiz 23, 1952, 143–145. (In Hebrew.)

Wernberg-Møller, Preben, The Contribution of the Hodayot to Biblical Textual Criticism, Textus 4, 1964, 133–175.

Whallon, William, Formulaic Poetry in the Old Testament, CL 15, 1963, 1–14.

—, Old Testament Poetry and Homeric Epic, CL 18, 1966, 113–131.

Yadin, Yigael (Y. Sukenik), Another Fragment (E) of the Psalms Scroll from Qumran Cave 11 (11QPs[a]) (with five plates), Textus 5, 1966, 1–10.

Young, George D., Ugaritic Prosody, JNES 9, 1950, 124–133.

—, The Present State of Ugaritic Studies, JKLF 2, 1953, 125–145.

D. MONOGRAPHS AND PAMPHLETS

Albrektson, Bertil, Studies in the Text and Theology of the Book of Lamentations: with a Critical Edition of the Peshitta Text, 1963.

Alt, Albrecht, Der Gott der Väter: Ein Beitrag zur Vorgeschichte der israelitischen Religion, 1929.

Bright, John, Early Israel in Recent History Writing: A Study in Method, 1956.

Childs, Brevard S., Memory and Tradition in Israel, 1962.

Gabor, Ignaz, Der hebräische Urrhythmus, 1929.

Gerhardsson, Birger, Memory and Manuscript, 1961.

Gevirtz, Stanley, Patterns in the Early Poetry of Israel, 1963.

Gottwald, Norman, Studies in the Book of Lamentations, 1962.

Guillaume, Alfred, Studies in the Book of Job with a New Translation. Edited by John MacDonald, 1968.

Jahnow, Hedwig, Das hebräische Leichenlied im Rahmen der Völkerdichtung, 1923.

Mowinckel, Sigmund, Real and Apparent Tricole in Hebrew Psalmic Poetry, 1957.

Nielsen, Eduard, Oral Tradition: A Modern Problem in Old Testament Introduction, 1954.

Noth, Martin, Das System der Zwölf Stämme Israels, 1930.

Patton, John Hastings, Canaanite Parallels in the Book of Psalms, 1944.

Pope, Marvin H., El in the Ugaritic Texts, 1955.

Rignell, Lars G., A Study of Isaiah Chapters 40–55, 1956.

Roth, Wolfgang M.W., Numerical Sayings in the Old Testament, 1965.

Tsevat, Matitiahu, A Study of the Language of the Biblical Psalms, 1955.

E. UNPUBLISHED MATERIALS

Ehlen, Arlis, The Poetic Structure of a Hodayah from Qumran; an Analysis of Grammatical, Semantic, and Auditory Correspondence in 1QH 3.19–36. Th.D. Dissertation. Cambridge: Harvard University, 1970.

Fitzgerald, Robert Paul, The Place of Robert Lowth's De Sacra Poesi Hebraeorum Praelectiones in Eighteenth Century Criticism. Ph. D. Dissertation. Iowa City, Iowa: The University of Iowa, 1964.

Freedman, David Noel, The Evolution of Early Hebrew Orthography: The Epigraphic Evidence. Ph.D. Dissertation. Baltimore: Johns Hopkins University, 1948.

Held, Moshe, Studies in Ugaritic Lexicography and Poetic Style. Ph.D. Dissertation. Baltimore: Johns Hopkins University, 1957.